Grammar Practice
for Upper Intermediate Students

with key

Debra Powell
with Elaine Walker and
Steve Elsworth

PEARSON
Longman

Contents

GRAMMAR

Nouns, pronouns, determiners and articles

Nouns, determiners, articles
1. Articles 4
2. Types of noun 6
3. Countable and uncountable nouns 7
4. Singular and plural nouns 9
5. *some*, *any*, *no*, *none*, etc. 11
6. *much*, *many*, *a lot*, etc. 13
7. *both*, *either*, *neither*, etc. 16
8. Pronouns 18
9. Possessive *'s*, possessive *of*, etc. 20

Check 1 Nouns, determiners, articles 22

Adjectives, adverbs and comparison

Adjectives and adverbs
10. Position and order of adjectives 24
11. Adjective or adverb? 26
12. Position and order of adverbs 28
13. Comparison of adjectives, adverbs and nouns 30
14. Comparative structures 32
15. *so ... that*, *such ... that*, *too*, *enough*, *very* 33
16. Adverbs of degree: *very*, *absolutely*, etc. 35
17. Sentence adverbs: *certainly*, *clearly*, etc. 37

Check 2 Adjectives and adverbs 38

Tenses

Present tenses
18. Present simple or continuous? 40
19. State verbs 42
20. Present perfect: *ever*, *never*, etc. 44
21. Present perfect: *just*, *already*, *yet*, etc. 46
22. Present perfect: *for*, *since* 48
23. Present perfect simple and continuous 50

Check 3 Present tenses 52

Past tenses
24. Past simple and continuous 54
25. Past perfect simple and continuous 56
26. *used to*, *would*, *be/get used to* 58

Check 4 Past tenses 60

Future forms
27. Future forms and meanings (1) 62
28. Future forms and meanings (2) 65
29. Other ways of talking about the future 67
30. Future in the past 68

Check 5 Future forms 70

Modal verbs
31. Ability and possibility 72
32. Degrees of certainty 74
33. Obligation and necessity 77
34. Advice, recommendations and criticism 80
35. Permission, requests, offers and suggestions 82

Check 6 Modal verbs 84

Sentence and text structure

Statements and questions
36. Basic sentence types 86
37. Question forms 88
38. Question tags and reply questions 90
39. Avoiding repetition: *so*, *neither*, *too*, etc. 91
40. Exclamations and emphatic forms 93

Check 7 Statements and questions 94

-ing forms and infinitives
41. Verb + *-ing* form or infinitive? 95
42. Verb + object + *-ing* form or infinitive? 97
43. Other uses of infinitives 99
44. Other uses of *-ing* forms 102
45. *doing*, (*to*) *do*, *being done*, (*to*) *be done*, etc. 104

Check 8 *-ing* forms and infinitives 105

Reported speech
46. Reported statements: tense changes 107
47. Reported statements: no tense changes 109
48. Reported questions, commands and requests 111
49. Reporting verbs 113

Check 9 Reported speech 115

Noun clauses
50. Noun clauses as object 117
51. Other uses of noun clauses 119

Check 10 Noun clauses 122

Relative clauses
52 Defining relative clauses ... 123
53 Non-defining relative clauses ... 125
54 *which* referring to a whole clause ... 127
55 Other ways to identify people and things ... 128
Check 11 Relative clauses ... 130

Linking words and structures
56 Compound and complex sentences ... 132
57 Adding and listing ... 133
58 Contrast and concession ... 134
59 Cause, reason, purpose and result ... 136
60 Time clauses ... 137
61 Common linking expressions in speech ... 139
62 Participle clauses: contrast, reason, result ... 140
63 Participle clauses: time ... 141
64 Past participle clauses ... 143
Check 12 Linking words and structures ... 144

Conditionals
65 The zero and first conditionals ... 146
66 The second conditional ... 147
67 The third conditional ... 149
68 *unless*, *provided* (*that*), *in case*, etc. ... 151
69 Mixed conditionals ... 152
70 *I wish*, *if only* ... 153
71 Other ways to express hypothetical meaning ... 155
Check 13 Conditionals ... 156

Changing sentence structure
72 Changing word order ... 158
73 The passive (1) ... 159
74 The passive (2) ... 161
75 The passive (3) ... 162
76 The causative: *have/get something done* ... 164
77 *there is/are* or *it is/they are*? ... 165
78 Emphasis: *It was ... that*, *What*, *All* ... 166
Check 14 Changing sentence structure ... 168

VOCABULARY

Prepositions
79 Prepositions of place and movement ... 170
80 Prepositions of time ... 172
81 Other prepositions ... 174
82 Prepositional phrases ... 175
Check 15 Prepositions ... 177

Words that go together
83 Adjective + preposition ... 178
84 Verb + preposition ... 180
85 Noun + preposition ... 182
86 Phrasal verbs ... 184
87 Confusing words (1) ... 186
88 *as*, *like* ... 187
89 Confusing words (2) ... 188
Check 16 Words that go together ... 190

Word formation
90 Prefixes ... 192
91 Forming adjectives: suffixes ... 193
92 Forming nouns: suffixes ... 194
93 *-ing* and *-ed* adjectives ... 195
94 Compound adjectives ... 196
95 Compound nouns ... 197
Check 17 Word formation ... 198

Appendices ... 199
Index ... 205
Answer key ... 209

Nouns, determiners, articles

1 Articles

Definite or indefinite meaning?
- We use the indefinite article *a/an* + singular countable noun to refer to any one of a kind or group, or when a noun is mentioned for the first time: *I'd like **an apple**. Anne's **a doctor**. I've got **a cold/headache**. I met **a** nice **girl** on holiday.*
- We use the definite article *the* + countable, uncountable or plural noun when the noun refers to something specific or unique, or to something already mentioned: *Let's go to **the park**. What's **the capital** of your country? **The weather's** awful. Which is the longest river in **the world**? **The boy** I met is called Andrew.*

General meaning
- We use zero article (no article) + plural countable noun or uncountable noun to make generalisations: *I like **cats** better than **dogs**. **Water** contains **oxygen**. Modern **life** is stressful.* (Not ~~The modern life is stressful~~.)
- We can also use *a/an* to refer to all examples of the same kind: ***A doctor** earns more than **a teacher**.* (= all doctors, all teachers)
- We can use *the* to refer to a whole class:
  - before singular nouns for species, inventions and musical instruments: ***The whale** is a mammal. Who invented **the computer**? I play **the piano**.*
  - before plural nationality adjectives and some adjectives with plural meaning: ***the** Americans   **the** Japanese   **the** rich   **the** old*
- We use *the* before superlative adjectives: ***the** best   **the** most expensive*

Other uses of articles
- We use *a/an* with expressions of quantity and frequency: ***a** half   **a** couple   **a** million   €2 **a** kilo* (= per kilo)   *50 km **an** hour* (= in an hour)   *twice **a** week*
- We use *the* with plural names of countries, oceans/seas, rivers, deserts, mountain ranges, groups of islands and regions: ***the** United States   **the** Pacific   **the** North Sea   **the** Thames   **the** Sahara   **the** Alps   **the** Maldives   **the** Middle East*
- We also use *the* with names of hotels, cinemas, theatres, museums and newspapers: ***the** Hilton   **the** Odeon Cinema   **the** National Theatre   **the** Natural History Museum   **the** Times*
- We use zero article with names of continents and most countries, states, cities/towns, mountains, lakes, streets/roads, parks, shops, restaurants and some magazines: *Europe   Spain   California   Paris   Mount Everest   Lake Ontario   Oxford Street   Hyde Park   Harrods   Hello Magazine*
- We also use zero article with meals, games, sports, subjects, languages, some illnesses and institutions (unless referring to a specific one): *lunch   chess   tennis   maths   Italian   sunburn   cancer   school   university   prison*

▶▶ *For prepositional phrases, see Unit 82.*

Grammar: *nouns, determiners, articles*

PRACTICE

1a Complete the sentences. Use *a*, *an* or *the*.

0   Have you seen ...*the*... newspaper? I can't find it anywhere.
1   I got my sister .... CD and .... new book for her birthday. I don't think she liked .... CD, though.
2   Is this .... first time you've stayed at .... Hilton?
3   She started her career as .... teacher but now she's .... journalist.
4   Is .... Nile or .... Amazon .... longest river in .... world?
5   I took .... bus and then .... train to the airport. .... bus was on time but .... train was late.
6   Several million visitors .... year are attracted to .... ski slopes on .... Alps.
7   I'll meet you outside .... post office. I'll be there in .... quarter of .... hour.
8   We lived in .... Netherlands before moving here. But before that we worked in .... Middle East.

1b Complete the essay. Use *the* or zero article (–).

Urban life past and present

(0) .... young people tend to think that (1) .... life was more difficult for (2) .... people in the past. Of course, (3) .... lives our parents led were different from (4) .... lives we lead today. For example, they couldn't rely as much on (5) .... modern technology as we do. When my parents were young, (6) .... computers were as big as a room and (7) .... mobile phone hadn't been invented yet!

On the other hand, I don't think there were as many social problems in those days. This is partly because (8) .... family was very important. For instance, (9) .... families took care of (10) .... old and weak so (11) .... homelessness wasn't (12) .... problem that it is today. In fact, in many ways (13) .... life was better in the past.

1c Complete the sentences. Use *a*, *the* or zero article (–).

0   In my opinion, ... education should be free.
1   .... education I got at school was excellent.
2   I'd like my children to have .... good education.

3   .... car is expensive to own and run but it's a reliable form of transport.
4   Unfortunately, ... car is a major cause of air pollution and global warming.
5   In some cities .... cars have been banned from the centre.

5

Grammar: *nouns, determiners, articles*

2 Types of noun

- There are two main types of noun: common nouns and proper nouns.
- A common noun is any noun that is not the name of a particular person, place or thing. Common nouns can be countable or uncountable: *a queen   boys   sugar*
- A proper noun names an individual person, place or thing and is spelt with a capital letter. Proper nouns include:
  - the names of people and titles when we are referring to specific people: *Helen   Mr Smith   the President (of France)   the Queen (of Sweden)*
  - places: *Thailand   Vancouver   the Tower of London*
  - nationalities and languages: *British   Turkish   Venezuelan*
  - days and months (but not seasons): *Monday   July*
  - titles of books, newspapers, films, paintings, etc: *Crime and Punishment   the Daily Telegraph   The Lord of the Rings   the Mona Lisa*
  - religions and festivals: *Buddhism/Buddhist   Christianity/Christian   Islam/Muslim   Easter   Ramadan*

▶▶ **See Appendix 1: Punctuation rules, page 199.**

PRACTICE

2 Re-write the sentences. Use capital letters where necessary.

0 I went to buckingham palace today. It was great.
I went to Buckingham Palace today. It was great.

1 It's open to visitors daily in the summer, from august to september.
....

2 I took the train to london and then the underground to victoria station. It's a short walk from there.
....

3 Fortunately, I speak german so I was able to join a group of tourists from germany, who were being shown round by a guide.
....

4 Have you met my sister jane? She's studying at the university of manchester.
....

5 She's coming home for christmas and then she's returning to manchester for new year's eve.
....

6 Would you like to come with us to see *titanic* at the odeon cinema on wednesday?
....

7 Did you hear about grace's promotion? She's taken over as head of the european division of the company.
....

8 That's great news! Does this mean she'll be moving to paris before the autumn?
....

Grammar: nouns, determiners, articles

3 Countable and uncountable nouns

- Countable nouns have a singular and plural form. Singular countable nouns can be used with *a/an*: *an appointment → two appointments*
- Uncountable nouns don't have a plural form and can't be used with *a/an*. They are followed by a singular verb. They refer to substances we think of as a mass or to abstract ideas: *bread   water   air   life   love   wealth   happiness*
- Some common uncountable nouns are: *accommodation, advice, beauty, behaviour, bread* (and other types of food), *English* (and other languages), *equipment, exercise, food, furniture, health, information, knowledge, luggage, maths* (and other subjects), *money, music, news, permission, progress, research, scenery, steel* (and other metals), *success, traffic, travel, trouble, water* (and other liquids), *weather, work*: *I'd like some **information**.*
- Some *-ing* words for activities are also uncountable: *dancing, running, swimming*: ***Swimming** is one of the best forms of exercise.*
- We can use countable noun + *of* to count many uncountable nouns:
  - *300 grams of cheese   a kilo of sugar   a litre of milk*
  - *a bottle of shampoo   a can of cola   a carton of juice   a cup of coffee   a glass of water   a jar of jam   a tin of olives   a tube of toothpaste*
  - *a bar of chocolate   a piece of advice/equipment/furniture   a handful of rice   a loaf of bread   a sheet of paper   a slice of bread   a spoonful of honey*
- Some nouns can be countable or uncountable, often with a change of meaning.

Uncountable noun	Countable noun
Beauty is only skin deep.	She's **a beauty**. (= a beautiful woman)
The napkins are made from linen **cloth**.	He wiped the table with **a** clean **cloth**.
Do you like your **coffee** black or white?	I'd like **a coffee**. (= a cup of coffee)
She has long dark **hair**.	There's **a hair** in my soup. (= one hair)
I don't eat **chicken**.	I bought **a chicken** for dinner.
I have **experience** in management.	I had **a** bad **experience** at work today.
Move over – I need more **room**.	There's **an** empty **room** next door.
There's plenty of **space** to study.	Sue cleared **a space** on her desk to work.
They're busy and haven't got **time**.	They had **a** good **time**.
He started **work** when he was fourteen.	He owns the collected **works** of Shakespeare.

You have beautiful **hair**.   There's **a hair** in my soup.

7

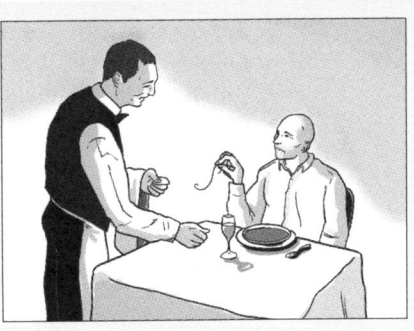

Grammar: *nouns, determiners, articles*

PRACTICE

3a Complete the conversations. Use the nouns in the box and *a/an* where necessary.

| cloth   cloth   experience   experience   glass   glass |
| noise   ~~room~~   room   university education |

0 **A:** Is there going to be enough ......**room**...... in the fridge for all this food?
   B: Don't worry – it's a large family-size fridge.
1 **A:** Could I have .... of water, please?
   B: Sure. Sorry. I've spilled it. Would you hand me .... to wipe it up, please?
2 **A:** I see you don't have ....
   B: No, but I have years of .... managing a business.
3 **A:** Nice suit. Is it silk?
   B: According to the label, it's made of fine woollen ....
4 **A:** I was really frightened last night. I was sure I heard .... downstairs.
   B: I had .... like that once and I called the police straightaway.
5 **A:** I need .... for the night. Have you got any vacancies?
   B: Yes, you're in luck. There's one free on the top floor.
6 **A:** What's happened? There's .... all over the floor.
   B: Oh, one of the kids kicked a football through the window again.

3b Complete the leaflet. Use the nouns in the box and *a/an* where necessary.

| appointment   classes   exercise   information   progress   swimming |
| ~~time~~   time   up-to-date equipment   valuable advice   work |

We're open from 7 a.m. to 10 p.m. so if you can't find (0) ......**time**...... to work out during the day, you can fit us in before or after you go to (1) .... However, do try and make (2) .... to consult one of our qualified instructors at (3) .... that's convenient for you. They will give you (4) .... about choosing the best exercise programme. Then once you start your programme, they will also help you make (5) .... towards becoming fitter and healthier.

Our gymnasium has a full range of (6) .... for running, cycling and weightlifting. Or, if you prefer (7) .... , try our Olympic size pool. We also have day and evening (8) .... in yoga and Pilates for those who would like a gentler form of (9) .... For more (10) .... about what we offer, you can phone, e-mail or drop by and see us!

4 Singular and plural nouns

- Most countable nouns have a singular and a plural form.
- To form the plural, we add -s to most nouns. There may also be other spelling changes: *event → events   tomato → tomatoes   opportunity → opportunities   knife → knives   wolf → wolves*
- Some nouns have an irregular plural: *child → children   foot → feet   man → men   mouse → mice   person → people   tooth → teeth   woman → women*
- Some nouns borrowed from other languages also have an irregular plural: *crisis → crises   phenomenon → phenomena*
- Some countable nouns have the same form in the singular and plural: *aircraft → aircraft   deer → deer   fish → fish   sheep → sheep*
- Some nouns end in -s in both the singular and plural: *crossroads → crossroads   means → means   series → series   species → species*
- Some nouns that end in -s are uncountable and are followed by a singular verb: *athletics, economics, maths, measles, news, physics:* **Maths is** *my best subject.*
- Some nouns are only plural and are followed by a plural verb. These include:
  - nouns ending in -s for things with two parts: *binoculars, glasses, jeans, pyjamas, scissors, shorts, trousers.* To count these nouns, we can use *a pair of*: *These* **jeans are** *too big for me.*   *This* **pair of jeans is** *too big for me.*
  - other nouns ending in -s: *belongings, clothes, congratulations, earnings, remains, outskirts, surroundings: Where* **are** *your* **belongings**?
- Some nouns can have a different meaning when they are in the plural.

Singular/Plural	Plural
She hurt her **arm**.	They carried **arms**. (= weapons)
Don't challenge his **authority**!	The **authorities** are worried about the problem.
Cheese has a high fat **content**.	The **contents** of the letter are a secret.
The **premise** of the novel is that there is life on other planets.	The company's **premises** are in the city centre.
Canada has vast natural **resources**, including oil.	He has considerable inner **resources**.
The operation restored his **sight**.	Let's go into town and see the **sights**.
You can go out on one **condition**: that you're home by midnight.	The **conditions** inside the prison were terrible.
Travel broadens the mind.	He wrote a book about his **travels** in the Far East.

- Collective nouns refer to groups of people: *army, audience, class, committee, community, company, crew, family, gang, government, group, orchestra, police, staff, team.* They can be followed by a singular or plural verb: *The school* **staff is** *excellent.* (= the group as a whole)   *Our* **staff are** *here to help.* (= each individual in the group)

▶▶ **See Appendix 2: Spelling rules, page 200.**

Grammar: *nouns, determiners, articles*

PRACTICE

4a Complete the sentences. Use the plural of the nouns in brackets.

0 There are ......*sheep*...... and ......*cows*...... grazing in the field. (sheep, cow)
1 There were .... , ... and .... aboard the doomed flight. (man, woman, child)
2 Technology has opened up new job .... in this field. (opportunity)
3 It was one of the best television .... of the last ten years. (series)
4 Before you serve the steaks, decorate with a few .... of lettuce. (leaf)
5 I've put the .... next to the .... and .... (glass, knife, fork)
6 The two .... faced each other across the river. (army)
7 Do you know how many .... of birds there are in the world? (species)
8 There were at least a thousand .... at the demonstration but nobody was carrying .... (person, arm)

4b Circle the correct answer.

There is little doubt that pollution (0) *is* / *are* contributing to changes in weather patterns. The melting of the polar ice is receiving a great deal of publicity but there are other (1) *phenomenon* / *phenomena* which we can also attribute to global warming. Plant and animal species (2) *is* / *are* losing their natural habitats and are in danger of extinction. Meanwhile, living (3) *condition* / *conditions* in many countries (4) *has* / *have* been affected by floods and droughts. Some say that governments (5) *is* / *are* not doing enough to solve the problem, while politicians claim they are doing the best they can with limited (6) *resource* / *resources*. In any case, we find ourselves at (7) *a* / *some* crossroads. Perhaps only a (8) *crisis* / *crises* will encourage us to change our habits.

4c Complete the news flashes. Use one word in each gap.

(0) ......*An*...... aircraft has gone down and news (1) .... now coming in about the crash. Rescue services have been sent to the area but the authorities (2) .... not releasing any more information about the accident at this point.

Fire has destroyed a home in South London. All the members of the family (3) .... safe but their belongings (4) .... been destroyed and they will be homeless for some time. The family (5) .... said they have no idea what caused the blaze. The police (6) .... treating the incident as suspicious.

Grammar: nouns, determiners, articles

5 *some, any, no, none*, etc.

- We use the following quantifiers with plural countable nouns and uncountable nouns: *some, any, a lot of, lots of, enough* and *plenty of*.
- We use *some* in affirmative sentences, requests and offers to mean 'not much/many' or 'a certain amount/number of': There are **some eggs** in the cupboard. Can I have **some** tea?
  Some can also mean 'a large number/amount of': It will be **some time** before we're ready.
- We use *any* in negative sentences and questions: I don't have **any time**. (not any = no) → I have **no time**. (Not ~~I don't have no time.~~) Do you need **any** more **information**? There was **hardly any traffic** on the roads. (hardly any = very little)
- Compare: Is there **any bread** left? (a neutral question) Is there **some bread** left? (I hope or expect the answer will be 'yes'.)
- In affirmative sentences, *any* means 'it doesn't matter which one': You can have **any item** on the list.
- *A lot of* and *lots of* refer to large quantities. They are informal. Other expressions include *loads of* (informal) and *dozens of*: I eat **a lot of fresh vegetables and fruit**. Do you have **lots of luggage**? Don't worry – there's **loads of time**. She's got **dozens of DVDs**.
- *Enough* means 'as much as we need'; *plenty of* means 'more than we need': Do we have **enough food**? They have **plenty of money**.

some/any/none + of before pronouns, etc.

- We can use *some/any/none of* before pronouns (*you, us*), possessives (*my, his*), *this/that*, etc.: **Some/None of us** left early. Were **any of his** friends there?
- We use *none of* to talk about three or more things or people. We can use a singular or plural verb. A singular verb is more common in formal writing: **None of my friends was/were** at the party.

some, any, none, enough, plenty as pronouns

- *Some, any, enough* and *plenty* can also be pronouns. *None* is always a pronoun: Would you like **some**? I haven't got **any**. 'Have you had **enough** to eat?' 'Yes, **plenty**!' There are **none** left.

someone/somebody, anyone/anybody, no one/nobody

- The differences between the pronouns *someone, anyone*, etc. are the same as those between *some, any*, etc.
- We use *someone/somebody, anyone/anybody* and *no one/nobody* to refer to people. The pairs of words mean the same: **Someone/Somebody** is at the door. **No one/Nobody** should leave the room.
- We use *something/anything/nothing* to refer to things or actions: There's **something** on your jacket. I'm not telling you **anything**. (= I'm telling you nothing.) **Nothing** happened yesterday.

Grammar: *nouns, determiners, articles*

PRACTICE

5a **Complete the sentences. Use *some*, *any*, *no* or *somebody*, *anybody*, etc.**

0 ......*Some*...... of us are going to a club tonight. Would you like to come?
1 I think there's .... at the door. Do you see .... ?
2 There was .... traffic on the roads so they got here very quickly.
3 Is there .... I can do to help with dinner? If not, I'll do my homework.
4 This town is really boring – .... ever happens here.
5 The loan went .... way towards paying her university fees.
6 There was hardly .... at the cinema – it was nearly empty.
7 Thank you for listening to me. Now, if .... has any more questions, we'll finish for today.
8 Please don't make .... noise. The baby's sleeping.

5b **Complete the e-mail. Use one word in each gap.**

I haven't heard from you for (0) ......*some*...... time so I thought I'd get in touch. There's hardly (1) .... time left until our exams and for weeks it seems as if I've done (2) .... but study. The teachers keep reminding us that (3) .... of the exams will be easy and no doubt they will be even more difficult than I expect. But there's (4) .... I can do except keep working.

When the exams are over, I'm going to take (5) .... time off and go on holiday with (6) .... people in my class. (7) .... of us care where we go as long as it's somewhere warm!

Anyway, why haven't I heard (8) .... from you? Are you seeing (9) .... these days? I was going out with (10) .... but that finished a few weeks ago. Just as well – I have (11) .... time for a social life at the moment and I won't have (12) .... until these exams are over!

5c **Complete the conversations. Use *some (of)*, *any (of)*, *no*, *none (of)*, *enough* or *plenty*. Sometimes more than one answer is possible.**

0 A: Oh, dear! Isn't there ......*any*...... money left?
   B: Yes, there is – a little. Why? Do you need to borrow ......*some*...... ?
1 A: .... us are happy about what you did.
   B: Sorry, but you gave me .... alternative.
2 A: Did you have .... trouble finding us?
   B: .... at all. I came straight here.
3 A: I'd love some tea. Have you got .... ?
   B: Sorry, there's .... left.

4 A: There aren't .... chairs for everyone.
   B: Don't worry! There are .... in the next room.
5 A: You can choose .... the books on the list. It doesn't matter which ones.
   B: Thanks. I've already read .... them.
6 A: Have you prepared .... food for the party?
   B: .... ! I'm sure people won't be able to eat it all and we'll probably have to throw .... away.

6 *much, many, a lot, etc.*

Quantifiers with plural countable nouns
- We use *many, a few, few, several* and *a large number of* with plural countable nouns.
- *Many* is mainly used in questions and negatives. In affirmative sentences it is more formal than *a lot of/lots of*: How **many times** have you been there?   There **aren't many fish** in this lake.   **Many people** travel to the city centre for work.
- *Too many* means 'more than we need': There are **too many violent programmes** on television these days.
- *A few* (= some) has a positive meaning: I've got **a few minutes** if you want to talk to me about it.
- *Few* (= almost none) has a negative meaning and is formal: **Few people** remember what happened.
- *Several* means 'more than a few but not a lot': I reminded him **several times** but he forgot.
- *A large number of* is formal. It is usually followed by a plural verb: **A large number of people were** at the party.

Quantifiers with uncountable nouns
- We use *much, a little, little* and *a great deal of* with uncountable nouns.
- *Much* is mainly used in questions and negatives. In affirmative sentences it is more formal than *a lot of/lots of*: How **much money** have you got?   I haven't got **much time** left.   After **much discussion** we arrived at a decision.
- *Too much* means 'more than we need': You added **too much water**.
- *A little* (= some) has a positive meaning: I can translate for you – I speak **a little German**.
- *Little* (= almost none) has a negative meaning and is formal: We have **little money** to waste on luxuries.
- *A great deal of* (= a lot of) is formal: There's **a great deal of work** to be done.

many/much, etc. + of
- We can use *many/much/a few/few/a little/little/several + of* before pronouns, articles, possessives, *this/that*, etc.: **Many of them** travel by train.   I'd like **a little of that**.   **Several of our** friends were at the party.
- We can also use *dozens/hundreds/thousands + of +* plural noun: **Thousands of people** gathered to watch the parade.

Grammar: *nouns, determiners, articles*

PRACTICE

6a Circle the correct answer.

0 **A:** He's a new artist and his work is attracting *a large number of /* (*a great deal of*) attention.
   B: That's right. (*A large number of*) / *A great deal of* visitors attended his last exhibition.

1 **A:** I have very *few / little* time – just *a few / a little* minutes.
   B: Don't worry. This won't take *much / many* time.

2 **A:** I have to buy *a little / a few* things at the supermarket.
   B: We only have *a little / a few* milk left. Would you get some while you're out?

3 **A:** I don't have *much / many* money with me. Could I borrow some, please?
   B: *How much / How many* would you like to borrow?

4 **A:** Do you get *much / many* visitors here in the winter?
   B: Not really. That's why *much of / many of* our staff are part-time.

5 **A:** There's *too much / too many* work here for one person to do.
   B: I know, and there are *too little / too few* people to help.

6 **A:** There's been *a great deal of / a large number of* interest in the house but no one's made an offer to buy it yet.
   B: I'm surprised. There aren't *many / much* places as nice as this in the area.

7 **A:** I don't know *how many / how much* people are likely to come to the meeting.
   B: I'm sure some won't be able to make it. *Few / A few* have already sent their apologies.

8 **A:** Is Anne here?
   B: I'm afraid she left an hour ago with *several / several of* her colleagues.

6b Complete the sentences. Use *a little*, *little*, *a few* or *few*.

0 There's ......*little*...... doubt in my mind that he's guilty.
1 We have .... time, so don't hurry too much.
2 I paid .... attention to what he was saying, I'm afraid.
3 She called to say she's going to be .... minutes late.
4 There's .... money left – in fact, we're virtually broke.
5 Unfortunately, there were very .... people in the audience.
6 Would you like .... more coffee?
7 There are .... more things I'd like to discuss.
8 All we can offer at the moment are low-paid jobs that .... people want.

Grammar: *nouns, determiners, articles*

6c Complete the sentences. Use *of* where necessary.

0 Much ....*of*.... the city was destroyed in the war but a great deal ....*of*.... it has been restored since then.
1 I've lived in this village for a number .... years.
2 I've never seen this many .... people at a local event.
3 Jane arrived at the meeting with a few .... her colleagues – several .... them had come to support her.
4 Much .... this work was started last year.
5 Very little .... his money was left after the taxes had been paid.
6 You may have to wait several .... months for the decision.
7 Hundreds .... people were killed when the earthquake struck.
8 Too much .... time has been spent on this problem.

6d Look at the results of a survey about what young people do after school. Then complete the text. Use one word in each gap.

Number of people interviewed: 60

19 years old: 70%   18 years old: 10%
17 years old: 5%   16 years old: 15%

Results of survey

		Yes	No
1	Do you take part in sporting activities?	48	12
2	Do you take advantage of extra tuition offered by your school/college?	40	20
3	Do you have a part-time job?	22	38
4	Are you a member of a school/college club or society?	10	50
5	Do you do volunteer work (work for which you don't get paid)?	4	56

We asked sixty students what activities they took part in after school or college. The students were aged sixteen to nineteen but a large (0) ....*number*.... were closer to nineteen years of age. On the whole, the students that we interviewed expressed a great (1) .... of interest in sports. Extra tuition in difficult subjects was also popular with (2) .... students although one third did not take advantage of this opportunity. (3) .... students had a part-time job but most said they preferred to concentrate on their studies.

Turning to the less popular activities, there wasn't a (4) .... deal of interest in joining school clubs. Although a (5) .... students said they were members of a club, more than 80% said they preferred to do other things. Volunteer work was the least popular activity and there was (6) .... interest in this activity; very (7) .... students said they did unpaid work after school.

15

Grammar: *nouns, determiners, articles*

7 both, either, neither, etc.

both (of), either (of), neither (of)
- We can use *both (of), either (of)* and *neither (of)* to talk about two people or things.
- *Both* means 'one and the other'. The pattern is: *both (of)* + plural noun + plural verb: **Both shoes have** holes in them. **Both of my parents are** teachers.
- *Either* means 'one or the other'. The pattern is: *either* + singular noun + singular verb OR *either of* + plural noun + singular/plural verb: *'What shall we go to see tonight?' 'Either film is fine. / Either of these films is/are fine.'*
- *Neither* means 'not one or the other'. The pattern is: *neither* + singular noun + singular verb OR *neither of* + plural noun + singular/plural verb: **Neither team is** winning. **Neither of her grandparents is/are** alive.
- We use *both/either/neither* + *of* before pronouns: **Both of us** can help you.
- We can use *both (of)/either (of)/neither (of)* + noun/pronoun after the verb: I bought **both T-shirts**. I don't like **either pair of** shoes. I called **neither of them**.
- We can use *both, either* and *neither* on their own: I've got two brothers and **both** are at college. **Neither** is married.

each (of), every
- We use *each/every* + singular noun + singular verb. We prefer *each* when we think of the people or things in a group separately and *every* when we think of them together: **Each member** of the family **contributes**. **Every room was** painted white.
- We use *each (one) of/every one of* + plural noun/pronoun/possessive + singular verb: **Each (one) of/Every one of the boys has** a job.
- We use *each* but not *every* to talk about two people or things: **Each tyre** on my bicycle has a puncture.
- We can use *each* as a pronoun, before a verb, after a verb and object, or after the verb *be*: They **each** left early. I gave them ten pounds **each**. The tickets are **each** worth twenty pounds.
- We use *every* but not *each* with *almost, nearly* and *not*: **Nearly/Almost every** child attended the party but **not every** one enjoyed it.

all (of), half (of), the whole (of)
- To talk about the complete amount or total number of people or things in general, we use *all*: **All living things** need oxygen to breathe. I hate **all violence**.
- To talk about the people or things in a specific group, we can use *all (of)*: **All (of) the people on the bus** were tired.
- We use *all (of)/half (of)/a quarter of*, etc. + uncountable noun + singular verb OR *all (of)/half (of)/a quarter of*, etc. + plural noun + plural verb: **All (of) the information was** useful. **All (of) the children are** here.
- We use *the whole* + singular countable noun + singular verb: **The whole world was** shocked by the catastrophe.
- We use *all/half (of)* + noun/pronoun: **All/Half (of) the food** was eaten.
- We use *all* and *whole* in some time expressions: *all* day/evening   the **whole** day/evening   *all* my life   my **whole** life
- Compare: **All** the people **are** leaving now.   **Everybody is** leaving now.

16

Grammar: *nouns, determiners, articles*

PRACTICE

7a Circle the correct answer.

0 *(All)/ Every* cats are born with blue eyes.
1 Wheat is grown on *all / every* continent except Antarctica.
2 *All / Each* person has a unique fingerprint and tongue print.
3 The giraffe, camel and cat are the only animals that move *both / either* their left feet and then *both / neither* their right feet when walking.
4 Only about *a tenth / a tenth of* the plants and animals that ever lived inhabit the earth today.
5 Honeybees kill more people than *each of / all of* the poisonous snakes in the world combined.
6 A worker bee produces less than a teaspoon of honey in its *all / whole* life.

7b Complete the sentences. Use the present simple of the verbs in brackets.

0 A: ......*Are*...... either of the twins good swimmers? (be)
   B: Yes, both of them ......*are*...... excellent swimmers. (be)
1 A: Which newspaper would you like to read?
   B: The *Times* or the *Guardian*. Either .... fine, thanks. (be)
2 A: .... every child .... a prize? (get)
   B: No, but each child who takes part .... a small gift. (get)
3 A: Who .... each person in the team responsible to? (be)
   B: Everyone .... to the Sales Manager. (report)
4 A: Where .... all the money I gave you? (be)
   B: Half of it .... still in my bank account. (be)
5 A: .... all of the things I asked you to get in the kitchen? (be)
   B: Yes. I put them away for you.

7c Complete the text. Use one word in each gap.

"I come from a large family. (0) ......*Both*...... my parents are doctors but they're retired now so (1) .... of them practises any longer. I have two sisters but I don't think (2) .... of them will go to university as they're (3) .... married and (4) .... of them has a child – one sister has a little boy and the other has a girl.

Because I'm my parents' only son, (5) .... person in the family expected I'd go to medical school – so that's what I did. When I graduated, my (6) .... family came to the ceremony. My parents (7) .... come from a large family so I have a lot of aunts, uncles and cousins – and almost (8) .... of them came to the ceremony too. Afterwards we had a party at our house. (9) .... guest brought something to eat and to my surprise, they'd (10) .... brought me a gift! The best part of the (11) .... day, though, was having (12) .... room in the house filled with family that I hadn't seen for ages."

17

Grammar: *nouns, determiners, articles*

8 Pronouns

Subject pronouns	Object pronouns	Reflexive pronouns
I	me	myself
you	you	yourself
he, she, it	him, her, it	himself, herself, itself
we	us	ourselves
you	you	yourselves
they	them	themselves

Subject and object pronouns
- We use subject pronouns before the verb in a clause or sentence. We use object pronouns after the verb or a preposition: *I left early.   My friend and I watched TV.   Come and see us.   Look at John and her!* (Not *Look at John and she!*)   *I have a problem and I'd like to talk to you about it.*

⚠ Notice this informal use of the object pronoun *me*: **Me** *and my family live in Glasgow.*

- *You* can mean 'people in general', including the speaker. *One* has a similar meaning but is formal: **You** *can't be too careful these days!   Great art makes* **one** *think.*
- *They* can mean 'people in general', excluding the speaker, or 'the authorities': **They** *say it's going to be a hot summer.*
- *They* and *them* can refer to a single person after *someone, anyone* and *no one*: **Someone** *said* **they** *would lock up after the meeting.   If* **anyone** *rings, tell* **them** *I'm in a meeting.*

Reflexive pronouns
- We use reflexive pronouns after a verb or preposition when the same person is the subject and object of the verb: *I've cut* **myself**.   *We bought them for* **ourselves**.
- When the subject and object are not the same, we can use *each other* or *one another*: *We bought them for* **each other/one another**.
- A few verbs are followed by a reflexive pronoun to form an idiom: **Behave yourself!**   *We* **enjoyed ourselves**.   *They* **helped themselves** *to sandwiches.*

⚠ These verbs don't normally take reflexive pronouns in English: *wash, shave, dress: Gerald* **shaves** *every morning.* (Not *Gerald shaves himself every morning.*)

- We can use a reflexive pronoun to emphasise the noun or pronoun before it. If the reflexive pronoun refers to the subject, it can come at the end of the sentence: **Amelia herself** *designed the house.   Amelia designed the house* **herself**.
- *by myself/himself*, etc. means 'alone': *I live* **by myself**. (= on my own)

one, ones
- We can use *one/ones* to avoid repeating a countable noun: *We missed the bus so we waited for the next* **one**.   *My favourite biscuits are the* **ones** *with chocolate chips.*

Grammar: *nouns, determiners, articles*

PRACTICE

8a **Complete the sentences. Use pronouns or *one another*.**

0 I'm hungry. I think I'll make ......*myself*...... something to eat.

1 A: Did you decorate the house .... ?
   B: Yes, we did most of it ....

2 The train was crowded so we decided to catch a later ....

3 I'm surprised they didn't do the job .... I suppose .... was too much work for ....

4 Isabel and Tyler are neighbours. They see .... nearly every day.

5 A: My wife and .... are going on holiday.
   B: Be sure you send my husband and .... a postcard.

6 .... say it's only through solitude that one gets to know ....

7 The washing machine switches .... off when it's done.

8 My sister and I always call .... during the holidays.

9 It was the King .... who gave the opening address.

10 Please help .... to another slice of cake. There's plenty left.

11 I hope Maria behaved .... at school today.

12 I don't know whether to buy the small blue glasses or the large green .... Please help .... to choose.

8b **Complete the texts. Use pronouns.**

"Any city can be dangerous but a little common sense will keep (0) ......*you*...... safe. Let's talk about how to take care of (1) .... when (2) ....'re travelling. If (3) ....'re walking, choose busy streets during the day and never walk through dark areas by (4) .... at night. Always go out with a friend at night – there's safety in numbers. If (5) ....'re using public transport, put handbags and packages on your lap – not on an empty seat where (6) .... can be grabbed by a passing thief. Finally, if your car breaks down and someone offers to help, don't unlock your car door – ask (7) .... to ring the police instead. (8) .... say you can never be too careful – and I'm afraid that's absolutely correct."

> It is important that one knows how to take care of (9) .... when travelling in a city.
>
> - When on foot, (10) .... should choose busy streets whenever possible during the day and avoid walking by (11) .... at night.
> - On public transport, handbags and packages should be kept on one's lap and not left by (12) .... on an empty seat.
> - Car doors should be kept locked. If one's car breaks down and a stranger offers to help, (13) .... should not be allowed to enter the car.
>
> Remember: (14) .... can never be too careful.

Grammar: **nouns, determiners, articles**

9 Possessive *'s*, possessive *of*, etc.

We can show the relationship of possession between nouns/noun phrases in several ways.

Possessive *'s*
- We usually use the possessive *'s* for people, groups of people and animals. We add *'s* to singular nouns and plural nouns that don't end in *-s*, and an apostrophe (') to plural nouns that end in *-s*: **Sarah's** shoes   the **government's** policy   the **cat's** whiskers   my **friend's** mother (one friend)   my **friends'** mothers (two or more friends)   **men's** clothing   **Liam and Chloe's** home
- We can omit the second noun when the meaning is clear from the context: when we are talking about where someone lives or works, or for some shops and businesses: *'Did you go to **John's** party?' 'No, I went to **Roger and Clare's**.'* (= Roger and Clare's party)   *We had dinner at **Barbara's**.* (= Barbara's house)   *He's going to **the chemist's**.* (= the chemist's shop)
- We can use *'s* or an apostrophe in some expressions with periods of time: *today's* weather   *yesterday's* newspaper   *this term's* results   *a week's* holiday   *three minutes'* silence
- When a proper name ends in *-s*, we can use *'s* or an apostrophe: *Charles'/Charles's* flat

noun + *of* + noun
- We usually use noun + *of* + noun to talk about things: *the back of the house* (Not ~~the house's back~~)   *the top of the mountain*
- We prefer *'s* when the first noun/noun phrase is much shorter than the second noun/noun phrase: *the school's rules regarding truancy and lateness* (Not ~~the rules regarding truancy and lateness of the school~~)
- We sometimes use *of* + *'s* together: *a cousin of my mother's* (= my mother's cousin)

noun + noun
- We often use noun + noun, especially when we are talking about parts of things: *the bathroom door*   *a computer screen*

PRACTICE

9a Circle the correct answer.

0 A: Have you heard *the news of yesterday* / *(yesterday's news)* about the plane crash?
   B: No. Where did it happen?

1 A: I've only read *the book's first chapter* / *the first chapter of the book* so far.
   B: Keep going. It's a really interesting story.

2 A: Are you going to *Jane's and Mark's* / *Jane and Mark's* wedding on Saturday?
   B: No, we're going to *Nathan and Alison's* / *Nathan's and Alison's*. They're *friends of my parent's* / *friends of my parents'*.

3 A: Have you got *the front door's key* / *the key of the front door* in your bag?
   B: No. Haven't you got it?

Grammar: *nouns, determiners, articles*

4 **A:** I've got a toothache. I have to go to *the dentist's / the dentists'*.
B: Good luck. When I tried to make an appointment, I had to wait for three weeks.

5 **A:** Do you know what *the university's policy on handing in late assignments / the policy on handing in late assignments of the university* is?
B: No, but why don't you ask the secretary?

9b Complete the sentences. Use the words in brackets.

0 I'm going to my ….*aunt's house*…. tonight. It's her eightieth birthday. (aunt / house)

1 The ……………………. to the film was positive. (audience / reaction)

2 Yesterday we celebrated my ……………………. . (parents / wedding anniversary)

3 They've closed the ……………………. for refurbishment. (women / changing room)

4 We spent the weekend at my ……………………. . It's a lovely place. (friend / cottage)

5 ……………………. are predicted to be even higher than ……………………. . (next year / sales figures, this year)

6 ……………………. is going to Leeds University next year. (James / daughter)

7 The ……………………. gave each child a small present. (boys / teacher)

8 The ……………………. are well known. (city / problems of crime and unemployment)

9 I'm taking ……………………. in ……………………. . (two weeks / holiday, a week / time)

10 Don't pull the ……………………. . It's cruel and besides, the dog might bite you. (dog / tail)

9c Complete the sentences. Use one word from each box in each sentence.

centre	children	computer	daughter	~~front~~	kitchen	table	top

city	friends	leg	page	party	~~queue~~	screen	window

0 They waited for ages to get to the ….*front of the queue*…. but the performance was worth the wait.

1 We invited our youngest ……………………. to the house for a ……………………. when she turned ten years old.

2 He opened the ……………………. to let out the smoke from the burnt roast.

3 Public transport will take you into the ……………………. , where you will find many shops and restaurants.

4 Before you start the test, write your name at the ……………………. .

5 That ……………………. is broken so don't put anything on the table or it will collapse.

6 She gets headaches if she stares at a ……………………. for many hours.

Check 1 Nouns, determiners, articles

1 Choose the correct answer A, B, C or D.

Violet Jessop was a stewardess on the White Star Line for (1) ...... years in the 1900s. In 1911 she was serving on the *Olympic* when it collided with another ship, *HMS Hawke*. (2) ...... ships were damaged but fortunately, (3) ...... on either ship lost their lives.

The following year Violet was serving on the *Titanic* when it struck an iceberg and sank. As we know, (4) ...... the passengers and (5) ...... lost their lives but Violet survived. In 1916, during (6) ...... First World War, Violet was working as a Red Cross nurse aboard *HMS Britannic* when it also sank after striking a mine. (7) ...... of those on board died. Violet was washed overboard and hit by one of (8) ...... ship's propellers but she managed to save (9) ...... by grabbing on to a life jacket as it floated past her.

Violet had never learned to swim. (10) ...... might say that Violet had (11) ...... luck because she was involved in three disasters at sea. On the other hand, for a non-swimmer with a career on the sea, it could be said she had (12) ...... of luck!

1 A plenty	B many of	C several	D several of
2 A Both	B Each	C Either	D Neither
3 A someone	B anyone	C no one	D everyone
4 A many	B many of	C much	D much of
5 A crew	B crews	C crew's	D a crew
6 A a	B some	C any	D the
7 A A great deal	B A large number	C A little	D Much
8 A a	B some	C any	D the
9 A her	B herself	C it	D –
10 A One	B Oneself	C She	D Herself
11 A few	B a few	C little	D a little
12 A enough	B much	C a large number	D a great deal

/ 12

2 Complete the sentences. Use *a*, *an*, *the* or zero article (–).

13 .... rich should do more to help .... poor.
14 .... travel adds .... interest and .... variety to .... life.
15 .... dictionary is .... important tool in learning .... language.
16 You should leave .... space between paragraphs.
17 .... horse has been domesticated for thousands of years.
18 Excuse me, but is there .... room for my luggage over there?
19 I don't have .... time now. Could we speak later?

/ 7

3 Correct the sentences.

20 A: Is thailand a buddhist country?
　 B: Yes, it is.
　 ....

21 A: What do you think of the president of france?
　 B: I'm not sure.
　 ....

22 A: I'd love to buy new furnitures for my home.
　 B: Perhaps one day you will.
　 ....

23 A: He felt like a King when he won first prize!
　 B: I bet he did!
　 ....

24 A: Is the binoculars yours?
　 B: Yes.
　 ....

25 A: Physics are my worst subject.
　 B: Really?
　 ....

26 A: Have you ever watched a game of american football?
　 B: No. Have you?
　 ....

/ 7

4 Complete the conversations. Use one word in each gap.

A: Have you got any money for the groceries?
B: I've got £50.
A: That's (27) .... ! We only need bread and milk.

A: I didn't understand (28) .... Johan said. Did you?
B: No, but don't pay (29) .... attention to him. Sometimes he (30) .... doesn't know what he means.

A: Where has (31) .... gone?
B: Home. They left a couple of hours ago.

A: Is the job finished yet?
B: Yes, (32) .... the work has been done.

A: Is everybody happy with the decision?
B: Not really. (33) .... of us has a different opinion about what we should do.

/ 7

5 Circle the correct answer.

34 A: We have *an hour's wait / an hours' wait* before the meeting.
　 B: As long as that?

35 A: I'm looking for a book on *the history of Turkey / Turkey's history*.
　 B: Try the third shelf down on your left.

36 A: I've got *three week's holiday / three weeks' holiday* this year.
　 B: I bet you're looking forward to it!

37 A: Don't leave your *belongings / belonging* unattended when you're at the airport.
　 B: Of course. I'll be careful.

38 A: How many of *the girl's mothers / the girls' mothers* came to the meeting?
　 B: Most of them, I think.

39 A: Are the children old enough to *dress / dress themselves*?
　 B: Not quite.

40 A: We're spending a week at *Helmut and Trudy's / Helmut's and Trudy's*.
　 B: That sounds like fun.

/ 7

Total: / 40

Self-check

Wrong answers	Look again at	Try CD-ROM
6, 8, 13, 14, 15, 17	Unit 1	Exercise 1
20, 21, 23, 26	Unit 2	Exercise 2
16, 18, 19, 22	Unit 3	Exercise 3
5, 24, 25, 37	Unit 4	Exercise 4
3, 27, 28, 29, 31	Unit 5	Exercise 5
1, 4, 7, 11, 12	Unit 6	Exercise 6
2, 32, 33	Unit 7	Exercise 7
9, 10, 30, 39	Unit 8	Exercise 8
34, 35, 36, 38, 40	Unit 9	Exercise 9

Now do **Check 1**

Adjectives and adverbs

10 Position and order of adjectives

- Adjectives can come before a noun (attributive adjectives). They can also come after linking verbs (predicative adjectives): *appear, be, become, feel, get, grow, keep, look, seem, smell, sound, stay, taste, turn*: She's an **intelligent woman**.   In the summer it **gets** very **hot**.   The leaves of the trees **turned red** and **brown** in autumn.
- Some adjectives can only come before a noun: *chief, elder, indoor, inner, live, main, only, outdoor, outer, principle*: It was a **live concert**.
- Some adjectives can only come after a verb:
  - *fine, ill, (un)well*: 'How is she?' '**She's fine**.'
  - *afraid, alike, alive, alone, asleep, awake*: He **was alone** and felt frightened.
  - *glad, sorry, upset*: You **seem upset**. What's wrong?
- If there is more than one adjective before a noun, this is the most common order:

Opinion	Size	Other qualities	Age	Shape	Colour	Origin	Material	Type
beautiful	large	cold	old	oval	brown	Chinese	wooden	electric

- We don't usually use commas between the adjectives before a noun:
  an ugly concrete building   a tiny round brass button   a difficult new theory   blue Italian ceramic tiles   expensive electronic equipment
- If there are two adjectives of the same type before the noun, we can join them with *and*. When there are more than two adjectives, we use commas and *and* before the last adjective. The order of adjectives is usually not important in these cases: *It's a **violent and shocking/shocking and violent** film.   She wants a **stable, warm and loving** relationship.*
- We always use *and* to join two colour adjectives and after linking verbs: *The boy wore a **red and blue** shirt.   It's **small and lightweight**.   I feel **cold and tired**.*

PRACTICE

10a Put the words in the correct order. Use commas where necessary.

0   unwell / is / James / feeling / today
    James is feeling unwell today.

1   hair / grey / to turn / Alice's / is beginning
    ....

2   that / delicious / beef stew / smells
    ....

3   you / I'll meet / main / entrance / outside / the
    ....

4   a(n) / have / Eric and Mary / indoor / swimming pool
    ....

24

5 the neighbours' / kept / me / party / awake / all night
....

6 about / Mark / something / upset / looks
....

7 they / gave me / round / photograph frame / a / silver-plated / gorgeous
....

8 carpet / a(n) / Mia / bought / old / beautiful / Chinese
....

9 a / Samuel / businessman / well-respected / is / and / wealthy
....

10 wore / silk / and / Julie / a / pink / brown / dress
....

10b Complete the letter. Use the words in the box. Put them in the correct order and add *and* where necessary.

> amazing / antique / Chinese
> black / gold / wooden
> charming / stone / whitewashed
> clean / linen / white
> enjoyable / restful
> ~~summer / fantastic~~
> Greek / small
> outdoor / traditional
> lovely / warm
> round / wooden

I must tell you about the (0) ....*fantastic summer*............ holiday we're having. We're staying in a(n) (1) .... house on a(n) (2) .... island. It's close to the sea, which at this time of year is (3) .... – the perfect temperature for swimming.

    The food here is very good. For lunch we usually go to a(n) (4) .... restaurant, sit in the garden at (5) .... tables with (6) .... tablecloths and treat ourselves to the local specialities. This evening we're going to a nearby taverna and then on to a live performance of music and dancing.

    The local shops are a lot of fun. You know I've been looking for something for my sitting room? The other day I was walking through the flea market and I saw a(n) (7) .... mirror with a(n) (8) .... frame. Of course, I bought it immediately – now all I have to worry about is getting it home on the plane!

    Speaking of the plane, we fly home in a couple of days. It's been a(n) (9) .... holiday and I'll be sorry to leave this island.

Grammar: *adjectives and adverbs*

11 Adjective or adverb?

- Adjectives describe a noun or pronoun: *There was a **magnificent view** from the top of the mountain.   The **view** was **magnificent**.   It was **magnificent**.*
- Adverbs describe verbs. We form many adverbs by adding *-ly* to an adjective: *bad → badly   easy → easily   economic → economically*
- Some words that end in *-ly* are adjectives, not adverbs: *friendly, lively, lonely, lovely, silly*. We can't make adverbs from them so we use an adverbial phrase: *in a friendly/lively/silly way*: *They greeted me **in a friendly way**.*
- Some adjectives and adverbs have the same form: *early, fast, free, hard, high, late, straight, wide*: *Let's catch the **early** train to London.   We arrived at the train station **early**.   There is snow all year round on some **high** mountains.   She threw the ball **high** into the air.*
- Some adjectives form two adverbs with different meanings: *free → free/freely   hard → hard/hardly   high → high/highly   late → late/lately   wide → wide/widely*: *You can get advice **free** from the local library.   I can breathe more **freely** now.   He works **hard**.   I **hardly** know him.   I came home **late** last night. I've been really tired **lately**.*

PRACTICE

11a Circle the correct answer.

0 Olivia's looking very (healthy) / healthily since she came back from her holiday.
1 Luke did very *good / well* in the exam.
2 I want you to answer the question *truthful / truthfully*.
3 Entering the war was a *political / politically* mistake.
4 The local team won the match *easy / easily*.
5 Since moving out of the family home, Alex has felt *lonely / in a lonely way*.
6 The teacher conducted the lesson *lively / in a lively way*.
7 I'll finish the report by Friday – it won't be *late / lately*.
8 He gave the door a *hard / hardly* push but it *hard / hardly* moved.

11b Complete the sentences. Use adverbs or adverbial phrases.

0 Amelia gave a confident presentation. She presented her ideas *confidently*.
1 Gavin gave me a sincere apology. He apologised ....
2 The children are noisy. They're playing ....
3 This building makes economic use of space. It uses space ....
4 Adrian's behaviour was sensible. He behaved ....
5 The match will be shown on national television. It will be shown ....
6 I know I was foolish. I don't know why I behaved so ....
7 My teacher has a friendly smile. She smiles ....
8 Michael is a fast driver. He drives ....

Grammar: adjectives and adverbs

11c Complete the conversations. Use the correct form of the words in the box.

> free (x2)   ~~hard~~ (x2)   high (x2)   late (x2)   wide

0   A: I can ....*hardly*.... believe it. I've passed my driving test!
    B: Why are you surprised? You worked ....*hard*.... and you deserved to pass it.
1   A: How much are the tickets?
    B: They're five pounds for adults but children can travel ....
2   A: Where have you been? I haven't seen you around ....
    B: Didn't I tell you? We've been on holiday. We stayed at a fabulous hotel .... in the mountains.
3   A: Let's go outside so that we can talk ....
    B: Why? Are you afraid of being overheard?
4   A: Do be careful. That solvent is .... flammable so you must keep it away from open flames.
    B: Don't worry. I'll put it outside in the garden shed.
5   A: Open your mouth .... , please. The tooth that's bothering you is right at the back.
    B: I know. Will this take long? I don't want to be .... getting back to work.

11d Complete the article. Use the correct form of the words in brackets.

THE LEAST SUCCESSFUL TOURIST

In 1977 Mr Nicholas Scotti of San Francisco flew to Italy to visit some cousins. The plane stopped (0) ....*briefly*.... (brief) in New York and Mr Scotti (1) .... (mistaken) believed he had arrived at Rome Airport. He got out of the plane but of course, his cousins were not there to greet him. Mr Scotti (2) .... (eventual) decided to try to find his own way to their address. On the journey he noticed that English was spoken (3) .... (wide). 'You can't escape from Americans,' thought Mr Scotti, a little (4) .... (sad). 'They're everywhere.'

   Mr Scotti did not speak much English himself so he (5) .... (polite) asked a policeman, in Italian, the way to the bus station. (6) .... (lucky), the policeman was from Naples and replied in the same language. After travelling around on buses for twelve hours, Mr Scotti was taken by a kind bus driver to a second policeman, who spoke to Mr Scotti in English. The policeman tried (7) .... (hard) to explain but Mr Scotti (8) .... (stubborn) refused to believe he was in New York. In the end, they took him to the airport in a police car. They didn't have much time so they had to drive very (9) .... (fast). 'You see,' said Mr Scotti (10) .... (confident), 'I know that I'm in Italy. This is the way that Italians drive.'

27

Grammar: *adjectives and adverbs*

12 Position and order of adverbs

Adverbs and adverbial phrases can come in different positions in a sentence: at the beginning, in the middle or at the end. The position depends partly on the kind of adverb/adverbial phrase and what we want to emphasise in the sentence.

Adverbs of frequency
- Adverbs of frequency (e.g. *always, often, rarely*) usually come before the main verb but after an auxiliary verb or the verb *be*: *We **sometimes meet** for lunch.   I have **always wanted** to go there.   I am **usually** in bed before midnight.*
- Some adverbs of frequency (e.g. *often, sometimes, occasionally*) can also come at the beginning or end of the sentence. The position at the beginning gives the adverb greater emphasis: *She helps me **sometimes**.   **Sometimes** she helps me.*
- Adverbial phrases of frequency can come at the beginning or end of a sentence, not in the middle: *I go shopping **on Fridays**.   **On Fridays** I go shopping.*

Adverbs of manner, place and time
- If there is more than one kind of adverb in a sentence, the order is usually manner, place, time: *I lived **happily in Singapore for many years**.*
- The most neutral position for adverbs/adverbial phrases of manner is at the end of a sentence: *They did their work **quietly**.   They did it **without a fuss**.*
- For greater emphasis, they can come at the beginning of the sentence: ***Slowly**, he opened the door.*
- Adverbs of manner ending in *-ly* can also come between the subject and the main verb for greater emphasis: *He **stupidly** went out without locking the door.*
- The most neutral position for adverbs/adverbial phrases of place and time is at the end of a sentence: *I bought these shoes **in a market**.   I saw Gina **yesterday**.*
- For greater emphasis, they can come at the beginning of the sentence: ***In Athens**, we stayed in the city centre. **In Crete**, we stayed at a hotel near the beach.*
- Some indefinite adverbs of time can come between the subject and main verb: *I **recently** changed my job.* (Not *I last month changed my job.*)

PRACTICE

12a Re-write the sentences. Put the words in brackets in the most neutral position.

0   Bianca is the last person to leave work. (always, in the evening)
     Bianca is always the last person to leave work in the evening.

1   Ross ran. (quickly, to the bus stop)

2   I worked in order to get good exam results. (for months, hard)

3   The children played. (happily, outside, today)

4   I thought you explained your ideas. (in the meeting, last week, very well)

5   She slept. (all afternoon, in the chair, soundly)

Grammar: *adjectives and adverbs*

12b Re-write the sentences. Put the words in brackets in the correct position.

0   We all know that if we eat and exercise, we will maintain an ideal weight. (healthily, regularly)
    We all know that if we eat healthily and exercise regularly, we will maintain an ideal weight.

1   As we become busier, many of us don't have the time to eat or exercise as often as we should. (at home and at work, sensibly)
    ....
    ....

2   Many fashionable diets promise you will see results without working to achieve them. (quickly, hard)
    ....
    ....

3   However, these diets involve cutting out certain types of food. (often, completely)
    ....
    ....

4   Many diet pills which advertisers claim have been tested are either dangerous or ineffective. (scientifically)
    ....
    ....

5   In fact, the only way to lose weight is to eat less and exercise more. (safely and permanently)
    ....
    ....

12c Complete the extract from a story. Use the words in the box.

| across the fields | always | badly | completely | directly |
| for some days | often (x2) | ~~recently~~ | slowly | suddenly |

After the lonely wet nights he had spent (0) ....*recently*...... , Inman felt half-dead. He stopped, put his boot on the roadside fence and looked out (1) .... The wound in his neck felt raw and hurt (2) .... He put his finger underneath the bandage and was surprised to find that the wound had healed over almost (3) ....

He calculated that he had been walking (4) .... His wound forced him to walk (5) .... and rest more (6) .... than he wished. He felt very tired and also rather lost, still trying to find a route that went (7) .... to his home in the Appalachian mountains. And the weather had been bad, with rain that came (8) .... , with thunder and lightning, day and night. Each farm he passed had two or three dogs and he was (9) .... forced to fight off their attacks. The constant danger from dogs and the Home Guards meant that he was (10) .... nervous travelling through the dark nights.

29

Grammar: *adjectives and adverbs*

13 Comparison of adjectives, adverbs and nouns

- To form the comparative and superlative of most short adjectives, we add *-er* (*than*) and *the* + *-est*. To form the comparative and superlative of longer adjectives, we add *more* (*than*) and *the most*: *Janet's* **brighter than** *her sister but her sister is* **more attractive**. *The Eiffel Tower used to be* **the tallest** *building in the world.*
- To form the comparative and superlative of adverbs ending in *-ly*, we add *more* (*than*) and *the most*. To form the comparative and superlative of adverbs that have the same form as the adjective, we add *-er* (*than*) and *the* + *-est*: *He drives* **more carefully than** *she does.* *I think Ashley works* **the hardest** *of all.*
- We can also use *less* (*than*) and *the least* with adjectives and adverbs: *Emily is* **less bright than** *her sister.* *They work* **the least efficiently**.
- Some adjectives and adverbs have irregular comparative and superlative forms:
  good/well → *better* → *the best* *bad/badly* → *worse* → *the worst*
  far → *farther/further* → *the farthest/furthest*
- We can use superlatives in these patterns:
  - *one of the* + superlative: *Anne is* **the best** *teacher I've ever had. She's also* **one of the most experienced** *teachers in the school.*
  - *the second/third* + superlative: *Coffee is* **the second most popular** *drink in the world.*
- We can also compare numbers and quantities. We can use:
  - *many/much* → *more* → (*the*) *most* (with countable and uncountable nouns): *There were* **more people** *at the performance on Tuesday than on Monday but* **most people** *came on Friday.*
  - *little* → *less* → *the least* (with uncountable nouns): *We have* **less time**.
  - *few* → *fewer* → *the fewest* (with countable nouns): *I made* **fewer mistakes**.

▶▶ See Appendix 2: Spelling rules, page 200.

PRACTICE

13a **Complete the conversation. Use the comparative or superlative form of the words in brackets.**

A: How are you enjoying the new house?
B: It's nice. It's (0) ....*more spacious*.... (spacious) than our old house and one of the (1) .... (good) things is having our own garden.
A: So it's much (2) .... (good) here than in London, then?
B: Well, I'm not sure. (3) .... (bad) thing about London was the pollution – and it's certainly (4) .... (polluted) here in the country. And I suppose it's (5) .... (stressful). I sleep (6) .... (soundly) here without all the noise. But I miss the cultural diversity of London. Shopping there was much (7) .... (interesting) than it is here. And the people here are (8) .... (varied) than they are in London. On the other hand, it's (9) .... (safe) here – London has the second (10) .... (high) crime rate in the UK!
A: Well, I know this is (11) .... (far) from London you've ever lived but it's one of the (12) .... (beautiful) places I've ever seen.

13b Complete the conversation. Use the comparative or superlative of *much/many*, *little* or *few*.

0 A: Why are you late?
B: Sorry. There was .... *more* .... traffic than usual this morning.

1 A: Doctors recommend eating .... salt.
B: I know. Salt's bad for you.

2 A: All these products are friendly to the environment but this one causes .... damage.
B: Can you prove that?

3 A: I wish there were .... hope that we will succeed.
B: Don't give up!

4 A: He has .... hobbies than his wife.
B: That's because he's always working.

5 A: A lot of people have read the book, you know.
B: Yes, that's true – but even .... have seen the film.

6 A: We have .... information about her life after she became successful than about her earlier life.
B: And I suppose we have .... information about her childhood.
A: That's right. We know almost nothing about it.

7 A: Who got .... marks in the test? Anke, Serena or Malcolm?
B: Anke, of course. She made .... mistakes. In fact, she only made one.

8 A: I'm so tired! I wish I had .... free time and .... work.
B: Well, can't you go away for a few days and relax?

13c Complete the memo. Use the comparative or superlative form of the words in brackets.

MEMO

The company's annual report shows that unfortunately, our sales figures were (0) .... *lower* .... (low) than those for the previous year. This is no surprise but what is (1) .... (alarming) is that a number of our (2) .... (old) clients have switched to another supplier. We are aware that there are (3) .... (expensive) suppliers than ourselves but cost may not be (4) .... (important) factor in our clients' decision to switch suppliers. One former client, for example, has said that their new supplier is not only (5) .... (efficient) but also offers a (6) .... (good) all-round service. Reports like these are (7) .... (worrying) than anything else. If we cannot compete (8) .... (effectively), then we will not survive. We have to make every effort to convince our clients that we can still give them (9) .... (good) value for their money than anyone else.

Grammar: *adjectives and adverbs*

14 Comparative structures

- We use *(just) as* + adjective/adverb + *as* to compare two equal things and *not as* + adjective/adverb + *as* to mean 'less ... than': *My house is **as big as** yours.*
- To express a big difference between two things, we can use:
  - *not nearly as* + adjective/adverb + *as*: *The exam **wasn't nearly as easy as** I thought it would be.*
  - *far/a lot/much* + comparative (+ *than*): *She's **far happier than** she used to be.*
  - *by far/easily* + superlative: *He's **by far the most charming** man I've ever met.*
- To express a small difference, we can use *a (little) bit/slightly* + comparative (+ *than*): *The coach is **slightly cheaper than** the train.*
- To compare quantities, we can use *(not nearly)* + *as much/many* + noun + *as* OR *far/a lot/much* + *more* + noun (+ *than*): *There **wasn't nearly as much information** on the Internet **as** I had hoped.   She made **a lot more mistakes than** me.*
- We can also use other expressions to compare things: *Her car is (**exactly**) **the same as** his.   I'm **almost as tall as** you are.   This painting looks (**very**) **similar to** the one over there.   Bobby's personality is (**very**) **different from** his sister's.*
- We use comparative + *and* + comparative to show that something is increasing or decreasing: *The city is growing **bigger and bigger**.*
- To say that one situation depends on another, we can use *the* + comparative + *the* + comparative: ***The harder** I try, **the better** I do.*
- Many expressions use the structure *the* + comparative + *the* + comparative: *'Can I bring a friend with me to the party?' 'Of course! **The more, the merrier**.'*

PRACTICE

14a Complete the sentences. Use the correct form of the words in brackets.

0 He's driving ....*much more quickly than*.... he should. (much / quickly)

1 Football is .... sport in Europe today. (by far / popular)

2 My car is .... yours but I think it's a .... car. (not / expensive, good)

3 I don't have .... you but I'm .... (nearly / much / money, far / happy)

4 Ted got .... Valerie did. (same / mark)

5 Audrey's personality is .... her brother's. (very similar)

6 The house looks .... the way it looked before it was painted. (completely / different)

7 He cared .... and .... about the band and eventually he decided to leave. (little, little)

8 .... I become, ... mistakes I seem to make. (old, many)

Grammar: *adjectives and adverbs*

14b Complete the article. Use the correct form of the words in brackets.

WEATHER ON OTHER PLANETS

If you think the weather on Earth is weird, the weather on other planets is (0) ...*far stranger*... (far / strange). Even though the sun shines (1) .... (much / weakly) on Mars than it does on Earth, Mars gets (2) .... (far / many) ultraviolet tanning rays. At the same time, the temperature on Mars is usually (3) .... (much / cold) than the temperature at our North Pole. That's warm, though, compared to Neptune's (4) .... (large) moon Triton, which scientists believe is (5) .... (cold) place in our solar system. Are you looking for somewhere (6) .... (a little / warm) than Mars? Then try Venus, where the sun is so hot that a picnic lunch would vapourise (7) .... (almost / quickly) you unpacked it. We might complain about the weather on Earth but it's (8) .... (by far / good) place to live in our solar system!

15 *so ... that, such ... that, too, enough, very*

so ... that, such ... that
- We can use *so* + adjective/adverb and *such* (+ *a/an*) + adjective + noun for emphasis: *You've been **so kind**! I've had **such a busy day**! They're **such nice people**. It was **such terrible weather**!*
- We can use *so* + adjective/adverb + *that* and *such* (+ *a/an*) + adjective + noun + *that* to describe cause and effect: *The box was **so heavy that** we couldn't lift it. It was **such a dull day that** we stayed indoors. They were **such beautiful songs that** I went out and bought the CD. It was **such hard work that** they felt exhausted.*
- We use *so* + *much/many/little/few* + noun + *that* to emphasise quantities or numbers: *There were **so many people** in the street **that** we couldn't move.*

too, enough, very
- *Too* has a negative meaning: 'more than you need'. *Enough* has a positive meaning: 'as much as you need'. We use them in these patterns:
  - *too* + adjective/adverb (+ *for someone*) (+ *to*-infinitive): *It's **too expensive**; I can't buy it. It's **too expensive for me**. The coffee is **too hot to drink**. Hurry up! You're walking **too slowly for us to catch** the train.*
  - *enough* + noun: *We have **enough money** – we can buy it.*
  - (*not* +) adjective/adverb + *enough* (+ *for someone*) (+ *to*-infinitive): *The weather isn't **warm enough for us to go** swimming.*
- We can use *very* to emphasise a positive or a negative quality. Compare: *It's **very** kind of you to help. The traffic is moving **very/too** slowly.*

33

Grammar: *adjectives and adverbs*

PRACTICE

15a Complete the conversations. Use *so*, *such* or *such a*.

0 A: It's ......*so*...... hot! Shall we go to the beach?
   B: No, there'll be ......*so*...... many people there today that it'll be awful.
1 A: Daniel has ......*such a*...... lovely voice!
   B: I agree. I didn't realise he could sing ......*so*...... well.
2 A: Why are you ......*so*...... late?
   B: It was ......*such a*...... good film that we stayed and saw it a second time.
3 A: These shoes were ......*such*...... poor quality that they're coming apart!
   B: So they weren't ......*such a*...... good bargain after all!
4 A: I feel ......*so*...... ill that I can't go to work.
   B: You've had ......*so*...... much time off that your boss will get annoyed.
5 A: We've had ......*such*...... awful weather that we're coming home early.
   B: That's a shame.

15b Re-write the sentences. Use the words in brackets.

0 He's not well enough to travel (so)
  He's so ill that he can't travel.
1 It was too cold for us to go swimming. (enough)
  It wasn't warm enough
   too
2 The old lady was so weak that she couldn't stand up. (too)
  ....
3 They're going so slowly that they'll never get there on time. (enough)
  They aren't going fast enough to get there on time
4 The music is too loud for me to hear you. (so)
  so that I can't hear you
5 The children are too young to travel long distances. (enough)
  aren't old enough

not + adj + enough for sth/sb to + inf

15c Complete the conversation. Use one word in each gap.

Doctor: What seems to be the problem?
Patient: I'm (0) ......*so*...... tired in the mornings that I can't get out of bed and in general, I haven't been feeling (1) ......*very*...... well.
Doctor: I see. Do you get (2) ......*enough*...... exercise?
Patient: Not really. I've joined a fitness centre but I'm having (3) ......*such*...... a busy time at work (4) ......*that*...... I don't have time to go there.
Doctor: And how's your diet?
Patient: I'm (5) ......*not*...... eating (6) ......*enough*...... fruits and vegetables – I don't really like them. And I eat (7) ......*too*...... much fast food.
Doctor: Yes, well, many of my patients come to see me because they're (8) ......*too*...... busy (9) ......*to*...... take care of themselves properly.
Patient: There's one more thing, doctor. Lately, I've been getting (10) ......*such*...... terrible headaches (11) ......*that*...... I have to lie down. I'm starting to feel (12) ......*really / so*...... worried about them.
Doctor: We can look into that. I'll book you in for some tests next week.

34

16 Adverbs of degree: *very*, *absolutely*, etc.

- Gradable adjectives and adverbs refer to qualities that we can grade or compare; they usually have a comparative and superlative form.
- We can use adverbs of degree to make gradable adjectives and adverbs stronger or weaker: *He's a **fairly good** painter but he needs to improve his technique. They work together **extremely efficiently**.*
- We can use *very* with all gradable adjectives and adverbs. We can use *extremely* and *really* with many of them: *very intelligent/badly   extremely hot/old-fashioned   really happy/colourful*
- Ungradable adjectives and adverbs refer to extreme qualities that we don't grade or compare; they don't usually have a comparative and superlative form. Compare these pairs of gradable and ungradable adjectives and adverbs: *angry – furious   badly – appallingly   big – gigantic   well – brilliantly   hot – boiling   important – essential   tired – exhausted*
- We can use *absolutely* and *really* to emphasise many ungradable adjectives and adverbs but we cannot make them weaker: *absolutely brilliantly   really awful*
- Some adverbs of degree tend to collocate with certain adjectives:
  - *utterly impossible/miserable/ridiculous/useless*
  - *highly amusing/improbable/skilled/successful*
  - *totally different/exhausted/satisfied/unnecessary*
  - *completely accurate/relaxed/free/satisfied/useless*
  - *entirely clear/happy/satisfactory/sure*
- The adverbs *quite* and *rather* can have different meanings, depending on how they are used:
  - *quite* (= fairly) + gradable adjective/adverb: *It's **quite good**.*
  - *quite* (= absolutely) + ungradable adjective/adverb: *The team played **quite brilliantly**.*
  - *rather* (= fairly) + negative gradable adjective/adverb: *She's **rather angry**.*
  - *rather* + comparative adjective/adverb: *Their last CD was **rather better** than this one.*
  - *rather* (= to a greater degree than expected) + positive gradable adjective/adverb: *That programme was **rather interesting**.*
- With a noun, we can use the following patterns: *It was **quite a pleasant** surprise. It was **rather a pleasant** surprise.   It was **a rather pleasant** surprise.*

PRACTICE

16a Circle the correct answer.

0 Your prediction was accurate. In fact, you were (absolutely)/ *extremely* right.
1 Carlos is an *extremely* / *absolutely* hard worker. He also works *absolutely* / *very* quickly.
2 It's *absolutely* / *really* cold outside. Shall we stay in?
3 Is it *very* / *absolutely* important that I go out tonight? I'm *absolutely* / *really* tired.

Grammar: *adjectives and adverbs*

4 She was *really / fairly* furious with him for leaving the baby alone.
5 If you follow the instructions, it's *absolutely / fairly* simple to assemble the bookcase.
6 Are you *absolutely / extremely* certain that the information is accurate?
7 Hygiene is *absolutely / extremely* important in places like hospitals.
8 He was *absolutely / very* devastated by the accident. Luckily, all of his friends responded *absolutely / very* sympathetically.
9 Budapest is a beautiful city with some *really / very* magnificent buildings.
10 You should go and see the exhibition at the museum. It's *absolutely / very* interesting.

16b Circle the correct answers. There may be more than one correct answer.

0 The meal is (*absolutely*) / *fairly* / (*really*) delicious.
1 The film we saw was *quite / totally / highly* amusing.
2 You've made *fairly / quite / very* a big mess.
3 I always have a(n) *absolutely / really / very* wonderful time when I go there.
4 He looked *entirely / very / utterly* ridiculous in those clothes.
5 They weren't *entirely / rather / utterly* happy with the results.
6 If you aren't *highly / completely / rather* satisfied with your purchase, we'll give you your money back.
7 They make a(n) *absolutely / extremely / very* attractive couple, don't you think?
8 She's a(n) *entirely / extremely / highly* successful surgeon.
9 Donna hates her new school. In fact, she is *utterly / highly / absolutely* miserable there.
10 There's a lot of traffic on the roads and I think it's *very / entirely / highly* improbable that they'll arrive on time.

16c Complete the conversations. Use *quite* or *rather*. Sometimes both are possible.

0 A: We're ......*quite*...... amazed at how quickly he's recovered from the illness.
B: I know. It's ......*rather*...... surprising but such a relief!
1 A: You look .... exhausted. How do you feel?
B: I've just had a rest but I'm still .... tired.
2 A: I think Sue behaved .... appallingly this evening. Don't you?
B: Well, you're over-reacting a little but she did behave .... badly.
3 A: The lead singer performed .... splendidly this evening.
B: She did perform .... well given that her reviews haven't been very positive.
4 A: Sula understands English .... well but she finds it difficult to speak.
B: True, but she did .... better than I expected on her last test.
5 A: I think Hong Kong is .... an amazing city.
B: Yes, and it's .... fascinating too.

Grammar: adjectives and adverbs

17 Sentence adverbs: *certainly, clearly,* etc.

- Sentence adverbs modify the whole sentence or clause. Some adverbs express how certain the speaker is: *certainly, definitely, probably, possibly*. In affirmative sentences, these adverbs usually come after the verb *be* or after the auxiliary. In negative sentences, they come before the auxiliary: *I'll **probably be** late for dinner tonight. I **certainly won't** be early.*
- Some adverbs often come at the beginning of the sentence and may be followed by a comma: *clearly, honestly, hopefully, luckily, naturally, obviously, personally, surely*: **Clearly,** *the situation is serious.* **Surely** *we should be doing more about environmental issues.*
- These adverbs can also come before the verb, after the verb *be* or after the auxiliary: *Figures **clearly show** a drop in sales.   The situation **is obviously** serious.*
- Some sentence adverbs help to organise a text or conversation. *Anyway* shows that the speaker is about to end a conversation, go back to an important topic or change to a new topic. *By the way* introduces a new idea or topic: **Anyway,** *as I said, he is arriving tomorrow.*   **By the way,** *have you seen my keys?*

PRACTICE

17a Re-write the sentences. Put the adverbs in brackets in the correct position.

0   I'm not sure where she is but she's still at work. (probably)
    I'm not sure where she is but she's probably still at work.

1   The disease was caused by lead poisoning. (possibly)
    ....

2   I didn't expect this to happen. (certainly)
    ....

3   She knew the money was stolen. (surely)
    ....

4   He's very attracted to you. (obviously)
    ....

5   There are no easy answers to the problem. (clearly)
    ....

17b Circle the correct answer.

A: You look like you've been enjoying yourself. Where have you been?
B: To see the new Bond film. It's (0) *naturally /* (probably) the best one yet.
A: I'm surprised. The reviews (1) *certainly / surely* haven't been very good.
B: (2) *Obviously / Personally,* I enjoyed it. You can't always trust the critics.
A: I suppose not. (3) *Anyway / By the way,* you've convinced me. I'm
    (4) *definitely / surely* going to see the film now.
B: (5) *Anyway / By the way,* I heard that you'd had an accident but that
    (6) *luckily / surely,* it wasn't anything serious. Is that right?
A: I'm afraid so. (7) *Fortunately / Hopefully,* I was wearing my seatbelt.
    (8) *Naturally / Personally,* I was shaken up but I'm fine now.

37

Check 2 Adjectives and adverbs

1 **Tick the correct sentence in each pair.**
   1a He was upset. ....
   1b He had an upset feeling. ....
   2a The sisters are alike. ....
   2b They are alike sisters. ....
   3a They are afraid children. ....
   3b The children are afraid. ....
   4a I wear often jeans to work. ....
   4b I often wear jeans to work. ....
   5a I submitted the report on Tuesday. ....
   5b I submitted on Tuesday the report. ....

   / 5

2 **Put the words in the correct order.**
   6 live / large / in / stone / a / my family and I / farmhouse
   ....
   ....

   7 gets / my country / rarely / in / it / this hot
   ....
   ....

   8 wanted / to go / always / to Paris / have / I
   ....
   ....

   9 new / our / blue / is / and / sofa / green
   ....
   ....

   10 she / camera / bought / digital / expensive / a(n) / new
   ....
   ....

   / 5

3 **Circle the correct answer.**
   11 A: What's the matter? You look absolutely *angry / furious*.
       B: I am. I've just had a fight with Dave.
   12 A: What time are you coming home this evening?
       B: Well, *hopefully / certainly*, I'll be home by seven – unless the traffic is bad.
   13 A: Whose gloves are these?
       B: They're *certainly / presumably* not mine. They're too small.
   14 A: Are you going to get a visa?
       B: I don't need one. If you're a member of the EU, you can travel *free / freely* between member states.
   15 A: The bill for the job seems high. Is it correct?
       B: Yes. We did the work as *economic / economically* as we could.

   / 5

4 **Complete the conversations. Use one word in each gap.**
   A: My favourite meal is steak and fried potatoes.
   B: I like it too but we really should eat (16) .... red meat than we do and (17) .... fresh vegetables. In fact, neither of us eats enough fresh vegetables!

   A: How was your tennis game?
   B: I played a (18) .... better today than yesterday but I didn't play (19) .... as well as I wanted to.

   A: I like my new English teacher.
   B: Why's that?
   A: She teaches in such a lively (20) .... that lessons are never boring.

   / 5

5 **Complete the second sentence so that it means the same as the first, using the word in bold. Use between two and five words.**
   21 When you study a lot, you get better marks. **more**
       The .... marks you get.
   22 Your coat and mine look almost the same. **similar**
       Your coat .... mine.
   23 This sentence is so complicated that I can't understand it. **too**
       This sentence .... to understand.

38

24 Your room is bigger than mine. **big**
My room .... yours.

25 Hilary is a more imaginative writer than anyone else in the class. **the**
Hilary .... in the class.

26 I didn't have time to think because things happened very quickly. **so**
Everything happened .... I didn't have time to think.

27 It's too cold to go swimming. **warm**
It .... to go swimming.

28 Radu got more right answers than anyone else. **mistakes**
Radu made .... anyone else.

/ 8

6 Choose the correct answer A, B, C or D.

New Message

It was (29) ...... to hear your news. We're having a (30) ...... wonderful time here in the Maldives! The weather's better (31) ...... we expected. In fact, it's such warm weather (32) ...... the locals are worried. Global warming is (33) ...... a serious topic here – these beautiful islands may soon disappear because of rising sea levels! (34) ...... , that would be a tragedy – the Maldives are as close to being a paradise (35) ...... you could imagine!

(36) ...... , on a happier note, there's a lot to do here. We've been snorkelling nearly every day. This is also a great place for whale and dolphin watching – there are over twenty different species in the waters here. Spinner dolphins are the (37) ...... species and it's (38) ...... easy to see them at certain times of day.

(39) ...... , I'm going to have to stay in the shade for a couple of days. I spent (40) ...... more time in the sun yesterday than I should have and I got sunburnt.

---

29 A good   B well
C better   D best

30 A highly   B very
C really   D completely

31 A as   B than
C that   D from

32 A than   B that
C so   D to

33 A absolutely B highly
C very   D quite

34 A Definitely B Obviously
C Possibly   D Luckily

35 A as   B than
C that   D what

36 A Anyway   B By the way
C Fortunately D Clearly

37 A common   B commonly
C more common D commonest

38 A absolutely B too
C highly   D very

39 A Naturally B Obviously
C Unfortunately D Certainly

40 A as   B nearly
C far   D very

/ 12

Total: / 40

✓ Self-check

Wrong answers	Look again at	Try CD-ROM
1, 2, 3, 6, 9, 10	Unit 10	Exercise 10
14, 15, 20, 29	Unit 11	Exercise 11
4, 5, 7, 8	Unit 12	Exercise 12
16, 17, 25, 28, 31, 37	Unit 13	Exercise 13
18, 19, 21, 22, 24, 35, 40	Unit 14	Exercise 14
23, 26, 27, 32, 38	Unit 15	Exercise 15
11, 30, 33	Unit 16	Exercise 16
12, 13, 34, 36, 39	Unit 17	Exercise 17

Now do **Check 2**

Present tenses

18 Present simple or continuous?

Present simple
- We use the present simple to talk about permanent situations: *I **live** in London but I **come** from Canada.*
- We also use the present simple:
  - for habitual actions or routines, or events or actions that happen regularly, often with a time expression or an adverb of frequency: *We **see** each other **every day**. She **always catches** the 8.00 train. It **snows** here **in the winter**.*
  - for a general truth or statement of fact: *Water **boils** at 100 degrees Centigrade. Cats **don't like** water.*
  - in instructions and directions: *To get to my house, you **take** the first turning on the left.*
  - in film reviews and plot summaries: *Bullock **gives** a plausible performance in the lead role. The thrills are non-stop as the bus **speeds** out of control.*
  - in sports commentaries to describe what is happening as the commentator speaks: *Beckham **passes** the ball to Cole – and he **scores**!*
- These adverbs of frequency and time expressions are often used with the present simple:
  - *never, hardly ever, rarely, seldom, occasionally, sometimes, frequently, often, usually, always*: *I **sometimes work** late.*
  - *every day/week, in the morning/evenings, on Mondays/Tuesday, once a week/year*: *I **get up** early **in the morning**.*

Present continuous
- We use the present continuous for activities and situations that are temporary: *I'**m** only **staying** here for a short time.*
- We also use the present continuous for:
  - actions in progress at the moment of speaking: *'What **are** you **doing**?' 'I'**m taking** a break.'*
  - situations that are changing: *Traffic **is getting** worse every year.*
  - annoying habits, with *always*: *You'**re always forgetting** your keys!*
- These time expressions are often used with the present continuous:
  - *always, still, currently* (usually after the auxiliary verb): *I'**m still working** for the same company.*
  - *at present, at the moment, (right) now*: *Janice **is living** in Madrid **at present**.*

▶▶ For adverbs of frequency, see Unit 12.
▶▶ See Appendix 2: Spelling rules, page 200.

Grammar: *present tenses*

PRACTICE

18a Circle the correct answer.

0 I (*usually drive*) / *'m usually driving* to work but this week I *take* / (*'m taking*) the bus because my car is at the garage.

1 Make sure you *lock* / *'re locking* the doors and windows before you leave the house.

2 She *plays* / *'s playing* tennis once or twice a week but she *doesn't play* / *isn't playing* this week because she's hurt her wrist.

3 A: Where *does Evan come* / *is Evan coming* from?
   B: I'm not sure, but his parents *live* / *are living* in New Zealand.

4 The film *begins* / *is beginning* with a death and *ends* / *is ending* with a dramatic car chase through the streets of New York.

5 And the Ferrari *takes* / *is taking* the last corner at high speed, *races* / *is racing* towards the finish line and *crosses* / *is crossing* it! What a race!

6 A: What *do you do* / *are you doing*?
   B: I *wait* / *'m waiting* for the bus. It *runs* / *'s running* late.

7 You *always leave* / *'re always leaving* the lights on! It doesn't matter how many times I *remind* / *'m reminding* you.

8 There is so much fast food available that people *forget* / *are forgetting* how to cook.

9 If you *don't watch* / *aren't watching* the television, would you turn it off?

10 According to recent research, too little sleep *causes* / *is causing* young people to gain weight.

18b Complete the information from a website. Use the present simple or continuous of the verbs in the box.

| gain | go on | learn | offer | organise | perform | remain | study | ~~take~~ |

This year the International School for Languages has about 100 part-time students who (0) ......***are taking***...... evening classes and a further 300 who (1) .... full-time. Many of them (2) .... a new language to improve their job prospects or to prepare for university. The European languages (3) .... very popular but Chinese and Japanese (4) .... in popularity.

The school (5) .... an excellent range of learning facilities and (6) .... social activities like excursions to local areas of interest.

Every year our students (7) .... extremely well in their examinations and many (8) .... to study at top universities in the country.

Grammar: *present tenses*

18c Complete the fact sheet. Use the present simple or continuous of the verbs in brackets.

> **GEOGRAPHY**
> The landscape (0) ......*rises*...... (rise) from the lowlands in the east to the Himalayas in the west. High plateaux and mountains (1) .... (occupy) one third of the area. The coastline on the Yellow Sea is flat at the mouths of China's two major rivers, the Yangtze and the Huanghe. Unfortunately, rapid industrialisation (2) .... (destroy) much of the plant and animal life in the country.
>
> **ECONOMY**
> Most people (3) .... (live) in rural regions. Rice production (4) .... (provide) enough food for the local population and surpluses are exported. However, the economy (5) .... (develop) rapidly and as a result, China (6) .... (open up) to world markets. China (7) .... (export) many inexpensive processed goods, including machinery and textiles, and income from foreign trade and tourism (8) .... (increase).

19 State verbs

- Action, or 'dynamic', verbs describe activities, e.g. *run, drive, listen, watch*. They can be used in the simple or continuous form.
- State verbs describe a state, not an activity. They cannot normally be used in the continuous form. They include:
  - mental/thinking verbs: *agree, believe, disagree, doubt, expect*, forget*, know, realise, remember*, suppose, think*, understand*
  - attitude verbs: *dislike, hate, like, love, need, prefer, want*
  - sense/perception verbs: *hear, see*, smell*, taste**
  - appearance, qualities: *appear*, look* (= seem), resemble, seem, sound*
  - being, possession: *be*, belong to, consist of, contain, have*, include, own, possess*
  - other verbs: *come*, cost, depend*, fit, matter, mean, owe, weigh**
- The verbs marked with an asterisk (*) can be used in the continuous form, but with a change of meaning: *I **think** you're right.* (= This is my opinion.) *I**'m thinking** of buying a new car.* (= I'm considering it.) *He**'s** nice.* (= It's one of his character traits.) *He**'s being** nice.* (= He's behaving in a nice way at the moment.)
- With verbs like *feel* and *look* (= seem), we can use either the simple or the continuous form with no change in meaning: *I **feel**/**'m feeling** ill.*

Grammar: *present tenses*

PRACTICE

19a Complete the sentences. Use the present simple or continuous of the verbs in the box.

| appear (x2) | be | ~~belong to~~ | come | have (x2) | taste | weigh |

0   Who ...*does*... that beautiful house on the hill ...*belong to*... ?
1   That soup .... delicious! What have you put in it?
2   My sister doesn't resemble me. For a start, she .... blond hair.
3   It .... that she's changed her mind about taking the job.
4   I can't believe you .... so unreasonable! What's wrong?
5   We .... lunch. Can I phone you back in half an hour?
6   Now all new cars .... with one year's free insurance.
7   Alex is working. He .... on stage in a play by Agatha Christie.
8   How much .... an adult African elephant .... ?

19b Complete the article. Use the present simple or continuous of the verbs in brackets.

Singer and songwriter James Sharp (0) ...*has*... (have) a new hobby – golf. He (1) .... (have) lessons every day and spends so much time on the course that his girlfriend, actress and model Sophie Clarke, (2) .... (think) of taking up the sport as well so she can spend more time with him!

What (3) .... he .... (think) of the rumours that he and Sophie are planning to get married? 'Every day I (4) .... (see) things written about me that aren't true. One day they say we're getting married and the next that I (5) .... (see) another woman. I just try to ignore all of it.'

James's new album came out last month and so far the critics have been positive. The album (6) .... (include) a mixture of familiar and new musical styles and (7) .... (contain) remixes of some old favourites. James is pleased with the reviews but it's his fans that (8) .... (matter) most to him. However, if they (9) .... (hope) for something that (10) .... (sound) like his last album, they may be disappointed.

So is James worried? Not at all. 'I need to grow as an artist and that (11) .... (mean) taking risks. I hope that never changes.'

Somehow, we (12) .... (not think) his fans will be disappointed.

Grammar: *present tenses*

20 Present perfect: *ever, never,* etc.

- We use the present perfect for states or for single or repeated actions that happened at an unspecified time in the past. The exact time is not important:
  Diana's been ill quite often recently.   I've seen the film but I haven't read the book.
- We often use expressions of frequency with the present perfect: *often, once/twice/several times, the first/second time, ever, never:* *They've visited Spain several times.   This is the first time I've met his parents.   Have you ever ridden a camel?   It's the best meal we've ever eaten.   She's never been to Belgium.*
- We use the past simple for finished events or actions that happened at a definite time in the past. We usually say when they happened, using expressions like *yesterday, last week/month/year, (two days) ago: I rang her last week from Tokyo.* Compare:
  I've been to Spain but I've never been to Portugal.   I went to Spain last year.
  'Have you ever eaten octopus?' 'Yes, I ate it when I was on holiday last year.'

⚠ Note the difference between *have been* and *have gone*:
  Richard's been to Spain. (= He went to Spain but he's back home now.)
  Richard's gone to Spain. (= He's in Spain now.)

▶▶ See Appendix 2: Spelling rules, page 200.

PRACTICE

20a Circle the correct answer.

0   We (spoke) / *'ve spoken* to them yesterday.
1   Katie *had / 's had* several jobs abroad and now she *went / 's gone* to Turkey to work for a large multinational.
2   There *were / have been* several major earthquakes in Japan recently. In fact, there *was / has been* a serious one about a week ago.
3   I'm afraid he isn't here. He *left / 's left* an hour ago.
4   *Did you see / Have you seen* any good films recently?
5   I *visited / 've visited* their offices a few days ago but not their factory.
6   They *never ate / 've never eaten* such spicy food before but they're enjoying it!
7   I *tried / 've tried* to contact her several times but the last time I *talked / 've talked* to her, she *put / 's put* the phone down on me.
8   That's the silliest article I *ever read / 've ever read*!
9   A: *Did you ever work / Have you ever worked* in an office?
    B: Yes, I *worked / 've worked* in one last year but I *didn't like / haven't liked* it.
10 They say it's the first time he *ever lost / 's ever lost* a game.
11 I *always dreamed / 've always dreamed* of becoming a doctor and I hope to study medicine.
12 She *only went / 's only been* to Manchester once before and she doesn't remember it well.

44

Grammar: present tenses

20b Complete the e-mail. Use the present perfect or past simple of the verbs in the box.

always / want	encourage	ever / have	find
happen	have	invite	meet (x2)	~~see~~	start (x2)

New Message

Dear Anna,

It seems like ages ago since I last (0) ....*saw*......... you! So much (1) .... recently that I don't know where to begin. First of all, I (2) .... someone special. His name is Steve and we're planning to get married. We (3) .... a little over a year ago at Gill's wedding.

Secondly, I (4) .... a new job as an editorial assistant for a local newspaper. I wasn't going to apply but Steve (5) .... me and much to my surprise, they (6) .... me for an interview! I (7) .... working there six months ago.

What else? We're busy planning the wedding but we still (8) .... time to take a holiday in Turkey last month. I (9) .... to go there and we (10) .... a great time.

Anyway, you'll be hearing from me again soon. I hope you're well – I really think this is the best year I (11) .... !

Love, Suzanne

20c Complete the second sentence so that it means the same as the first, using the word in bold. Use between two and five words.

0   This is the saddest film I have ever seen.   **never**
    I ....*have never seen*.......... such a sad film.

1   She has never done anything like that before.   **ever**
    It's the first time she .... anything like that.

2   This is Sean's first time in a helicopter.   **flown**
    Sean .... in a helicopter before.

3   Andy and Rachel are still on holiday in Italy.   **gone**
    Andy and Rachel .... to Italy on holiday.

4   I have been to Russia once before.   **second**
    This .... I have been to Russia.

5   We still remember the times we spent together.   **forgotten**
    We .... the times we spent together.

6   I went to the exhibition at the National Gallery last week.   **been**
    I .... the exhibition at the National Gallery.

7   You have never told anyone the story before, have you?   **ever**
    Is this the first time .... anyone the story?

45

Grammar: *present tenses*

21 Present perfect: *just, already, yet,* etc.

- We use the present perfect for recently completed single actions, when the result of the action is important in the present: *I've broken my leg.* (Result: I can't walk.)
- We often use *just, already* (= sooner than expected) and *yet* (= up to now) for emphasis. Notice the word order: *The taxi has just arrived. She's already told them what happened. They've finished their work already. Have you already eaten? Have they finished yet? He hasn't seen the film yet.*
- We can also use *recently* (= a short time ago): *Have you spoken to them recently?*
- We use the past simple for a completed past action which does not affect the present. Compare: *Have you had a good holiday?* (You've just returned from your holiday.) *Did you have a good holiday?* (You returned from your holiday some time before this question.)

⚠ In American English, people often use the past simple instead of the present perfect:

British English	American English
They**'ve** just **arrived**.	They just **arrived**.
I**'ve** already **eaten**.	I already **ate**.
Have they **come** yet?	**Did** they **come** yet?

PRACTICE

21a Complete the sentences. Use the present perfect or past simple of the verbs in brackets.

0   A: *Have you spoken* .... to Jim recently?
     B: I *spoke* .... to him last week. (you / speak, speak)

1   I .... Claire. We .... at the end of term party. (already / meet, meet)

2   Harriet .... me anything yet but her sister .... me yesterday that Harriet's expecting a baby. (not tell, tell)

3   Look! I .... all my exams! I'm so relieved because I .... them all last year. (pass, not pass)

4   My parents .... They .... in a taxi about five minutes ago. (just / arrive, arrive)

5   A: .... your wallet yet?
     B: Yes, I .... it under the sofa this morning. (you / find, find)

6   Someone .... the window – there's glass everywhere. They .... it last night. (break, break)

7   Nathan .... his hand so he can't write. He .... it last week playing tennis. (hurt, hurt)

8   If you're looking for Carol, I .... her. I .... her a few minutes ago in the canteen. (just / see, see)

21b Complete the conversations. Use the words in brackets and *just, already, yet* or *recently*.

0 A: Would you like something to eat?
   B: No, thanks. *I've just had lunch.* (I / have / lunch)

1 A: Is Tony here?
   B: I'm sorry. .... (you / miss / him)

2 A: .... (you / taste / the chocolates?)
   B: Yes, and they're delicious.

3 A: Why are we hurrying?
   B: We're late. .... (the film / start)

4 A: Why is all this laundry still here?
   B: .... (they / not repair / the washing machine)

5 A: .... (you / finish / your homework?)
   B: No, but it won't take me much longer!

6 A: Congratulations! .... (I / hear / the news)
   B: Thanks. We're delighted.

7 A: Would you like a coffee?
   B: No, thanks. .... (I / have / three cups)

8 A: I hear Gemma isn't well. .... (you / see / her?)
   B: No, not for a few days. Perhaps we should drop by.

21c Complete the e-mail. Use the present perfect or past simple of the verbs in brackets.

Dear Javier,

I'm sorry I (0) *haven't been* (not be) in touch recently but I (1) .... (be) really busy. I (2) .... (go) to my third job interview this morning but unfortunately, no one (3) .... (offer) me a job yet. I (4) .... (look) everywhere and I (5) .... (fill in) dozens of application forms. Still, I'm not discouraged. Some things take time.

In fact, I'm really enjoying myself here. I (6) .... (already / see) *Cats* and I (7) .... (just / buy) tickets for the next Madonna concert – I (8) .... (stand) in line for an hour this afternoon but it was worth it. Also, I like the family I'm staying with – they (9) .... (give) me lots of advice about finding work and last night they even (10) .... (take) me out for a meal. We talk all the time and as a result, my English (11) .... (already / improve) a lot. Anyway, someone (12) .... (just / come) to the door. I hope it's the pizza I (13) .... (order) an hour ago. I'll write more often in future – I promise.

Farida

Grammar: *present tenses*

22 Present perfect: *for, since*

- We use the present perfect with *for* and *since* to talk about states, events or actions that began in the past and continue up to now. We use *for* + a period of time and *since* + a point in time: ***for*** *a month/three years/ages* ***since*** *2004/yesterday/I was four:* **We've known** *each other* **for years/since 1997**. (Not ~~We know each other for years~~.)

- We use the past simple for states, events or actions that began and ended in the past. We can use *for* to talk about a finished period of time. Compare:
  She**'s been** a doctor **for twenty years**. (She's still a doctor.)
  She **was** a doctor **for twenty years**. (She isn't a doctor now.)
  '*How long* **has** *he* **been** *in the army?*' '**For five years.**' (He's still in the army.)
  '*How long* **was** *he in the army?*' '**For five years.**' (He isn't in the army now.)

- To talk about an unfinished time period, we use the present perfect with expressions such as *today, this morning/week*. We use the past simple for a finished time period. Compare: **Have** *you* **been** *busy this morning?* (It's still morning.) **Were** *you busy this morning?* (It's now afternoon or evening.)

PRACTICE

22a Re-write the sentences. Use the words in brackets.

  0 It's weeks since we last saw one another. (seen)
    We *haven't seen one another for weeks* .

  1 When did you get married? (been)
    How long .... ?

  2 They haven't seen their parents for two weeks. (since)
    It's two weeks ....

  3 I'm tired because the last time I slept was two days ago. (for)
    I'm tired because I ....

  4 When Owen left his job, he began to feel more relaxed. (felt)
    Since Owen left his job, ...

  5 Vanessa hasn't been to the cinema for months. (since)
    It's months ....

  6 I started working as a waiter and quit a month later. (for)
    I ....

  7 It's many years since they visited their grandparents. (for)
    They ....

  8 How long have Belinda and Roderick been married? (get)
    When ....

  9 She met them when she was a child. (known)
    She ....

  10 They're angry because the last time they got paid was two months ago. (been)
    They're angry because they ....

Grammar: *present tenses*

22b Complete the conversations. Use the present perfect or past simple of the verbs in brackets. Sometimes more than one answer is possible.

0 A: ...*Have you had*... (you / have) a busy day today?
   B: Not really. I ...*finished*... (finish) writing my essay this morning and then I ...*went*... (go) windsurfing.

1 A: .... (you / talk) to Hunter today?
   B: No. He .... (not come) in to work this morning. He .... (be) ill since Tuesday.

2 A: Sales .... (increase) in the first three months of this year and the prediction is that they will continue to rise.
   B: Excellent news!

3 A: Where .... (you / be) last night? I .... (wait) for hours.
   B: Sorry, I should have rung. I .... (be) at work.

4 A: .... (the package / arrive) yesterday?
   B: No, and it .... (not arrive) this morning either. Perhaps it'll come later this afternoon.

5 A: I .... (not see) Catherine today. What about you?
   B: I'm seeing her tomorrow.

22c Complete the texts. Use the present perfect or past simple of the verbs in the box.

| be   catch (x2)   collect   drop   introduce   keep |
| not see   phone   ~~study~~   suggest |

Carrie and I (0) ...*studied*... together at university for three years. We (1) .... in touch but I (2) .... her for ages. To my surprise, she (3) .... me last week and (4) .... we meet for lunch today. I (5) .... the bus to town this morning but although I (6) .... here for over an hour, there's no sign of her. I hope she's all right.

We're here this morning in Marylebone Road in London, where traffic police (7) .... these cameras a year ago to catch drivers who break the law. Since then, the police (8) .... thousands of motorists on camera and (9) .... many thousands of pounds in fines. Officials claim that traffic congestion (10) .... by almost 20% since the cameras were installed.

Grammar: *present tenses*

23 Present perfect simple and continuous

Present perfect simple	Present perfect continuous
We use the present perfect simple:	We use the present perfect continuous:
to describe an activity that is complete: *I've read several books about windsurfing.* (I've finished them.)	to describe an activity that is incomplete: *I've been reading a book about windsurfing.* (I haven't finished it yet.)
to emphasise the result or consequence of a completed action: *We've already seen that film.* (We don't want to see it again.)	to focus on an activity, not the result or consequence of that activity: *'You look tired. What have you been doing?' 'I've been working hard.'*
to say how often something has happened: *He's read that book twice.*	to emphasise how long an activity has been going on: *He's been reading that book for over two weeks.*
to describe a permanent state: *She's lived here for six years.* (This is her home now.)	to describe a temporary state or activity: *She's been living here for six months.* (But she intends to move.)

⚠ We don't use the present perfect continuous with verbs describing an action that lasts a short time: *begin, break, finish, start, stop: He's started a new job.* (Not *He's been starting a new job.*)

▶▶ For state verbs, see Unit 19.
▶▶ See Appendix 2: Spelling rules, page 200.

PRACTICE

23a Circle the correct answer.

0 You'd better put some boots on. It *'s rained* / *('s been raining)* all week and it's very muddy outside.

1 I *'ve e-mailed* / *'ve been e-mailing* him several times but he *hasn't answered* / *hasn't been answering* any of my messages.

2 We *'ve expected* / *'ve been expecting* them to arrive since last Thursday.

3 *Have you finished* / *Have you been finishing* your project yet? You *'ve worked* / *'ve been working* on it for ages.

4 Kevin *'s looked* / *'s been looking* for a job since he finished school but he's still unemployed.

5 Audrey *'s learnt* / *'s been learning* to play the guitar since she was a child and now she *'s started* / *'s been starting* piano lessons too.

6 They *'ve watched* / *'ve been watching* a film on television all evening. It's their favourite film and they *'ve seen* / *'ve been seeing* it three times.

7 Daniel *'s moved* / *'s been moving* house five times in the last five years!

8 I *'ve asked* / *'ve been asking* him to repair the television for ages. In fact, I *'ve asked* / *'ve been asking* him twice this week already.

Grammar: *present tenses*

23b Complete the conversations. Use the present perfect simple or continuous of the verbs in brackets.

A: You look hot. What (0) ...*have you been doing*... (you / do)?
B: I (1) .... (run).
A: In this heat? How far (2) .... (you / run)?

A: You look pleased about something. What (3) .... (happen)?
B: I (4) .... (just / pass) my driving test.
A: Congratulations! You deserve to pass. You (5) .... (practise) for months, haven't you?
B: That's right. My father (6) .... (give) me lessons.

A: Where (7) .... (you / be)?
B: At the doctor's. I (8) .... (not feel) well lately. I'm tired and a bit run-down.
A: I'm sorry to hear that. (9) .... (you / work) too hard?
B: I hope that's all it is but the doctor (10) .... (do) some tests and she'll let me know the results soon, I hope.

A: You look frustrated. What's the matter?
B: I (11) .... (try) to learn my lines for the play but I'm finding it difficult. I (12) .... (only / manage) to learn the first scene so far.
A: Can I help in any way?

23c Complete the article. Use the present perfect simple or continuous of the verbs in the box.

| avoid | do | eat | invite | lose | make | order |
| pay off | set | stick | watch |

They (0) ...*have set*... the date, picked the dress and are making the final preparations for the big day. Lyndsey Young (1) .... also .... sure she will look her best when she marries Ben O'Neill later this week.

For the past five months, she (2) .... to an exercise programme in which she (3) .... forty or fifty minutes of exercise a day. She (4) .... also .... her diet. She (5) .... high-calorie foods and (6) .... lots of fruit and vegetables instead. Thanks to all of her hard work, she (7) .... nearly ten kilos. Lyndsey's efforts (8) .... and she looks fabulous. The couple (9) .... huge amounts of food and beverages for the wedding, which will take place at a secret location, but sources say that Lyndsey and Ben (10) .... only family and close friends to the wedding. The stage is set for what will surely be the wedding of the year.

Check 3 Present tenses

1 **Complete the sentences. Use the present simple, present continuous, present perfect simple, present perfect continuous or past simple of the verbs in brackets.**

1 Anthony isn't usually easy to get on with but he .... very co-operative these days. (be)
2 What .... of her? Will she be easy to work with? (you / think)
3 I can't talk now. We .... a meeting. I'll ring you later. (have)
4 Jessica .... back from work and she's exhausted. (just / come)
5 I .... Bertha for ages. Where is she? (not see)
6 He .... his car. Someone bought it last week. (already / sell)
7 How long .... that you're going to have a baby? (you / know)
8 She .... unemployed for a long time but thankfully, she's got a job now. (be)
9 I .... to contact them for days but they .... any of my calls yet. (try, not return)
10 I .... his latest book but I .... it yet. (read, not finish)
11 Terry .... the kitchen all morning. He must be exhausted! (paint)
12 I .... preparing dinner yet so I'd better hurry. (not start)

/ 12

2 **Circle the correct answer.**

The Tower of London (13) *survived / has survived* centuries of warfare but it could vanish from sight in the twenty-first century, experts (14) *warned / have warned* yesterday. The ancient fortress, which (15) *dominates / has dominated* the city skyline for almost a thousand years, could be placed on a United Nations list of endangered landmarks because developers (16) *put up / are putting up* new buildings in the area and a number of high-rise buildings (17) *ruin / are ruining* views of the famous World Heritage site, according to the UN's cultural body UNESCO.

British officials have until the end of the month to show UNESCO that they can save the Tower. If not, the Tower could be put on UNESCO's World Heritage in Danger list. UNESCO inspectors (18) *visited / have visited* London last year after they received a damning report that the City of London (19) *doesn't appear / isn't appearing* to do enough to protect the setting of some of Britain's important sites. Other buildings under threat (20) *include / are including* Westminster Abbey and the Houses of Parliament.

/ 8

3 Complete the article. Use the present simple, present continuous, present perfect simple or present perfect continuous of the verbs in brackets.

According to research, the demand for alternative medicine (21) .... (rise) recently and approximately 20 per cent of the UK's population regularly (22) .... (turn) to alternative treatments when they (23) .... (be) ill. Consequently, more and more British doctors (24) .... (offer) their patients choices of treatment these days and many of them (25) .... (usually / combine) alternative treatments with conventional medicine.

Although alternative medicine (26) .... (become) increasingly popular, doctors (27) .... (disagree) about whether or not the treatments are effective. Of course, people (28) .... (use) alternative medicine for hundreds of years but many practitioners of conventional medicine (29) .... (claim) that so far they (30) .... (not see) any convincing proof that alternative treatments are safe or effective.

Today, the most widely practised alternative treatments are acupuncture, aromatherapy, massage and herbal medicine but other forms of treatment (31) .... (also / gain) in popularity.

What about you? (32) .... (you / ever / try) an alternative treatment? If so, was it successful? Send your views and experiences to:

/ 12

4 Complete the second sentence so that it means the same as the first, using the word in bold. Use between two and five words.

33 How long have you lived in this house? **move**
   When .... to this house?

34 I started cooking an hour ago. **been**
   I .... an hour.

35 I haven't seen Vasily for a few days. **since**
   It's a few days ....
   Vasily.

36 She paid back the money she owed me very quickly. **already**
   She .... the money she owed me.

37 A minute ago Katsu told me he has got a new job. **just**
   Katsu .... me he has got a new job.

38 They started working this morning and they are still working. **been**
   They .... this morning.

39 They have never been to Paris before. **ever**
   This is the first time .... to Paris.

40 When did you meet your wife? **known**
   How long .... your wife?

/ 8

Total: / 40

Self-check

Wrong answers	Look again at	Try CD-ROM
16, 17, 22, 23, 24, 25, 26, 29, 31	Unit 18	Exercise 18
1, 2, 3, 19, 20, 27	Unit 19	Exercise 19
14, 18, 30, 32, 39	Unit 20	Exercise 20
4, 6, 12, 21, 36, 37	Unit 21	Exercise 21
5, 7, 8, 13, 15, 33, 35, 40	Unit 22	Exercise 22
9, 10, 11, 28, 34, 38	Unit 23	Exercise 23

Now do **Check 3**

53

Past tenses

24 Past simple and continuous

- The past simple describes actions which are complete. We use the past simple for:
  - a past action or a sequence of past actions: *I **woke up** very early. Then I **got** dressed, **had** breakfast and **left** the house.*
  - a state, event or action that lasted for a period of time in the past: *The Smiths **owned** a farm in the north of the country.* *It **rained** for several days and nights. The students **waited** for a month to get their exam results.*
  - a habit in the past: *When we **were** children, we often **went** to the cinema.*
- The past continuous describes states, events or actions which are temporary or incomplete. We use the past continuous:
  - to emphasise that a past event continued for some time: *It **was raining** all night.*
  - to describe an action in progress at a particular time in the past, or a temporary past situation or event: *We **were watching** TV at nine o'clock last night.*
  - to describe two or more past actions happening at the same time: *He **was cooking** the dinner while she **was talking** to him.*
  - to set the scene in a story: *We set off early. Before long the sun **was rising** above the distant hills and the birds **were singing** their morning chorus.*
  - to talk about something we were planning or expected to happen: *We **were planning** to move to Canada but decided to stay here instead.*

▶▶ For future in the past, see Unit 30.

- We use the past simple and the past continuous with *when* and *as/while* to talk about a past action or event that was interrupted. Notice when we use a comma: *They **arrived** while we **were having** dinner.* *While we **were having** dinner, they **arrived**.* *We **were having** dinner when they **arrived**.* *When they **arrived**, we **were having** dinner.*

⚠ Sometimes we can use either the past simple or the past continuous, depending on what we want to emphasise. Compare: *I **lived** there for five years.* (I don't live there now.) *I **was living** there for five years.* (This emphasises that my residence there was temporary/the period of time I lived there.)

PRACTICE

24a Circle the correct answer.

It (0) (*happened*)/ *was happening* in June 1985. It was summer and we (1) *relaxed / were relaxing* in the garden. My mother (2) *read / was reading* a book and my uncle (3) *dozed / was dozing* peacefully in the sun. We children (4) *looked / were looking* for worms and insects. And then he (5) *arrived / was arriving*. He was a handsome man with piercing eyes and he (6) *looked / was looking* straight at my mother. Her face (7) *went / was going* pale.

'Arthur, I (8) *thought / was thinking* you were dead!' she said.

Grammar: *past tenses*

Jussi and I (9) *met / were meeting* while we (10) *lived / were living* in London. I (11) *rented / was renting* a room in a house in North London and he (12) *stayed / was staying* with friends who'd offered to put him up. We both (13) *had / were having* temporary jobs – at one time he (14) *waited / was waiting* on tables in a café and I (15) *washed / was washing* dishes in a small restaurant. Anyway, we (16) *got on / were getting on* really well and before long we (17) *planned / were planning* to go on a long holiday together. That (18) *was / was being* before the accident.

I (19) *sat / was sitting* in my taxi reading the morning newspaper when the alarm in the bank across the street (20) *went off / was going off*. I (21) *looked / was looking* up and (22) *saw / was seeing* two masked men running towards me. There was confusion everywhere. Police cars (23) *raced / were racing* towards the bank while pedestrians (24) *ran / were running* away from it. I (25) *turned / was turning* the key in the ignition when the masked men (26) *forced / were forcing* their way into my taxi and (27) *told / were telling* me to drive off. It was the scariest thing that had ever happened to me.

24b Complete the extract from a story. Use the past simple or continuous of the verbs in brackets. Sometimes both tenses are possible.

As I (0) ......*was going*...... (go) to sleep, I (1) .... (tell) myself that I would avoid the man who was sharing the room. I (2) .... (sleep) deeply when I was suddenly woken by a loud noise. To judge from the sound, my companion must have jumped down from the upper berth to the floor in a single movement. I (3) .... (hear) him trying to open the door; it (4) .... (open), and then I (5) .... (hear) him running at full speed down the passage, leaving the door open behind him. The ship (6) .... (roll) a little and I (7) .... (expect) to hear him fall but he (8) .... (run) as though for his life. The door (9) .... (swing) open and shut with the movement of the ship and the sound (10) .... (annoy) me. I (11) .... (get up) and (12) .... (close) it and (13) .... (find) my way back to my berth in the darkness. I (14) .... (go) to sleep again but I have no idea how long I slept.

25 Past perfect simple and continuous

Past perfect simple
- We use the past perfect simple:
  - to describe an event or action that happened before another past event or action. The past perfect simple makes it clear that one action or event was completed before the second one started. Compare: *When I arrived, the train **had left**.* (= The train left before I arrived.) *When I got there, the train **left**.* (= The train left as I was arriving or immediately after I arrived.)
  - to describe an event or action that happened before a particular time in the past: *It was June 1991. Ann and Michael **had** just **got** married.   It was midnight and the children **had gone** to bed hours ago.   By nine, most of the workers **had arrived**.*
- We use the past perfect simple with many of the adverbs and expressions we use with the present perfect: *just, already, yet, for, since, ever, never, it was the first/second time, it was the most …* : *Blake and Julie **had just left** and there was nobody at home.   Sophie and Austin met again at the reunion. They **hadn't seen** each other **for several years**.   **It was the first time** in his life he'**d felt** truly happy.*
- We often use the past perfect simple in clauses with *when, before, after, until, as soon as* and *by*. When the sequence of events is clear, we can also use the past simple: *When we **finished/'d finished** the meal, I made some coffee.   **As soon as** I **told/'d told** her the news, I regretted it.*

Past perfect continuous

Affirmative	I/you/he/she/it/we/they **had been waiting**
Negative	I/you/he/she/it/we/they **hadn't been waiting**
Question	**Had** I/you/he/she/it/we/they **been waiting**?

- We use the past perfect continuous:
  - to emphasise how long an event or action lasted: *It **had been raining** for three days when the dam burst.*
  - to describe an action whose effects, results or consequences were clear in the past: *I'**d been moving** house and I was tired and dirty.*

PRACTICE

25a Circle the correct answer.

0   It was only four o'clock but everyone *already left* / (*had already left*) the office.
1   He *was* / *'d been* in hospital for days before I *heard* / *'d heard* about the accident.
2   I could tell they *did* / *'d done* something wrong because they were looking guilty.
3   By the time she *was* / *'d been* ten years old, she *already appeared* / *'d already appeared* in a West End play.
4   The performance *just started* / *had just started* when we *arrived* / *'d arrived*.
5   Max *never left* / *had never left* home before without telling me where he was going.
6   By nine that evening, most of the guests *already left* / *had already left* the party.

25b Complete the sentences. Use the past simple or past perfect continuous of the verbs in brackets.

0   Everyone ....*felt*........ exhausted because they ....*'d been working*........ all day. (feel, work)

1   She .... paint on her hands because she .... the kitchen. (have, decorate)

2   After they .... for several hours, they .... to stop for a rest. (drive, decide)

3   We .... there for many months before we .... to notice the problems. (not live, begin)

4   .... long before the train .... ? (you / wait, arrive)

5   I .... for months but I still .... enough money to buy a new car. (save, not have)

6   We .... them to arrive for several hours when they finally .... into the drive. (expect, pull)

25c Complete the first part of an article. Use the past simple or past perfect simple of the verbs in brackets.

Pirate of the Caribbean

Black Sam Bellamy was an original pirate of the Caribbean. In 1984 Black Sam's ship, the *Whydah*, (0) ....*became*........ (become) the first pirate ship ever recovered from the sea. According to experts, Sam was probably a democratic leader because divers (1) .... (find) gold ornaments on the ship which were cut into pieces so they could be shared with the crew.

Black Sam (2) .... (leave) England and (3) .... (sail) to America in the early 1700s. We don't know much about the life he (4) .... (leave) behind. We do know that he was dark and handsome and that he (5) .... (wear) his long black hair tied in a ponytail.

By 1715 Black Sam (6) .... (already / meet) his lover, Maria Hallett, in Cape Cod, Massachussetts. While living in Cape Cod, Black Sam (7) .... (hear) of a fleet of Spanish treasure ships which (8) .... (sink) in the Caribbean earlier that year. He (9) .... (decide) to look for the sunken treasure but he (10) .... (need) a ship to do so. He (11) .... (persuade) a friend, Palgrave Williams, to buy him one. Black Sam (12) .... (go) looking for the lost treasure but when he (13) .... (not find) it, he (14) .... (turn) to piracy.

Grammar: *past tenses*

25d Complete the second part of the article. Use the past simple, past perfect simple or past perfect continuous of the verbs in brackets.

By 1717 Black Sam and his crew (0) **had captured** (capture) over fifty ships but none was as large or as rich as the slave ship, the *Whydah*. In April of 1717 the *Whydah* (1) .... (just / sell) a cargo of slaves and was returning to London when Black Sam (2) .... (begin) to chase her. By the time he (3) .... (capture) her, he (4) .... (chase) her for three days.

At last Black Sam (5) .... (find) the wealth he (6) .... (look) for and he (7) .... (decide) to sail back to Cape Cod. But the *Whydah* (8) .... (sail) into a storm and strong winds (9) .... (drive) her towards land. The ship (10) .... (strike) rocks a hundred yards from the shores of Cape Cod and (11) .... (sink). Two men (12) .... (swim) to shore but Black Sam wasn't one of them.

According to legend, Black Sam (13) .... (travel) home to meet Maria Hallett. Some people believe he (14) .... (decide) to propose marriage. They also say Maria (15) .... (wait) for his return and was watching from the cliffs of Cape Cod when the *Whydah* (16) .... (go) down. Was Maria saddened to lose her lover – or was she glad to be rid of such a dangerous man? No one knows.

26 *used to, would, be/get used to*

- We use *used to* to talk about past states: *She **used to have** long hair but she cut it. **Did** they **use to live** here? I **didn't use to like** fish but I do now.*
- We use *used to* or *would* to talk about habits or repeated actions in the past: *When we were children, we **used to/would go** out together. My grandmother **used to/would bake** a cake every weekend. We **never used to do/would never do** our homework until Sunday evening.*
- When we use *would* to talk about a past habit, we must use a past time reference. *Used to* can be used with or without a past time reference: *Before I got this job, I **used to/would go** out a lot. I **used to go** out a lot. (Not I would go out a lot.)*
- We use *be/get used to* + noun/pronoun/-*ing* form to talk about something that is or becomes normal because we have experienced or done it before. Compare: *I **used to eat** a lot of junk food.* (= I don't eat a lot any more.) *I'**m getting used to eating** fresh vegetables.* (= I'm becoming accustomed to eating fresh vegetables.)
- We can use *be/get used to* in various tenses: *She **isn't used to** living in a small village but she'**s getting used to** it. When my parents were young, they had to get up at five every morning. However, they **were used to** getting up early so it didn't bother them. Don't worry about the noise; you'**ll get used to** it!*

PRACTICE

26a Complete the sentences. Use the correct form of *used to* or *would*. Use *would* wherever possible.

0   When I was a child, I ......*would*...... dream of travelling round the world.
1   She .... have lots of free time before she started working here.
2   In the summer holidays we .... go to the beach nearly every day.
3   Before Harry moved here, he .... take the bus everywhere but now he needs a car.
4   They .... drink coffee but recently they've got into the habit of drinking several cups a day.
5   A: .... you .... have a beard?
    B: Yes, but it .... bother me so I got rid of it.

26b Complete the texts. Use the correct form of *used to* or *be/get used to*.

"I (0) ......*used to*...... be several kilos heavier than I am now. That's because I (1) .... hate exercising. But now I (2) .... working out at the gym regularly and I've lost a lot of weight. I (3) .... being fit and healthy and I never want to be overweight again."

"We live in London now but we (4) .... live in a small town. When we moved here, I (5) .... the noise of the traffic and I missed the country. However, I (6) .... city life now and I like it!"

26c Complete the essay. Use the correct form of *used to*, *would* or *be/get used to* and the verbs in the box.

| be   complete   go   have (x2)   light   ~~pack~~ |
| rush   spend   stop   walk |

Some of my happiest memories are of summer holidays with my family. Every year we (0) ...*would pack*... our suitcases and drive off to the seaside. Some years we (1) .... halfway and spend the night in a motel. But usually we (2) .... the journey in a day.

As soon as we arrived, we (3) .... down to the sea. The beach was rocky and for the first few days we had to walk carefully because we (4) .... over the sharp stones with our soft winter feet. We had lots of friends whom we saw only in the summers so we (5) .... a lot of time with them. During the day we (6) .... swimming and at night we (7) .... a fire on the beach, chat and listen to the waves.

By the end of the holidays, we (8) .... great suntans and our feet (9) .... hard from running over the rocks. We (10) .... mixed feelings about leaving. We didn't want to leave our friends behind but at the same time we looked forward to going home.

Check 4 Past tenses

1 **Circle the correct answer.**
   1 When I was a child, we *often used / would often* sit in the garden on summer evenings.
   2 As soon as she put the phone down, she *started / had started* to cry.
   3 I *used to / would* own a house in the country but I sold it.
   4 We waited until we had finished work and then we *took / had taken* a break.
   5 They *didn't used to live / weren't used to living* in a flat but they don't mind it now.
   6 It was now evening and we *were driving / had been driving* all day.
   7 Where *did you use to / would you* work before you got this job?
   8 Giles and Max *used to argue / were used to arguing* but they get along fine now.

   / 8

2 **Complete the conversation. Use the past simple or continuous of the verbs in brackets.**
   A: I (9) .... (phone) you this morning but you (10) .... (not answer). What (11) .... (you / do)?
   B: I (12) .... (hear) the phone but I (13) .... (have) a shower. Anyway, what (14) .... (you / want)?
   A: Well, last night I (15) .... (clear) out my desk when I (16) .... (find) these old photos. Do you want them?

   / 8

3 **Complete the extract from a story. Use the past simple, past perfect simple or past perfect continuous of the verbs in the box.**

   | arrive   go   only / be   rain   smell   talk |

   It was a beautiful morning. It (17) .... in the night and the next morning the air (18) .... fresh. No one was awake, though, because we (19) .... to bed late the night before. Our cousins (20) .... unexpectedly that evening and we (21) .... for most of the night. By eight o'clock in the morning we (22) .... in bed for three hours.

   / 6

60

4 Complete the article. Use the past simple, past continuous, past perfect simple or past perfect continuous of the verbs in brackets.

A Japanese businessman recently made medical history by surviving without food and water in near-freezing weather for about three weeks.

Mr Mitsutaka Uchikoshi, 35, climbed up Mount Rokko in western Japan for a barbecue party with friends but decided to come back down on his own. While he (23) .... (walk) down the mountain, he (24) .... (slip) in a stream and (25) .... (break) his pelvis. Until he (26) .... (become) unconscious, he survived by sipping the remains of a bottle of barbecue sauce that he (27) .... (carry) with him at the time of the accident.

When searchers (28) .... (rescue) him, he (29) .... (appear) to be in a coma. His pulse was almost undetectable and his body temperature (30) .... (drop) to 32 degrees. He (31) .... (also / lose) a lot of weight. Doctors (32) .... (treat) Mr Uchikoshi for hypothermia, multiple organ failure and blood loss. By the time he was rescued, he (33) .... (miss) for twenty-five days.

Remarkably, he (34) .... (recover) fully. One of his doctors said, 'He was frozen alive and survived. If we can understand why, it opens up all sorts of possibilities for the future.'

/ 12

5 Complete the texts. Use the correct form of *used to* or *be/get used to* and the verbs in brackets.

I (35) .... (hate) working at weekends but I (36) .... it now and I don't mind it any more.

I can't (37) .... the idea that my daughter is grown up. I still think of her as a child. I remember how I (38) .... (hold) her in my arms when she was a baby.

My wife and I (39) .... (never / go) abroad for our holidays. We (40) .... (spend) our summers in Cornwall.

/ 6

Total: / 40

Self-check

Wrong answers	Look again at	Try CD-ROM
4, 9, 10, 11, 12, 13, 14, 15, 16, 23, 24, 25, 28, 29, 32, 34	Unit 24	Exercise 24
2, 4, 6, 17, 18, 19, 20, 21, 22, 26, 27, 30, 31, 33	Unit 25	Exercise 25
1, 3, 5, 7, 8, 35, 36, 37, 38, 39, 40	Unit 26	Exercise 26

Now do **Check 4**

Future forms

27 Future forms and meanings (1)

will, shall
- We use *will*:
  - for statements of fact or general predictions about the future: *We'll have a break at six.   The President will outline his policy tomorrow.   They'll be here soon.*
  - for decisions we make at the time of speaking: *'Would you like to come with us to the theatre tonight?' 'All right. I'll join you.'*
  - in offers, promises and requests: *I'll do that for you.   Will you help me, please?*
  - with verbs like *believe, doubt, expect, hope, suppose* and *think,* and adverbs like *perhaps, probably* and *definitely*: *I expect they'll be here soon.   Do you think they'll win?   They probably won't come by taxi.*

- We use *shall*:
  - with *I* or *we* in offers and suggestions: *Shall I come with you?   Shall we go out?*
  - in place of *will* in more formal English, especially written English: *We shall make every effort to deal with your complaint.*

be going to
We use *be going to*:

- for things we expect to happen based on present evidence: *Look at that plane. It's going to land.*

- for intentions, when we have already decided to do something: *They're going to visit Madame Tussaud's when they're in London.*

> ⚠ Compare *will* and *be going to*: *Student numbers are going to fall over the next five years.* (The speaker is thinking of present trends and has evidence for the statement.)   *Student numbers will fall over the next five years.* (This is the speaker's opinion or belief.)

Present continuous
We use the present continuous for future events we have planned and arranged. The time reference must be stated or clear from the context: *I'm meeting her for lunch tomorrow.*

> ⚠ Compare the present continuous and *be going to*: *I'm visiting my aunt in hospital tomorrow.* (The speaker has arranged to do this.)   *I'm going to visit my aunt in hospital tomorrow.* (This is the speaker's intention.)

> ⚠ With *go* and *come* we prefer the present continuous to *be going to*: *I'm going to university next year.*

Present simple
We use the present simple:

- to talk about timetables and schedules: *The plane leaves at eight fifteen.*

- to refer to the future in clauses of time and condition after *if, unless, when, after, before, as soon as, until* and *by the time*: *We'll phone you when we get there.*

Grammar: future forms

PRACTICE

27a Complete the conversation. Use *will* or *be going to* and the verbs in brackets.

A: Have you decided what you (0) ....'re going to do.... (do) this weekend?
B: Well, Mark phoned last night and he (1) .... (visit) us at the weekend.
A: Really? I'd like to see him. I think I (2) .... (phone) him tonight and arrange something.
B: Why not? We're planning to spend the day at the beach on Saturday. I hope the weather (3) .... (be) warm enough. The weather forecast says it (4) .... (be) a nice weekend – apparently, there's warm weather coming in from Europe later on this week. And then on Saturday night we (5) .... (see) a film.
A: Well, I've got nothing planned so I (6) .... (join) you on Saturday morning if that's OK.
B: Sure. I (7) .... (pick) you up from your flat after breakfast.
A: Great! And what about the film? What time (8) .... (you / see) that?
B: We (9) .... (see) the early show at six and after that we (10) .... (probably / go) somewhere for a meal.
A: Sounds good. I (11) .... (see) you on Saturday!

27b Complete the conversations. Use the present continuous or *be going to* and the verbs in brackets. Use the present continuous wherever possible.

A: I (0) ....'m going to ring.... (ring) Suli. Would you like me to tell her anything?
B: Tell her I've spoken to Ned and I (1) .... (meet) him for lunch tomorrow.

———

A: Where (2) .... (you / go)?
B: Home. (3) .... (you / come) with me?

———

A: Shall we go to the cinema tonight?
B: I (4) .... (take) Alice out for dinner. I've booked a table at a nice restaurant and I (5) .... (ask) her to marry me.

———

A: That child on the bicycle isn't looking where he's going. Oh, dear! He (6) .... (crash) into the wall if he's not careful!
B: You're right. Look! He's hurt himself. He (7) .... (need) stitches for that cut on his leg.

———

A: Could you help me decorate the living room this afternoon?
B: Sorry, I can't. I (8) .... (play) tennis with Tom. We've already booked the court.
A: I hope you're playing indoors. It's nice now but they say it (9) .... (rain) later today.

Grammar: *future forms*

27c Complete the e-mail. Use the present simple or continuous of the verbs in brackets.

9.00 am	Leave Brighton	6.00 pm	Supper
10.30 am	Madame Tussaud's and guided tour	7.30 pm	*Phantom of the Opera*
12.00 pm	Lunch	10.30 pm	Leave Victoria Station
1.00 pm	Free	12.00 am	Arrive Brighton

New Message

The coach (0) ......*leaves*........ (leave) Brighton at nine and we (1) .... (arrive) at Madame Tussaud's at ten thirty. When we get there, we (2) .... (go) on a guided tour – it's all been arranged for us. After that we (3) .... (have) lunch somewhere nearby and in the afternoon we can do what we like – some of us (4) .... (go) shopping. If you (5) .... (not want) to do that, there'll be lots of other things we can do in London. We (6) .... (meet) up in the evening for something to eat and then we (7) .... (take) the Underground to Piccadilly Station. We can walk from there to the theatre. *Phantom of the Opera* (8) .... (start) at seven thirty and (9) .... (finish) at ten. At ten thirty the coach (10) .... (leave) Victoria Station for Brighton.

27d Complete the sentences. Use *will, shall, be going to*, the present simple or continuous and the verbs in brackets.

0   If you ......*see*........ Pete, would you tell him I'm looking for him? (see)
1   A: .... Luis and Sondra round for a meal? (we / invite)
    B: That's a good idea.
2   I think things .... better after a good night's sleep. I'm sure you .... so bad in the morning. (look, not feel)
3   What's wrong? You look as if you .... (cry)
4   They .... on Saturday morning and they .... back for three weeks. They booked the holiday months ago. (leave, not come)
5   I .... any more work today. My train .... in half an hour. (not do, leave)
6   Zoe .... round the world when she .... school. (travel, finish)
7   The President .... the nation at two this afternoon. (address)
8   We .... our computer system later this year. We don't know exactly when the work .... but we hope it .... finished by the end of the summer. (change, start, be)

28 Future forms and meanings (2)

Future continuous	will be + present participle: *I'll be doing*
Future perfect simple	will have + past participle: *I'll have done*
Future perfect continuous	will have been + present participle: *I'll have been doing*

Future continuous
- We use the future continuous:
  - for an activity that will be in progress at a point in time or for a period of time in the future: *This time tomorrow we'll be sitting on a plane.   I'll be studying in the library all evening.*
  - for intentions or events that are fixed or expected to happen: *They'll be going to town tomorrow to do some shopping.   He'll be arriving at six.*
  - to talk about a future activity without expressing deliberate intention: *She'll probably be running her own company in a few years' time!*
- Compare the future continuous and future simple *(will)*: *I'll go and see Ethan tomorrow.* (a deliberate intention or promise)   *I'll be seeing Ethan tomorrow so I can give him your message.* (an action that will happen anyway, one not specially planned)

Future perfect simple
- We use the future perfect simple for an action that will be completed before a particular time in the future, often with *by* or *by the time* + present simple: *I'll have finished this job by Friday.   We'll have cooked dinner by the time you get here.*

Future perfect continuous
- We use the future perfect continuous with *for* to emphasise the duration of a state or action which will probably continue after the time mentioned: *We'll have been living here for two years in January.*

PRACTICE

28a Complete the conversations. Use the future simple (*will*) or future continuous of the verbs in brackets.

A: Would you like to come for lunch on Saturday?
B: Unfortunately, I (0) ...'ll be working... (work) all day on Saturday.
A: That's too bad. I (1) .... (phone) you on Sunday.
   (2) .... (you / be) in?

A: Do you ever think about what you (3) .... (do) in ten years' time?
B: Sometimes I imagine I (4) .... (have) a much more interesting job and I (5) .... (earn) a lot of money. But to be honest, I think I (6) .... (probably / work) here, doing the same job as now.

A: I'm taking the car so I (7) .... (give) you a lift tonight.
B: Thanks. I (8) .... (play) tennis until seven but I
   (9) .... (be) back shortly after that.

Grammar: *future forms*

28b **Write sentences. Use the future continuous, future perfect simple or future perfect continuous.**

What will life be like in fifty years' time?

0   we / use / energy that doesn't harm the environment
    We'll be using energy that doesn't harm the environment.

1   scientists / discover / life on other planets
    ....

2   the Earth's climate / become / much hotter than it is today
    ....

3   we / not use / fossil fuels like coal and oil
    ....

4   doctors / not find / a cure for the common cold
    ....

5   people / live / on the moon for several years / by then
    ....

6   the Internet / replace / television / as our main source of entertainment
    ....

28c **Complete the interview. Use the future simple (*will*), future continuous or future perfect of the verbs in brackets.**

Interviewer: Today we're talking to Professor Marjorie Brown about life in the future. Let's start with homes. Professor, what will our homes be like?

Professor: Well, they might not look very different from homes today but (0) *there will certainly be* (there / certainly / be) differences. In twenty years' time homes (1) .... (become) smaller. This is because more and more people (2) .... (live) in crowded cities. However, designers (3) .... (undoubtedly / find) ways of making small homes more comfortable. For example, the homes of the future (4) .... (have) walls that can be moved so that space can be used in different ways. Scientists (5) .... (also / invent) glass that can change from transparent to black. Transparent glass lets light and heat in and out. Black glass keeps it in. This (6) .... (help) us to control the temperature of our homes.

Interviewer: (7) .... (there / be) any other changes to the way we live?

Professor: Yes, one major change. Experts predict that by 2024 humans (8) .... (live) on the moon. One can only imagine what homes there (9) .... (look) like! And I think that by then many of us (10) .... (take) at least one holiday in space and maybe even to the moon. Imagine that.

29 Other ways of talking about the future

- We use *be* + *to*-infinitive to talk about formal plans or arrangements, instructions and prohibitions: *The Queen **is to arrive** at 10.00 to begin the ceremony.   You **are to be** there no later than eight o'clock.*
- We use *be due* + *to*-infinitive to talk about events that we expect to take place at a fixed time, e.g. with timetables: *The bus **is due to arrive** any minute.*
- We use *be (just) about* + *to*-infinitive or *be on the point of* + *-ing* form to talk about events that we expect will happen very soon: *We're (just) **about to leave**.   I think he's **on the point of asking** her to marry him.*
- Some verbs refer to the future: *plan/hope/intend* + *to*-infinitive: *The company **plans to build** a new supermarket.   I **hope to study** law next year.*

PRACTICE

29a Complete the second sentence so that it means the same as the first, using the word in bold. Use between two and five words.

0   You must pay your fees before classes begin.   **are**
    You ......*are to pay*...... your fees before classes begin.

1   Dylan isn't going to spend the night here.   **intend**
    Dylan .... the night here.

2   The judges will announce the winner any moment now.   **about**
    The judges .... the winner.

3   The President will announce his resignation very soon.   **point**
    The President is .... his resignation.

4   Elizabeth thinks she will travel to Africa next year.   **hopes**
    Elizabeth .... to Africa next year.

5   Charles isn't going to write his essay tonight.   **plan**
    Charles .... his essay tonight.

6   They must not begin without me.   **are**
    They .... without me.

7   The police are going to stop the search very soon.   **about**
    The police .... the search.

8   Clarissa is having her operation in three weeks.   **due**
    Clarissa .... her operation in three weeks.

29b Complete the conversations. Use the correct form of the words in the box.

> be / about / make   be / due / open   be / on the point of / call
> hope / find   hope / have   intend / finish   intend / pay
> ~~not be / come~~   not be / due / arrive   not plan / go

A: You've got school tomorrow so you (0) ......*are not to come*...... home any later than ten.
B: Oh, all right.

Grammar: *future forms*

A: I hear you're expecting a baby. Congratulations!
B: Thank you. My husband (1) .... a girl this time but I don't mind as long as it's healthy. And now there's another baby on the way, we're moving into a bigger house.
A: That's a big decision. Have you seen anywhere you like?
B: Yes. In fact, we (2) .... an offer for a house near where we live now.

A: We've been waiting for ages. What time is the bus supposed to be here?
B: I'm afraid it (3) .... for another twenty minutes.
A: I'm so cold I (4) .... a taxi. What do you think?
B: I don't mind. But how (5) .... you .... ? I don't have that much money with me.

A: What's happening with the new hospital?
B: Well, they say it (6) .... next month but I don't think that's likely.
A: I think you're right. I'm sure everyone (7) .... projects like these on time but they never do.

A: What are you going to do next year when you finish college?
B: Well, I (8) .... a job. I (9) .... to university for at least another year.

30 Future in the past

When we are talking about the past, we sometimes need to refer to events that were still in the future at that point. To do this, we use the same forms we use to refer to the future but we make the verbs past.

Future	Future in the past
am/is/are going to ▶▶ See Unit 27.	was/were going to: We **were going to travel** by car but we changed our minds.
Present continuous ▶▶ See Unit 27.	Past continuous: I left work early as I **was meeting** a friend.
will ▶▶ See Unit 27.	would: I had met the man I knew I **would marry**.
am/is/are + to-infinitive ▶▶ See Unit 29.	was/were + to-infinitive: The guests **were to arrive** before the Queen.
am/is/are + due + to-infinitive ▶▶ See Unit 29.	was/were + due + to-infinitive: The bus **was due to arrive** at ten so I waited in the café.
am/is/are + about + to-infinitive ▶▶ See Unit 29.	was/were + about + to-infinitive: I **was about to ring** you.

PRACTICE

30a Circle the correct answer.

0 All the way there I knew we (*were going to*) / *were about to* be late.
1 The film *was due to* / *was about to* be released in October.
2 He looked as if he *was crying* / *was going to cry* at any moment.
3 When they last saw her, she *would get* / *was getting* married the following day.
4 The ceremony *was to* / *was about to* take place at the palace but they were forced to change the venue.
5 The instant they met, they knew they *were due to* / *were going to* be friends.
6 I *was going to* / *was to* move to London but decided against the idea.
7 We took our seats because the film *would* / *was about to* begin.
8 Liam *was going to buy* / *was buying* a new car but in the end he decided not to.
9 I always thought I *was to* / *would* be famous one day.
10 Hailey *was to* / *was about to* go out when the phone rang.

30b Complete the conversation. Use the correct form of the words in brackets.

A: What happened? I thought you (0) ....*were going*.... (go) on holiday yesterday.

B: We were – and then everything went wrong. We'd made all the arrangements and a taxi (1) .... (take) us to the airport but just before it (2) .... (be / due / arrive), we heard there was terrible traffic on the roads and they were advising people not to use the motorway. So when the taxi came, we told the driver we (3) .... (go) to the train station instead of the airport. He dropped us off and we got onto the train. But as it (4) .... (be / about / pull away), it broke down and we were stuck at the station. We were sure we (5) .... (be) late but eventually, another train arrived and we got to the airport. We (6) .... (be / just about / check in) when we heard that they'd changed the departure time of our plane – it (7) .... (not leave) for another twenty-four hours! So we put our bags back on the train and here we are!

A: What a nightmare! I hope you intend to make a complaint.

B: Of course. I (8) .... (plan / be) on a beach right now and instead I'm waiting for another taxi.

Check 5 Future forms

1 Complete the sentences. Use *will*, *be going to* or the present continuous and the verbs in brackets.

1 I .... to the concert this evening with Andy. What about you? (go)
2 I think you should know: I .... Ben you borrowed his car without asking him. (tell)
3 You look as if you .... Are you ill? (faint)
4 We .... anything special at the weekend. I expect we .... at home. (not do, stay)
5 .... me lift this, please? It's heavy. (you / help)

/ 5

2 Circle the correct answer.

6 The book *was due* / *was about* to be published six months ago.
7 She *was going to move* / *was moving* house but changed her mind.
8 After she graduates, she *is about* / *intends* to travel round the world for a year.
9 According to the invitation, we *are* / *are due* to be there no later than seven.
10 I always thought that one day I *was writing* / *would write* a best-selling novel.

/ 5

3 Complete the second sentence so that it means the same as the first, using the word in bold. Use between two and five words.

11 We were getting ready to leave when we got the call. **about**
We .... when we got the call.
12 Avril is leaving her job very soon. **point**
Avril is .... her job.
13 According to the schedule, the project will finish next year. **due**
The project .... next year.
14 You must not write on the question paper. **are**
You .... on the question paper.
15 When are they going to get married? **plan**
When .... married?
16 I had arranged to meet Liz for lunch but she cancelled. **meeting**
I .... Liz for lunch but she cancelled.
17 I was about to ring you when you rang me. **going**
I .... you when you rang me.
18 We expected to see them at the concert. **would**
We thought we .... them at the concert.

/ 8

70

4 Circle the correct answer.

WIND POWER

If the British government gets its way, the 'fuel' of the future (19) *will / is about to* be the air we breathe. The government (20) *is on the point of using / plans to use* electricity from wind farms to help meet its targets for renewable energy. With government approval, private firms (21) *will have built / are to build* offshore wind farms in the southeast of England. One of these, the London Array wind farm, (22) *will be / will have been* the largest in the world when it (23) *is / will have been* completed. Together, the London Array and Thanet wind farms (24) *will produce / are producing* enough electricity to power a million homes.

London Array have not yet announced when they (25) *begin / will begin* construction of the wind farm. However, they expect that they (26) *will be completing / will have completed* it by 2010 or 2011. The smaller wind farm in Thanet (27) *is going to supply / will be supplying* electricity to about 240,000 homes by 2008.

However, the farms are controversial. Developers (28) *were hoping / would hope* to build a third farm in the Lake District but the government rejected their plans because they are concerned about the effect of the farm on the countryside and on tourism.

Environmentalists say we (29) *will have to / are having to* do much more than build wind farms in the future. Otherwise, climate change (30) *will have / will be having* a devastating effect on the environment.

/ 12

5 Complete the conversations. Use the present simple, future simple (*will/shall*), future continuous, future perfect simple or future perfect continuous and the verbs in brackets.

A: I'd love to read that book.
B: I think I (31) .... (finish) it by the weekend and then you can borrow it.
A: Really? Thanks.

A: I (32) .... (take) the car to work tomorrow. Would you like a lift?
B: Thanks, that would be great.
A: I (33) .... (leave) the house at seven thirty so I can collect you shortly afterwards.
B: That's fine. The bus I usually catch (34) .... (leave) at seven.

A: Why don't you come to our place this evening at nine? The children (35) .... (go) to bed by then.
B: Thanks, I will. (36) .... (I / bring) a DVD?
A: Good idea. (37) .... (you / eat) or should I prepare some food?
B: Oh, please don't bother. I (38) .... (have) dinner with my parents tonight.
A: Fine. I (39) .... (work) all day and I probably (40) .... (not feel) like cooking.

/ 10

Total: / 40

✓ Self-check

Wrong answers	Look again at	Try CD-ROM
1, 2, 3, 4, 5, 19, 22, 23, 24, 25, 29, 30, 34, 36, 40	Unit 27	Exercise 27
26, 27, 31, 32, 33, 35, 37, 38, 39	Unit 28	Exercise 28
8, 9, 12, 13, 14, 15, 20, 21	Unit 29	Exercise 29
6, 7, 10, 11, 16, 17, 18, 28	Unit 30	Exercise 30

Now do **Check 5**

Modal verbs

> **REMEMBER!**
> The modal verbs are: *can, could, may, might, will, would, shall, should* and *must*.
> - We use a modal verb with a main verb to express ability, obligation, etc.
> - After modal verbs, we use the infinitive without *to*: *I **can speak** English.*
> - Modal verbs don't add *-s* after *he/she/it*: *He **can** drive.   She **might** come.*
> - In questions and negative sentences, we don't use the auxiliary *do*: ***May** I come in?*
> - Modal verbs don't have past, perfect or future forms, or participle forms. We use other verbs instead: *They **had to** leave early yesterday.   We **haven't been able to** find suitable accommodation.   **Will** you **be able to** get here next week?   **Having to** take exams is a bore!*
> - These verbs and expressions have similar meanings to modal verbs: *be able to, manage to, have (got) to, need to, be allowed to* and *ought to*.

31 Ability and possibility

- To talk about general ability or possibility in the present, we use *can* or *be able to*. *Be able to* is more formal and less common than *can*: *I **can speak** French fluently but I **can't speak** Spanish.* (general ability)   *You **can buy** the tickets online or at the box office.* (possibility)   *We **aren't able to/'re unable to take** your call at the moment.*
- To talk about general ability in the past, we use *could/couldn't* or *was/were (not) able to*: *She **could/was able to read** when she was very young but she **couldn't/ wasn't able to write** until she was older.*
- To talk about the ability to do something on a single occasion in the past, we use *was/were able to* + infinitive, not *could*: *He didn't understand but I **was able to explain** the problem to him.* (Not *I could explain the problem to him*)
- To talk about the ability to do something in the future, we use *can* or *will be able to* + time expression: *I **can/'ll be able to come** and see you **tonight**.*
- We use *will be able to*, not *can*, to talk about an ability we will have or a skill we will acquire in the future: *I'**ll be able to drive** by next summer so we can hire a car.*
- We use *can/could* to talk about typical behaviour or events: *It **can rain** a lot at this time of year.   He **could be** charming when he wanted to be.*
- We use *could have* + past participle to talk about an unfulfilled possibility in the past: *I **could have gone** on holiday but I decided not to.*
- For grammatical forms that are not possible with *can*, we use *be able to*: *They like **being able to work** at home.   I'd like **to be able to help** you.   We'**ve been able to work** much faster since we got the computer.*
- The verbs *succeed* and *manage* suggest that something is achieved with difficulty: *Did you **succeed in finding** a hotel?   We **managed to get** home at last.*

Grammar: *modal verbs*

PRACTICE

31a Circle the correct answers. There may be more than one correct answer.

A: My father's really fit for his age. He plays tennis a lot and he (0) *can* / *could* / *will be able to* run quite a distance.

B: I wish my father were the same! He (1) *can* / *could* / *was able to* play tennis well a few years ago but not any longer. Sometimes I worry about his health. He was so ill a year ago that he (2) *can die* / *could die* / *could have died* but fortunately, he's all right now.

A: Perhaps I should introduce him to my father and they (3) *can* / *are able to* / *manage to* play tennis together.

A: Where have you been?

B: I had an important letter to post. Luckily, I (4) *could get* / *was able to get* / *could have got* to the post office just as it was closing.

A: Congratulations! I hear you passed your driving test. Was it difficult?

B: I had lessons for months and I (5) *can't* / *couldn't* / *wasn't able to* pass a driving test. But then I found a good instructor and I (6) *could* / *managed to* / *succeeded in* pass on my third attempt!

A: That's great news. Personally, I love (7) *being able to* / *been able to* / *can* drive.

A: (8) *Can you* / *Will you be able to* / *You could* come to the party tomorrow?

B: I think so. I (9) *was eventually able to* / *eventually managed to* / *eventually succeeded in* arranging a lift.

A: I thought you might have to work.

B: I (10) *can* / *'ll be able to* / *'ve been able to* get so much more done since I got the new computer that I (11) *can* / *be able* / *could have* take some time off.

A: Great! I'm sure someone (12) *will be able to* / *will succeed in* / *being able to* give you a lift home.

31b Complete the second sentence so that it means the same as the first, using the word in bold. Use between two and five words.

0 We got lost but we managed to find our way home using a map. **were**
We got lost but we ......*were able to find*...... our way home using a map.

1 I am afraid it is not possible for him to see you now. **unable**
I am afraid he .... you now.

2 You will have the ability to understand Spanish after a few lessons. **able**
You .... Spanish after a few lessons.

3 Lucy is often bad-tempered when she is working under pressure. **can**
Lucy .... when she is working under pressure.

4 They managed to persuade Francis to join them. **succeeded**
They .... Francis to join them.

5 Joan managed to get to the bank just before it closed. **was**
Joan .... to the bank just before it closed.

6 Alex had the opportunity to leave work early but he decided to stay on. **have**
Alex .... work early but he decided to stay on.

73

Grammar: *modal verbs*

32 Degrees of certainty

- To show how certain we are that something is true or will happen in the present or future, we use *may, might, could, must, can* and *can't*.
- We use *may* (*not*), *might* (*not*) and *could*, but not *couldn't*, to talk about something we think is possible now or in the future: *They **may/might/could take** a trip to the States next summer. She isn't in the office but she **may/might/could be working** at home. She **may/might not be feeling** well.*
- We don't use *can* to talk about future possibility: *There **may/might/could be** snow this evening.* (Not ~~There **can be** snow this evening.~~)
- We use *must* or *have to* when we are certain something is true in the present. *Have to* is informal: *He isn't at home. He **must be** on his way here. There **has to be** some mistake! You **have to be joking**!*
- We use *can't* when we are certain something is impossible: *You **can't be** hungry! You've only just had lunch!*
- To talk about something which is possible in theory, we use *can* or *could*: ***Can/Could there be** life on Mars? I suppose you **can/could go** by train.*

⚠️ Compare: *We **may/might not get** there on time.* (= Perhaps we'll be late.)
*We **can't/couldn't** possibly **get** there on time.* (= We'll certainly be late.)

- To speculate about the past, we use *may/might/could/must/can't/couldn't have* + past participle OR *may/might/could/must/can't/couldn't have been* + present participle.
- To talk about the possibility that something happened, we use *could/may* (*not*) / *might* (*not*) *have* + past participle OR *could/may* (*not*)/*might* (*not*) *have been* + present participle: *They **may/might not have had** time to finish the job. He didn't answer the phone – he **could/may/might have been sleeping**.*
- When we are certain something happened, we use *must have* + past participle OR *must have been* + present participle: *It's wet. It **must have been raining**.*
- When we are certain something didn't happen, we use *can't/couldn't have* + past participle OR *can't/couldn't have been* + present participle: *He **can't/couldn't have committed** the robbery. He was with me.*

PRACTICE

32a Circle the correct answer.

0 Her new car looks expensive. It (*must*)/ *can't* have cost a fortune!
1 They *might / can't* have gone home. I don't see them anywhere.
2 Surely he *mustn't / can't* still be alive after all this time!
3 Our car broke down and we *couldn't / may not* have enough money to pay for the repairs.
4 Many accidents *could / must* be prevented with a little care.
5 She *couldn't / might not* want to come with us.
6 Mr Morris *must / can't* be nearly ninety years old but he doesn't look it.
7 I don't know where Bernard is – he *must / could* be playing tennis with Carrie.
8 They're going whitewater rafting. They *have to / may* be mad to do such a thing!

Grammar: *modal verbs*

32b Correct the incorrect sentences.

0 That mustn't be the right answer. You've made a mistake.
   That can't be the right answer.

1 She's wearing a nurse's uniform. She can be a nurse.
   ....

2 I don't know if Dominic's here – he must be outside.
   ....

3 She isn't here and she hasn't rung. She can have forgotten our appointment.
   ....

4 He spoke to me about it this morning so he could have forgotten about it.
   ....

5 I think it can rain this afternoon – it's very cloudy.
   ....

6 A: Why didn't she come to the party last night?
   B: I don't know. She might be feeling tired.
   ....

7 Mickey can be going out. He's wearing a coat and boots.
   ....

8 That mustn't have been Davina you saw last night. She's abroad.
   ....

9 Our neighbours can be going away. Their cases are packed and there's a taxi waiting for them.
   ....

10 Some scientists believe there can be life on other planets.
   ....

32c Complete the second sentence so that it means the same as the first, using the word in bold. Use between two and five words.

0 It's lunchtime and I'm sure you're hungry. **must**
   It's lunchtime so ....*you must be*........... hungry.

1 It's possible that we'll get a reply in a few weeks. **could**
   We .... a reply in a few weeks.

2 Perhaps Sandy is playing golf this afternoon. **might**
   Sandy .... golf this afternoon.

3 I'm certain Emily realises that she's made a mistake. **must**
   Emily .... that she's made a mistake.

4 I'm sure they're out because they aren't answering the phone. **be**
   They aren't answering the phone so they .... at home.

5 It's possible that the man I saw her with was her brother. **could**
   The man I saw her with .... her brother.

6 I'm certain Richard's new car cost around £20,000. **must**
   Richard's new car .... around £20,000.

7 I'm sure Suzanne was running to catch the bus when I saw her. **must**
   Suzanne .... to catch the bus when I saw her.

Grammar: *modal verbs*

32d Complete the article. Use the correct form of the verbs in brackets.

WHAT HAPPENED TO THE DINOSAURS?

Many people think that because the dinosaurs died out so many years ago, we (0) ..*may never know*.. (may / never / know) what really happened to them. In fact, there are several theories.

Some scientists claim that a single event (1) .... (might / kill) these enormous reptiles. They believe that a large asteroid (2) .... (must / collide) with the Earth about 65 million years ago and that the impact resulted in dramatic climate change. There is some evidence for this theory: in the Yucatan peninsula in Mexico there is an enormous crater measuring ten to sixteen kilometres across, which (3) .... (may / be) caused by an asteroid strike.

Other scientists say that this theory (4) .... (can't / be) the whole truth and that a single event – even one as cataclysmic as an asteroid strike – (5) .... (can't / cause) all the dinosaurs to die out at once. They think that in future other evidence (6) .... (might / provide) us with important clues about conditions on Earth at the time of the great extinctions. They speculate that intense volcanic activity (7) .... (may / cause) the Earth's climate to change and this (8) .... (could / destroy) the dinosaurs' natural habitats.

And finally, a large number of scientists think that the dinosaurs (9) .... (may not / die out) at all. They claim that today's birds (10) .... (could / be) the descendants of the dinosaurs – and there is some very persuasive anatomical evidence to back up their claim. If you would like to find out more about the subject, there are a number of very interesting websites:

33 Obligation and necessity

Obligation, lack of obligation and prohibition

- To say it is important or essential to do or not to do something, we use *must/mustn't* and *have (got) to*.
- *Must/mustn't* is used:
  – when the speaker feels that an action is necessary: *I **must ring** Adele today. She's expecting to hear from me.   We **mustn't be** late for the film.*
  – by someone in authority, e.g. a parent or teacher: *You **must hand in** your homework by Friday.   You **mustn't talk** to your father like that!*
  – in written rules, instructions and notices: *All visitors **must report** to Reception.*
- We use *have (got) to* when an action is necessary because someone else requires it or because of a rule or law. *Have got to* is more informal than *have to*. *Have to* and *have got to* are more common than *must* in speech: *I **have to be** at the hospital at four.   We'**ve got to pay** for the tickets in advance.*
- We use *have to*, not *have got to*, for habits. *Have got to* can only be used for single actions: *I **have to catch** the bus to work every day.   I **have to**/'**ve got to catch** the bus to work today.*
- We usually use *have to*, not *must*, in questions: ***Did** you **have to get** a visa?* But we can use *must* when we query an order: ***Must** I really **be** home by midnight?*
- We use *mustn't* when it is important not to do something: *You **mustn't wait** here.* (= You aren't allowed to wait here.)
- We use *don't have to* when there is no obligation to do something: *You **don't have to wait**.* (= There is no obligation but you can wait if you wish.)
- For grammatical forms that are not possible with *must*, we use *have to*, not *have got to*: *I **had to get** a prescription from the chemist.   I don't like **having to tell** my parents where I'm going.*
- To talk about the future, we use *must/have (got) to/will have to* + time expression: *I **must e-mail** them **tomorrow**.   We'**ll have to get** there **before five**.*

Necessity and lack of necessity

- To express necessity and lack of necessity, we use *need to, needn't, don't need to, didn't need to* and *needn't have* + past participle.
- *Need* is a main verb and is followed by *to*-infinitive: *Everyone **needs to eat** a balanced diet.   You **don't need to come** if you're busy.   **Do** I **need to bring** anything with me?   I **needed to see** the boss.   If he gets the job, he'**ll need to buy** some new clothes.*
- We use *needn't* and *don't need to* to talk about lack of necessity in the present or future. *Needn't* is more formal: *You **needn't come**/**don't need to come** if you don't want to.* (= It isn't necessary to come.)
- Compare these ways of talking about lack of necessity in the past: *We **didn't need to get up** early because we had no morning classes.* (= We didn't get up early because it wasn't necessary.)   *We **needn't have got up** early. Our morning class was cancelled.* (= We got up early but it turned out that it wasn't necessary to do so.)

⚠ *Don't have to* and *don't need to* are very similar and can usually be used interchangeably: *It's Saturday tomorrow so you **don't have to**/**don't need to get up** early.   She e-mailed me so I **didn't have to**/**didn't need to phone** her.*

Grammar: *modal verbs*

PRACTICE

33a **Circle the correct answer.**

0 You *mustn't* / *don't have to* touch that! You'll hurt yourself.

1 I *'ve got to* / *have to* be at work every morning at nine but I think I'm going to be late today!

2 The children will be safe with me so you *don't need* / *needn't* worry.

3 The £55 passport fee *must* / *need* accompany your application.

4 *Did you have to* / *Must you* have a new engine put in when the car broke down?

5 Larry *doesn't have* / *doesn't need to* pick me up from the airport. I'll take a taxi.

6 Most people hate *must* / *having to* do the ironing.

7 We *mustn't* / *don't have to* hurry. There's plenty of time.

8 You *needn't have worried* / *didn't need to worry* so much. We were quite safe.

9 He *must have forgotten* / *had to forget* all about the appointment.

10 We *mustn't* / *won't have to* meet again tomorrow – I can finish the job on my own.

11 They'd given us a key to let ourselves in so fortunately, they *didn't need to wait* / *needn't have waited* up for us.

12 When we were children, we didn't have e-mail so we *must* / *had to* write letters.

33b **Complete the sentences. Use the correct form of *must* or *have to* and the verbs in brackets.**

0 She ……*had to leave*…… at eleven o'clock because the last bus left at twenty past. (leave)

1 You ……………………………… in a hostel. You can stay with us. (stay)

2 He ……………………………… to the station because he was late. (run)

3 Attention, please! All accidents ……………………………… reported to the safety officer. (be)

4 I don't like ……………………………… everything my boss tells me. (do)

5 They ……………………………… late tonight. They can finish the job tomorrow. (work)

6 I ……………………………… my parents. I'm really worried about them. (ring)

7 ……………………………… a uniform when you were at school? (you / wear)

8 You ……………………………… late for English classes. Otherwise, the teacher will lock you out. (be)

9 Barbara ……………………………… for a new car because her parents gave her one for her birthday. (save)

10 Aidan gets ill all the time. He ……………………………… a doctor three times so far this year. (see)

11 You ……………………………… to switch off all electric appliances before you leave the building. (forget)

12 Why ……………………………… so suddenly? Was anything wrong? (they / leave)

Grammar: *modal verbs*

33c Complete the second sentence so that it means the same as the first, using the word in bold. Use between two and five words.

0 There was very little petrol left so it was necessary to buy some. **had**
   We ...*had to buy some petrol*... as there was very little left.

1 It is important that you make an effort to be on time. **got**
   You .... an effort to be on time.

2 It is not necessary to buy any more food for the weekend. **need**
   We .... any more food for the weekend.

3 They weren't obliged to be home before midnight during the week. **have**
   They .... home before midnight during the week.

4 If you park your car on a yellow line, you will get a parking ticket. **must**
   You .... your car on a yellow line or you will get a parking ticket.

5 It wasn't necessary to spend so much money on Moira's present but I did. **spent**
   I .... so much money on Moira's present.

6 He has been forced to cancel five appointments this month. **had**
   He .... five appointments this month.

7 Was it necessary for her to book tickets for the concert in advance? **need**
   Did .... tickets for the concert in advance?

33d Complete the conversation. Use the correct form of *must*, *have to* or *need*. Sometimes more than one answer is possible.

A: Hi. Where are you going in such a hurry?
B: I (0) ...*have to*... post this letter and after that I (1) .... get something to eat before my driving lesson. I'm starving.
A: I didn't know you were learning to drive. How's it going?
B: Fine. I've thought for a long time I really (2) .... learn and when we moved out of the city, I (3) .... start taking lessons – the public transport in the village where I'm living is terrible. But enough about me. Where are you off to?
A: I'm running a little late too. I (4) .... catch a train to London because I have a job interview and I (5) .... be late because I really (6) .... get a job and start earning some money.
B: I know. I (7) .... get a job earlier this year to pay for these driving lessons. It wasn't fair to ask my parents for the money.
A: Lessons are really expensive. I was lucky – I (8) .... have any because my brother taught me.
B: Lucky you! Did you pass first time?
A: No, I failed and I (9) .... take a second test. I can't tell you how nervous I was the second time but I (10) .... worried because I passed it without any difficulty.
B: All I can say is I hope I (11) .... take more than one test. The sooner I finish these lessons, the better!

79

Grammar: *modal verbs*

34 Advice, recommendations and criticism

- We use *should/shouldn't* or *ought (not) to* to give advice or to say that something is or isn't a good idea in the present or future. *Should* is more common than *ought to*, especially in questions: *You **should/ought to try** to lose some weight.   Children **shouldn't/ought not to be** allowed to stay up late at night.   We **should/ought to be leaving** soon.   **Should** we **ask/Ought** we **to ask** them for permission?*
- We often use *should* and *ought to* with *I think* and *Do/Don't you think ... ?*: **Do you think** *I* **should/ought to call** *him?*   **Don't you think** *we* **should/ought to be leaving***?*
- To give strong advice and to make recommendations about a course of action in the present or future, we use *must/mustn't*: *You **must work** harder or you'll never succeed.   You **must come** over for a meal.*
- We use *had better (not)* + infinitive without *to* to give strong advice or a warning: *You**'d better be** on time for the interview.   You**'d better not tell** Lance about it.*
- We use *should/shouldn't/ought (not) to have* + past participle OR *should/shouldn't/ought (not) to have been* + present participle to express criticism of someone's behaviour in the past: *I **ought to have called** my parents last night.   He **shouldn't have been wasting** time like that. He **should have been working**.*

PRACTICE

34a Tick the correct sentences and correct the incorrect sentences. There are five incorrect sentences, excluding the example.

0   You should to watch the programme. It's fascinating. ......*should watch*......
1   You ought have called her to say you're sorry. ....
2   We really must try to take a holiday abroad this year. ....
3   I better not go out tonight. I'm exhausted. ....
4   I oughtn't to have eaten so much – I feel sick. ....
5   They should have call their parents earlier. ....
6   You were out enjoying yourself when you must have been studying. ....
7   You'd better to ask your mother if you can go out tonight. ....
8   Should we eat before we go out tonight? ....

34b Complete the sentences. Use the correct form of *must* or *should* and the verbs in brackets. Use *must* wherever possible.

0   It's your own fault you're tired. You ......*shouldn't have gone*...... to bed late last night. (go)
1   You .... and see us one evening. We'd love to see you. (come)
2   She .... a bath right now. We've got to leave in ten minutes! (have)

80

3 They .... him what happened. Now he'll never get over it. (tell)
4 Marcus and Wanda .... that new Japanese place. It's the best restaurant in town. (try)
5 You .... when I came into the room, not talking. (work)
6 I .... that suit. It was a waste of money. (buy)
7 You .... to your mother in that tone of voice ever again. (speak)
8 Do you think I .... my hair or .... I .... it as it is? (dye, leave)
9 You really .... us soon, Jeremy. We'd love to see you. (visit)
10 Why aren't they at the gym? They .... hard for the championship. (train)

34c Re-write the advice. Use *must, mustn't, should* or *shouldn't*.

GOLDEN RULES FOR TANNING SAFELY

0 It is very important to use your common sense when tanning.
1 It is very important not to sunbathe more than once a day.
2 It is not a good idea to have more than ten tanning sessions in two weeks.
3 We strongly recommend that you wear protective goggles and keep your eyes closed if you use a sun bed.
4 It is very important to use a sun cream that protects you against ultraviolet rays.
5 It is a good idea to use skincare products after tanning as well.
6 It is very important to check with your doctor that it is safe to tan if you are taking medication.

0 You *must use your common sense when tanning* ....
1 You ....
2 You ....
3 You ....
4 You ....
5 You ....
6 You ....

35 Permission, requests, offers and suggestions

Permission

- To talk about permission or lack of permission in the present or future, we use *can/can't, am/is/are (not) allowed to* and *may (not)*: You **can/are allowed to park** your car here.   You **can't/aren't allowed to keep** pets in the hostel.   You **may stand** or **sit**, whichever is more comfortable.

- *May (not)* and *must (not)* are sometimes used in notices and written rules: Each player **may look** at the cards once.   Travellers **may not bring** meat products into the country.   Candidates **must not start** writing until the examiner tells them to.

- To talk about permission or lack of permission in the past, we use *could/couldn't* and *was/were (not) allowed to*. Compare: At school we **could/were allowed to eat** in the playground but we **couldn't/weren't allowed to eat** in the classrooms. (general permission)   We **were allowed to bring** food into the classroom for the end of year party. (permission on a particular occasion) (Not We *could bring* food into the classroom for the end of year party.)

- To ask for permission, we use *can, could* (more polite) or *may* (formal). We don't use *be allowed to*: **Can/Could I borrow** your pen?   **May we wait** inside?
To give permission, we can answer: *Yes, sure/all right/of course/certainly*.
To refuse permission, we can answer: *(No,) I'm sorry, you can't*.

⚠️ We can use *couldn't* but not *could* to talk about permission on a particular occasion in the past: Last night I **was allowed to go** out with my friends but I **couldn't/wasn't allowed to stay** out late.

Requests
To make a request, we use:

- *Can I/you ... ?* or *Could I/you ... ?* (more polite): **Can I have** a drink of water, please?   **Could you help** me lift this box?

- *Will you ... ?* or *Would you ... ?* (more polite): **Would you phone** me later?

- *Would you mind + -ing?* or *Would you mind if I + past simple* (very polite): **Would you mind closing** the door?   **Would you mind if I opened** the window?

Offers
To make an offer, we use:

- *Shall I/we ... ?* (polite): **Shall I carry** that for you?

- *Would you like ... ?*: **Would you like** a sandwich?

- *I'll/Let me* (informal): **I'll make** some breakfast.

- *Can/Could I ... ?* or *May I ... ?* (more formal): **Can I help** you?   **May I take** your coat?

- *I/We can/could* (polite): '*I can't answer this question.*' '*I could help you if you like.*'

Suggestions
To make suggestions, we use:

- *Shall we ... ?*: **Shall we go** out for dinner?

- *We can/could* (more polite): **We could see** a film this afternoon.

- *Why don't we ... ?/Let's* (informal): **Why don't we have** a game of tennis?

- *What/How about + -ing?* (informal): **What about having** dinner at my place next week?

Grammar: *modal verbs*

PRACTICE

35a Circle the correct answer. Then match the questions (0–6) and the responses (a–g).

0 (May) / Shall I use your phone? **b**
1 Shall / Will I make sandwiches for lunch? ☐
2 Will / Would you mind if I turned the heating up? ☐
3 Will / Might you wait here for me, please? ☐
4 Shall / Let me do that for you. ☐
5 Could / Shall I borrow £10 until tomorrow? ☐
6 May / Will I leave my bag here? ☐

a I'm sorry, but no one is allowed to leave unattended luggage.
b Of course. Dial 9 for an outside line.
c No, thanks. I've already had something to eat.
d I can't lend you anything, I'm afraid. I haven't been to the bank.
e Actually, it's quite warm in here, don't you think?
f Thanks. I could use some help.
g OK. How long will you be?

35b Complete the conversations. Use the correct form of the words in the box.

| be / allow / smoke   could not / keep   how about / go   I / can / get |
| I / can / have   ~~I / may / come~~   I / may / park   I / shall / take |
| you / would / like   you / would / mind / take off |

Lin: I understand you have a room to let. (0) ......*May I come*...... in and look around?
Jen: Of course. (1) .... your coat? And (2) .... something to drink?
Lin: No, thanks. I can't stay long. So, are there any house rules?
Jen: Not really. Oh, (3) .... your shoes, please? What else? Let's see ... No one (4) .... in the house – I'm a non-smoker. And pets are a problem. The last person who rented the room had a cat but I'm allergic to cats so she (5) .... it here.
Lin: That's not a problem. I don't smoke and I don't have any pets – but I do have a car. (6) .... it on the drive if I take the room?
Jen: Yes, of course. I don't have a car so that's not a problem.
Lin: Thank you. In the last place I stayed, I had to park my car on the street – that was a nuisance.

―――――

Jen: Hi. Come in. (7) .... you anything?
Bob: (8) .... a cold drink, please? So, how was your day?
Jen: Good. I think I've found someone who wants to rent the spare room.
Bob: That's great news. (9) .... out for a pizza to celebrate?

83

Check 6 Modal verbs

1 **Circle the correct answer. In one question all answers are correct.**

A: I saw someone in my class cheat in our last exam and I didn't say anything. What do you think I (1) *should / ought / need* to do now?

B: I think you (2) *should say / should have said / had better say* something at the time. You (3) *could / may / might* talk to a teacher in confidence now but it (4) *could / may / might* be too late for the school to take action. Whatever happens, I don't think you (5) *could / may / should* be too hard on yourself.

/ 5

2 **Complete the conversations. Use one word in each gap.**

A: (6) .... don't we watch a film at my place this evening?
B: Good idea. I've got a new DVD. (7) .... I bring it?

A: I'm sorry, but you (8) .... only have one piece of hand luggage.
B: But the last time I flew I (9) .... allowed to bring two bags onto the plane.
A: I'm afraid the regulations have changed.

A: I don't feel well. I've got a headache.
B: You'd (10) .... not go to work today then.
A: Would you (11) .... ringing the office for me?

A: How's your new job?
B: It's good. I don't like (12) .... to travel to London three days a week but I do like (13) .... able to work from home the rest of the time.

/ 8

3 **Complete the sentences. Use the correct form of *must* or *need* and the verbs in brackets.**

14 You .... any money with you if you don't want to. I have plenty. (bring)

15 You .... here. If you do, they'll tow your car away. (park)

16 I .... myself – we'd already met. (introduce)

17 They .... early tomorrow – they can lie in for a change. (get up)

18 You really .... the film – it's brilliant! (see)

19 She bought three bottles of milk but she .... There was plenty in the fridge. (do)

20 You .... to ring me. Otherwise, I'll worry about you. (forget)

/ 7

84

4 Complete the article. Use one word in each gap.

When scientists dug up the fossilised bones of a camel in the Arctic, they (21) ....n't believe their eyes. How was it possible that animals whose descendants usually live in hot desert areas were (22) .... to survive in the cold Canadian north? But these bones suggest that thousands of years ago the Arctic can't have (23) .... as cold and barren as it is today and somehow, the camels (24) .... able to find food and survive.

Scientists know that the Earth's climate goes through cycles of warmer and cooler periods but they haven't been able (25) .... find out why these occur. They are sure that something (26) .... affect the amount of heat the Earth receives from the sun. One suggestion is that in the past a thick cloud of ash and gas from a volcanic eruption might (27) .... blocked out the sun's heat, causing the Earth to cool. Another theory is that the Earth's irregular orbit (28) .... have taken it farther away from the sun. Either of these events could (29) .... had a great impact on the climate.

(30) .... we be in for another ice age? Some scientists believe that under normal circumstances, we would now be due for a cooling period. Against this, the greenhouse effect is warming the planet so the Earth (31) .... get warmer or cooler in the long term – no one (32) .... be certain.

/ 12

5 Complete the second sentence so that it means the same as the first, using the word in bold. Use between two and five words.

33 The hills are often cold at night. **can**
   The hills .... at night.

34 I wish I could speak Japanese. **able**
   I would like .... Japanese.

35 He had the opportunity to go to university but decided not to. **could**
   He .... to university but decided not to.

36 I was able to open the door only after pushing really hard. **succeeded**
   I .... the door only after pushing really hard.

37 Would you advise me to call them? **should**
   Do you .... them?

38 It wasn't necessary for her to work at the weekend. **have**
   She .... at the weekend.

39 Shall I make us something to eat? **to**
   Would .... us something to eat?

40 Let's go somewhere different tonight. **going**
   How .... tonight?

/ 8

Total: / 40

Self-check

Wrong answers	Look again at	Try CD-ROM
13, 21, 22, 24, 25, 32, 33, 34, 35, 36	Unit 31	Exercise 31
4, 23, 26, 27, 28, 29, 30, 31	Unit 32	Exercise 32
12, 14, 15, 16, 17, 19, 20, 38	Unit 33	Exercise 33
1, 2, 5, 10, 18, 37	Unit 34	Exercise 34
3, 6, 7, 8, 9, 11, 39, 40	Unit 35	Exercise 35

Now do **Check 6**

Statements and questions

36 Basic sentence types

- In English, a sentence must have a subject and a verb. The verb may be followed by an object, a complement and/or an adverbial. The subject tells us the topic of the sentence. The object tells us the person or thing affected by the verb. Subjects and objects can be nouns, noun phrases, pronouns or -*ing* forms.

Subject	Verb	Object
My brother Jon	has bought	a beautiful sports car.
He	loves	showing off his new car.

- Intransitive verbs don't have an object. They can be followed by adverbials (an adverb or a prepositional phrase): *Sales rose **in January**. They rose **sharply**.*
- Transitive verbs have an object (+ adverbial).

Subject	Verb	Object	Adverbial
Jon	bought	the car	last week.

- Some transitive verbs can have two objects. Two patterns are possible:

Subject	Verb	Direct object + *to/for* + Indirect object / Indirect object + Direct object
Marian's mother	baked	a cake for her daughter / her daughter a cake.
She	posted	the cake to her daughter / her daughter the cake.

- When the direct object is a pronoun, we usually put the pronoun first: *Marian's mother baked **it** for her daughter. She posted **it** to her daughter.*
- Some transitive verbs have a complement after the object. This tells us more about the object and can be an adjective, noun phrase or prepositional phrase.

Subject	Verb	Object	Object complement
I	find	the room	cold.
Harriet and Ivan	called	their baby	Quentin.
They	took	the bags	to the car.

- Linking verbs like *be, become, feel, get, look, seem* and *smell* are followed by a complement, not an object:

Subject	Verb	Subject complement
The meal	smells	really delicious.
Your coat	is	in the wardrobe.

- Adverbials can come before the subject or verb, or after the verb, object or complement: ***Unfortunately**, we **soon** realised how difficult the work would be. She posted the letter **yesterday**.*
- We can use conjunctions to join sentences: *He missed supper **and** he's starving.*

Grammar: *statements and questions*

PRACTICE

36a Decide if the underlined words are direct or indirect objects, complements or adverbial phrases.

> ### The Least Sudden Wedding
> Octavio Guillen met (0) <u>a young girl</u> in 1900. Her name was (1) <u>Adriana Martinez</u>. He proposed (2) <u>two years later</u> and when she accepted, he gave (3) <u>her</u> (4) <u>a ring</u> and announced (5) <u>their engagement</u> to their families. Octavio and Adriana finally married (6) <u>in Mexico</u> in 1969. They were (7) <u>in their eighties</u> and they had been (8) <u>engaged</u> for sixty-nine years!

0 direct object   1 ....   2 ....
3 ....   4 ....   5 ....
6 ....   7 ....   8 ....

36b Put the words in the correct order. Some sentences have two clauses separated by a dash (–). Begin these sentences with the clause given first.

0 Larry Page / met / Serge Brin – when / graduate students / were / they / at Stanford University
   Larry Page met Serge Brin when they were graduate students at Stanford University.

1 although / at first / disliked / they / one another – they / to work together / soon / started ....

2 started / Page and Brin / in a friend's garage / the Google business / in 1998 ....

3 had been working on / since 1996 / they / a search engine called 'Backrub' ....

4 when / to work together / started / Page and Brin – they / in making money / interested / weren't ....

5 to share / they / with the world / wanted / their ideas ....

6 today / use / Google / millions of people – is / worth several billion dollars / and / the company ....

87

Grammar: *statements and questions*

37 Question forms

Yes/No questions

Auxiliary/ Modal verb	Subject	Verb	Completion	Short answers
Are	you	coming	with me?	No, I'm not.
Can	you	help	her?	Yes, we can.
Did	Tim and Mia	report	the robbery?	Yes, they did.
Has	he	done	his homework?	No, he hasn't.

Wh- questions

Question word	Auxiliary/ Modal verb	Subject	Verb	Completion
Where	are	you	going	now?
How	will	I	tell	her the news?
Who	do	they	work	for?

- Prepositions usually go at the end of a *wh-* question: *What are you listening to?*
- Notice these questions with *what* and *how*:
  - What + noun: **What colour** *is it?*   **What subjects** *are you studying?*
  - How + adjective/adverb: **How big** *is it?*   **How often** *do you see them?*
  - How + much/many: **How much** *are the tickets?*   **How many** *sisters do you have?*
- Compare *what* and *which*: **What's** *your favourite colour?* (There are many colours.) **Which** *colour do you prefer, red or blue?* (There is a limited number of colours.)

Subject/Object questions

Who, what, which, whose and *how much/many* can be the subject or object of a question.

Subject	Object
Who married Linda? **I** married her.	**Who** did Linda marry? Linda married **me**.
What will happen? **Nothing** will happen.	**What** will you do? I will do **nothing**.
Whose car is the Fiat? **The Fiat** is Jon's.	**Whose car** do you like? I like **Jon's car**.
How many guests came to the wedding? **150 guests** came.	**How many guests** did you invite? I invited **150 guests**.

Negative questions

- We make questions negative by adding *not* to the auxiliary or modal verb.
- We use negative *yes/no* questions to ask for confirmation, express surprise or annoyance: **Doesn't** *the room look nice?* (= I think it looks nice.)   **Haven't** *you finished that yet?* (= You should have finished.)
- We use negative *wh-* questions to ask for information, make suggestions or criticise past actions: **Who hasn't** *got a cup of coffee?*   **Why don't** *we go out for a meal?*   **Why didn't** *you do as I asked?*

▶▶ *See Appendix 1: Punctuation rules, page 199.*

Grammar: *statements and questions*

PRACTICE

37a Write questions.

0 They're leaving for the theatre. *Are they leaving for the theatre?*
1 He should fix the car this weekend. ....
2 She's looked everywhere for her keys. ....
3 Conrad wants to borrow this book. ....
4 They'd given the money to Vince. ....
5 You were watching a play last night. ....
6 She'll have finished the book by then. ....

37b Write questions for the underlined answers.

0 A: *How much money have you got?* B: I've got <u>ten pounds</u>.
1 A: .... B: The new carpet is <u>red</u>.
2 A: .... B: I enjoyed <u>Maths</u> most.
3 A: .... B: They play <u>three times a week</u>.
4 A: .... B: He bought <u>a dozen</u> eggs.
5 A: .... B: <u>Eva</u> met Keith at the cinema.
6 A: .... B: Eva met <u>Keith</u> at the cinema.
7 A: .... B: I borrowed <u>Julie's</u> electric guitar.
8 A: .... B: Paul left <u>the newspaper</u> on the sofa.

37c Complete the conversations. Write negative questions. Use the words in brackets.

0 A: Hurry or you'll be late. *Weren't you late yesterday?*
   (you / be / late / yesterday)
   B: No, I wasn't. I was on time.

1 A: I've got some spare copies. ....
   (who / have got / one)
   B: I haven't. Could you give me one, please?

2 A: We're going to be late! ....
   (why / you / get / ready / sooner)
   B: I was busy. Anyway, I don't see the problem – we're only a few minutes late.

3 A: You're washing the car! ....
   (you / have got / anything better to do)
   B: No, I haven't. And besides, I enjoy washing the car.

4 A: There's no room on the mantlepiece for that vase.
   .... (why / you / put / it / here)
   B: That's a good idea. I'll do that.

5 A: The car has been running well since we had it serviced.
   .... (the garage / do / a great job)
   B: Yes, they certainly did. You'd think it was a new car.

Grammar: *statements and questions*

38 Question tags and reply questions

Question tags
- We form question tags with an auxiliary/modal verb + pronoun. We use negative question tags after positive statements and positive question tags after negative statements: *You're coming tonight,* **aren't you?** *The Browns* **live** *here,* **don't they?**
- The question tag with imperatives is *will you*: **Close** *the door,* **will you?**
- The question tag with *Let's* is *shall we*: **Let's** *go for a walk,* **shall we?**
- We use *they* in question tags after *someone, everyone,* etc. and *it* in question tags after *nothing, something* and *everything*: **Someone** *rang earlier,* **didn't they?** **Nothing** *ever happens here,* **does it?**
- We use question tags:
  – to invite agreement (our voice goes down): *'We haven't met before,* **have we?'** (= I don't think we've met.) *'No, we haven't.'*
  – as 'real' questions when we aren't sure if something is true (our voice goes up): *'You like fish,* **don't you?'** *'Yes, I do. / No, I don't.'*

Reply questions
- We use reply questions to show that we are interested in or surprised by what someone is saying: *'You left your bag here.'* **'Did I?** *How silly of me!'*
- We use a positive question after a positive statement and a negative question after a negative statement: *'I'll finish it for you.'* **'Will you?** *Thanks.'* *'I* **haven't** *been well.'* **'Haven't you?** *I'm sorry.'*

PRACTICE

38a Complete the questions. Use question tags.

0 Put that cat down, ...*will you*...... ?
1 I'm too thin to wear that dress, ... ?
2 We haven't finished yet, ... ?
3 Let's have some lunch, ... ?
4 You won't leave, ... ?
5 Jane left a message, ... ?
6 Everyone is here now, ... ?
7 You don't eat meat, ... ?
8 Something fell on the floor, ... ?

38b Complete the conversations. Use reply questions.

0 A: I left my ring by the sink.   B: ......*Did you?*......
1 A: There won't be any problems.   B: ....
2 A: You said you'd ring me.   B: ....
3 A: I couldn't get anyone to help me. B: ....
4 A: He isn't sure how to do this.   B: ....
5 A: She plays the guitar.   B: ....

6 A: They've left their front door open. B: ....
7 A: There aren't any messages for you. B: ....
8 A: I can speak several languages. B: ....

38c Complete the conversations. Use one or two words in each gap.

A: Put the screwdriver down over there, (0) ...*will*...... you?
B: Sure. No problem. You've done this before, (1) .... you?
A: Of course. I put up all the shelves in my last house.
B: (2) .... you? But someone helped you, (3) .... they?

A: Let's see the new Bond film this evening, (4) .... we?
B: Great idea! I've seen every Bond film they've ever made.
A: (5) .... you?

A: You haven't got a pencil I could borrow, (6) .... you?
B: I think so. Here you are. Now have a look at page five, (7) .... you?
A: Thanks. I see what you mean. That calculation can't be right, (8) .... it?

39 Avoiding repetition: *so, neither, too,* etc.

- We can use the following structures to avoid repeating the same words when we add more information to a statement:
  - *so/neither/nor* + auxiliary/modal verb + subject: *Jan was upset and **so was I**.* (= I was also upset.)   *I can't sing and **neither can Kate**.* (= Kate can't sing either.)
  - subject + auxiliary/modal verb + *too*: *Jake's taken a year off work and **I have too**.*
  - subject + negative auxiliary/modal verb + *either*: *I won't come and **my brother won't either**.*

- We can use these structures to agree with someone:
  - '*I've enjoyed myself.*' '**So have I.** / **I have too.**'
  - '*I don't have any money.*' '**Neither/Nor do I.** / **I don't either.**'

- To answer a question, we can use *I'm afraid/believe/expect/hope/think* + *so* and *I don't think/expect so* or *I hope not*: '*Is she very ill?*' '**I'm afraid so.**'   '*Is Helen joining us later?*' '**I think so.**'   '*Will we get paid this week?*' '**I don't think so.**'   '*Has everything been destroyed?*' '**I hope not.**'

- To answer questions beginning with *Shall we ... ?*, we use '*Yes, let's. / No, let's not*: '**Shall** *we stop for a meal?*' '**Yes, let's.**'

- We often shorten sentences to avoid repetition:
  - when we ask and answer questions: '*Have you ever studied abroad?*' '*No, I haven't. **Have you?***' (= No, I haven't studied abroad. Have you studied abroad?) '*I can't speak Mandarin. **Can you?***' (= Can you speak Mandarin?)
  - when we respond to statements, requests, etc.: '*It must be time for lunch.*' '*I think **it is**.*' (= It is time for lunch.)   '*Please help yourself.*' '*Thanks, **I will**.*' (= I will help myself.)
  - in clauses: *I said I would finish by nine and **I did**.* (= I did finish by nine) *I'd be there if **I could**.* (= if I could be there)

Grammar: *statements and questions*

PRACTICE

39a **Complete the conversations. Use one word in each gap.**

A: Will you be working this weekend?
B: I hope (0) ....*not*.... . I could do with a rest.
A: (1) .... could I. Maybe we should go away together for a few days.

A: Have you seen Axel recently?
B: I'm afraid (2) .... I haven't seen him for days.
A: (3) .... have I. I wonder if he's avoiding us.

A: Do you understand what the boss wants us to do?
B: I think (4) ....
A: Well I (5) ....n't and neither (6) .... Eleanor.

A: Haven't we met before?
B: I don't (7) .... so. I'm afraid I don't recognise you.

A: I haven't seen the new animated film.
B: I haven't (8) .... Shall we go this weekend?

A: You should try that new Italian restaurant. It's really good.
B: I (9) .... We were there at the weekend.

39b **Complete the conversations. Use the words in brackets.**

0   A: I've never been abroad. (either)   B: *I haven't either.*
1   A: I haven't had anything to eat yet. (neither)   B: ....
2   A: I'm very fond of Linda. (so)   B: ....
3   A: I disagreed with her suggestion. (too)   B: ....
4   A: I don't like the new teacher. (nor)   B: ....
5   A: I'm going to Italy this summer. (so)   B: ....
6   A: I don't like horror movies. (neither)   B: ....
7   A: I couldn't get in touch with Greg. (either)   B: ....
8   A: I'll order the vegetarian option. (too)   B: ....

39c **Cross out the words in italics that are not necessary. Don't change the meaning of the sentence.**

0   A: I wish you were here!   B: I'd be there if *I could* ~~be there~~.
1   A: Have you had lunch yet?   B: No, but *I'm going to have lunch* in a minute.
2   A: I think we should stop somewhere for something to eat.
    B: Yes, I think *we should stop somewhere for something to eat*.
3   A: Please sit down.   B: Thank you, *I will sit down*.
4   She promised she would pick me up at six and *she did pick me up at six*.
5   I offered to pay for the tickets and *I did pay for them*.
6   I won't be attending the conference. *Will you be attending the conference?*

40 Exclamations and emphatic forms

- Exclamations express strong feelings. They are formed in the following ways:
  - *That* + verb + adjective: *'I've won the lottery!' 'That's amazing!'*
  - adjective + noun/pronoun: *Lucky you!   Poor Ian!   Silly me!*
  - *How* + adjective (+ subject + verb): *How interesting!   How ill she looked!*
  - *What* (+ adjective) (+ *a/an*) + noun (+ subject + verb): *What a day!   What a wonderful view!   What enormous trees!   What dreadful weather we're having!*
- Exclamations are also formed in other ways:
  - *so* + adjective/adverb or *such* (+ *a/an*) (+ adjective) + noun: *It's **so** hot!   This is **such** a good book!   Vera and Bob are **such** nice people!*
  - negative questions: **'Wasn't** *that film terrible?'* *'Awful!'*
  - question word + *on earth* … ?: **What on earth** *are you doing?*
  - question words with *-ever: however, whatever,* etc: **Whatever** *can he mean?* **However** *will I manage without you?*
  - *do* in imperatives and in sentences where there is normally no auxiliary verb: ***Do** sit down.   She **does** work hard.   I **do** like Janice.*

▶▶ See Appendix 1: Punctuation rules, page 199.

PRACTICE

40a Complete the conversations. Use the words in the box.

| didn't | do | how | however | lucky you | ~~so~~ | that | what | why on earth |

0 A: Why didn't you call? We were ....*so*............ worried!.   B: I'm sorry.
1 A: Harry's been in an accident.   B: .... awful!
2 A: I think I've lost my passport.   B: ....'s terrible!
3 A: I've just won a holiday in New York!   B: ....!
4 A: .... a fantastic holiday that was!   B: Wasn't it great?
5 A: .... didn't you ask me to help?
   B: I thought you were busy.
6 A: .... they make a good job of the report?   B: Very good!
7 A: .... did he get that job?
   B: He must know the right people.
8 A: .... have another piece of cake.
   B: Thank you. It's delicious.

40b Re-write the sentences.

0 How beautiful this view is!   What *a beautiful view this is* ....!
1 What strange birds they are!   How .... the birds are!
2 What rude children they have!   They ....!
3 Her poems are so difficult!   What .... she writes!
4 She's so beautiful!   She's .... woman!
5 It's such a complicated problem!   The problem ....!

Check 7 Statements and questions

1 **Put the words in the correct order. Some sentences have two clauses separated by a dash (–). Begin these sentences with the clause given first.**

1 good / the meal / look / although / didn't / very – was / tasty / it / quite

....
....

2 call / why / you / didn't / me – you / as soon as / arrived / at the hotel / ?

....
....

3 you / have / here / been waiting / for a long time / ?

....
....

4 is / leaving / Sylvia / next month – I / so / and / am

....
....

5 the bus / left / Lance / his briefcase / on / yesterday

....
....

/ 5

2 **Circle the correct answer.**

6 A: I haven't seen Janice here before.
B: *Haven't you? / Have you?* She comes here often.

7 A: I posted *to her the letter / the letter to her* last week.
B: And she still hasn't received it?

8 A: *Do you / Don't you* look nice today!
B: Thank you. I'm wearing a new suit.

9 A: I'll clean the car this afternoon – it's filthy!
B: *Will you? / Won't you?* That would be great.

10 A: Sam is *a such / such an* easy person to be around!
B: Do you think so?

/ 5

3 **Complete the e-mail. Use one word in each gap.**

Dear Sebastian,

I'm so sorry to hear you've got the flu! (11) .... rotten luck!

We went out for dinner last night as planned. Flora couldn't make it and (12) .... could Miles but everyone else was there. I arrived late and (13) .... did Sath but it didn't spoil the evening. We all had (14) .... fun!

I spoke to Danielle and she said that you haven't sent (15) .... a copy of the report yet. I know you'd have sent it if you (16) .... have. Let me know if you need help, (17) .... you?

I (18) .... hope you feel better soon. Let's arrange another meal when you're well, (19) .... we? (20) ....n't you think that new Italian restaurant will be nice?

Regards, Albena

/ 10

Total: / 20

Self-check

Wrong answers	Look again at	Try CD-ROM
1, 5, 7, 15	Unit 36	Exercise 36
2, 3, 8, 20	Unit 37	Exercise 37
6, 9, 17, 19	Unit 38	Exercise 38
4, 12, 13, 16	Unit 39	Exercise 39
10, 11, 14, 18	Unit 40	Exercise 40

Now do **Check 7**

-ing forms and infinitives

41 Verb + -ing form or infinitive?

- Some verbs are followed by an *-ing* form. The *-ing* form often describes an activity: We **enjoyed seeing** you last week.   I **miss going** to the beach every day.
- Some verbs are followed by a *to*-infinitive. The *to*-infinitive often describes an intention or a future event: I **hope to see** you soon.   They **promised not to tell** her.
- Some verbs can be followed by either an *-ing* form or a *to*-infinitive with no change in meaning: We **prefer travelling/to travel** by train.   The baby **started crying/to cry**.
- Sometimes there is a difference in meaning between *like + -ing* and *like + to*-infinitive: I **like swimming**. (This is something I enjoy doing.)   I **like to finish** all the boring jobs first and then focus on more creative work. (I don't (necessarily) like the boring jobs but I prefer to do them first.)
- Some verbs can be followed by an *-ing* form or a *to*-infinitive with a change in meaning. Compare:

The car **needs washing**. (= Someone needs to wash the car.)	He **needs to get up** early (= It's necessary for him to get up early.)
I **regret upsetting** her. (= I'm sorry that I upset her.)	I **regret to inform** you that you didn't get the post. (= I'm sorry but I have to tell you that you didn't get the post.)
I **remember speaking** to her last night. (= I remember that I spoke to her.)	I **remembered to speak** to her. (= I remembered and then I spoke to her.)
We **stopped talking** when she came in. (= We were talking but when she came in, we stopped talking.)	We **stopped to have** a cup of tea. (= We stopped what we were doing in order to have a cup of tea.)
We **tried living** in the United States for a while but we didn't like it. (= We lived in the United States for a while to see if we would like it but we didn't.)	They **try to exercise** every day. (= They make an effort to exercise every day.)
He **went on working** until he was in his seventies. (= He didn't stop working until he was in his seventies.)	After her studies she **went on to become** a successful surgeon. (= She became a successful surgeon after she had finished her studies.)

- *Would like*, *would prefer* and *would love* are always followed by a *to*-infinitive, not an *-ing* form: I'**d prefer to travel** by train. (Not I'd prefer travelling by train.)
- We use the infinitive without *to* after:
  - modal verbs: I **must go**.   You **shouldn't tell** him.
  - *had better* and *would rather*: We'**d better go**.   I'**d rather stay** here.
  - *Let's* and *Why not ... ?*: **Let's have** something to eat.

▶▶ See Appendix 3: Verbs followed by -ing form, page 201; Appendix 4: Verbs followed by to-infinitive, page 201; Appendix 5: Verbs followed by -ing form or to-infinitive page 201.

Grammar: -ing forms and infinitives

PRACTICE

41a Complete the sentences. Use the correct form of the verbs in brackets.

0 The architect expects *to complete* the building in April. (complete)
1 I really didn't mean .... you. (offend)
2 Zac gave up .... several years ago. (smoke)
3 We managed to avoid .... an accident. (have)
4 Have you finished .... your essay yet? (write)
5 I chose .... German rather than French. (learn)
6 Young children enjoy .... round the house. (help)
7 Geraldine is hoping .... law at Cambridge. (study)
8 My new job will mean .... all over the world. (travel)
9 Dmitri and Ursula have postponed .... married for a few months. (get)
10 Magnus refused .... any money for the work he'd done. (accept)

41b Circle the correct answer.

0 *I'd like to go* / (*I like going*) on holiday to a different place every summer.
00 (*I'd like to go*) / *I like going* somewhere different this summer. Any ideas?
1 I regret *to tell* / *telling* you that your contract will not be renewed.
2 I regret *to tell* / *telling* you about it because it upset you.
3 He stopped *to have* / *having* coffee because it kept him awake at night.
4 He stopped *to have* / *having* a coffee and then he went back to work.
5 I know you're tired but please try *to concentrate* / *concentrating* for a few more minutes.
6 I'm going to try *to drink* / *drinking* warm milk before I go to bed; it might help me sleep better.
7 Alice went on *to act* / *acting* until she was forced to retire because of her health.
8 Although Alice started out in television, she went on *to act* / *acting* on the stage.
9 He remembered *to close* / *closing* the windows so the rain didn't get in.
10 He remembered *to close* / *closing* the windows so he was surprised to find them open when he got home.

42 Verb + object + *-ing* form or infinitive?

verb + object + *to*-infinitive
- Some verbs must be followed by an object before the *to*-infinitive: *Water came into the boat and **caused it to sink**.*   *They **forced him to tell** them the secret.*
- Some verbs can be followed by an object before the *to*-infinitive, or an *-ing* form with no object: *They don't **allow visitors to park** their cars here.*   *They don't **allow parking** here.*
- Some verbs can be followed by an object, depending on the meaning of the sentence. Compare: *I **expect to be** on time.* (= I expect that I will be on time.) *I **expect you to be** on time.* (= I expect that you will be on time.)

verb + object + infinitive without *to*
- *Make* and *let* are followed by object + infinitive without *to*: *You can't **make me tell** you – it's a secret!*   *Some people **let their children do** whatever they like.*
- *Help* is followed by object + infinitive with or without *to*: *I **helped her** (**to**) **carry** her cases.*

verb + object + *-ing* form
- Some verbs are followed by object + *-ing* form: *I **caught him looking** in my desk. I couldn't **stop her biting** her nails.*

see, hear, watch, etc.
- Verbs of perception (e.g. *see, notice, look at, watch, hear, listen to, feel, smell*) can be followed by object + *-ing* form, or infinitive without *to*. Compare:
*I **watched him play** football.* (= I watched him during the whole game.)
*I **watched him playing** football.* (= I watched him for a period of time while the game was in progress.)
The *-ing* form is more common. The difference in meaning between the two forms is often small: *I can hear the birds **sing/singing** in the mornings.*

▶▶ See Appendix 6: Verbs followed by object + to-infinitive, page 201.

PRACTICE

42a Circle the correct answer.

0 They wouldn't *allow / forbid /* (*let*) him go out with his friends.
1 Les *assisted / helped / taught* me set up the new computer.
2 Their parents make them *staying / to stay / stay* home on weekdays.
3 They wouldn't *allow / let / make* us to go into the building.
4 What *caused / forced / made* you change your mind?
5 The factory *lets / makes / allows* eating in the canteen only.
6 Bad health *forced / let / made* him to leave his job.
7 She *likes / expects / imagines* to finish the project by January.
8 I was shocked to see her *going / to go / go* through my bag.

Grammar: *-ing* forms and infinitives

42b Join the sentences. Use the *-ing* form or *to*-infinitive.

0   Several cars collided on the motorway. Poor weather conditions caused this.
    Poor weather conditions caused several cars to collide on the motorway.

1   Motorists should avoid that section of the motorway. Police are advising this.
    ....

2   Injured people are getting to hospital. Rescue services are helping them.
    ....

3   People might panic. Police are anxious to stop this.
    ....

4   People can call a special number for more information. Police are encouraging this.
    ....

5   Motorists should not approach the scene of the accident. Police are preventing this.
    ....

42c Complete the extract from a story. Use the correct form of the verbs in brackets. Sometimes more than one form is possible.

  She invited me (0) ......*to sit*...... (sit) down and then she excused herself from the room. I heard her (1) .... (make) the tea in the kitchen and listened as she set out the cups and saucers. The room had begun (2) .... (feel) a little odd and I regretted (3) .... (take) off my jacket. I noticed the fire (4) .... (begin) to die down in the grate, watched the second hand (5) .... (move) slowly round the clock face and wondered how long it would be before she would allow me (6) .... (leave).
  A few minutes later I heard the tea trolley (7) .... (roll) on its wheels through the kitchen and then into the sitting room, where I was waiting. I started (8) .... (drink) the tea she had poured for me and she let me (9) .... (continue) in silence. I felt her (10) .... (watch) me and looked up quickly, hoping to catch her (11) .... (stare) at me, but she was looking instead at the cup of tea in my hand. Nervously, I sipped some more. It tasted slightly of bitter almonds but I carried on (12) .... (drink) it to be polite. At last I finished the unpleasant brew and set my cup down in the saucer.
  'Would you like me (13) .... (pour) you another cup?' she asked.
  'No thank you,' I said, reaching unsteadily for my briefcase. 'I must be going if I expect (14) .... (be) home in time for dinner.'

43 Other uses of infinitives

adjective + *to*-infinitive
We can use the *to*-infinitive:

- with adjectives such as *(un)able, certain, determined, keen, (un)likely, ready, sure* and *(un)willing*. The infinitive often refers to a future event: *They aren't **willing to do** it.   She's **determined to win**.   It's **certain to rain** tomorrow.   He's **sure to be** late again.*

- with adjectives such as *afraid, amazed, ashamed, delighted, disappointed, glad, happy, sad, sorry* and *surprised*, to describe feelings: *I'm **pleased to meet** you. We were **sorry to hear** your news.*

- with adjectives such as *careless, good, kind, nice* and *wrong*, to express an opinion or make a judgment. We can also use *it + be +* adjective *(+ of someone) + to*-infinitive: *She was **wrong to do** that.   It was **wrong** (**of her**) **to do** that.*

- after adjectives such as *difficult, easy, exciting, expensive, fun, hard, impossible* and *interesting*, to describe an action or activity. We can also use *it + be +* adjective *(+ for someone) + to*-infinitive: *This language is **easy to learn**.   It's **easy to learn** this language.   The article is **impossible to understand**.   It's **impossible for us to understand** the article.*

noun/pronoun + *to*-infinitive
We can use the *to*-infinitive:

- to refer to an event in the future. The pattern is noun + *be* + *to*-infinitive: ***My ambition is to be*** *a doctor.   **His first thought was to ring** us.*

- with nouns such as *attempt, chance, decision, desire, effort, intention, opportunity, plan* and *time*, to complete their meaning: *I finally made **a decision to leave** my job.*

- to give more information about a noun: *Let's find **a place to eat**.* (= Let's find a place where we can eat.)   *We had **a long journey to make**.* (= We had a long journey that we had to make.)

- with *something, anything, somewhere*, etc.: *Is there **anywhere** (for us) **to sit down**? There's **nothing to do** in this place.*

- with *the/first/second/last/only/best*, etc.: *She was **the only person to succeed**.* (= She was the only person who succeeded.)   *It was **their first attempt to climb** Mount Everest.*

- to describe purpose. The pattern is *for* + noun + *to*-infinitive: *I left the window open **for the cat to get out**.* (= so that the cat could get out)

▶▶ For *to*-infinitive after *too* and *enough*, see Unit 15. For infinitive of purpose, see Unit 59.

Grammar: -ing forms and infinitives

PRACTICE

43a Complete the conversations. Use the correct form of the verbs in the box.

| agree be (x2) ~~go~~ keep leave look love |
| spend stay travel understand work |

A: Aren't you ready (0) ......*to go*...... yet?
B: I'm sorry (1) .... you waiting. I'll be ready in fifteen minutes.
A: All right, but please hurry. It's not polite (2) .... late for dinner and we have a long way (3) ....

A: You hate your job. Why don't you leave?
B: Look, it's not hard (4) .... why I stay here. My ambition is (5) .... sales manager and I've made a decision (6) .... here for another year because it'll be good for my career.

A: I think we should find somewhere (7) .... the night. It's getting late.
B: It's expensive (8) .... in a hotel. Where do you suggest?
A: I don't know, but I brought a guidebook for us (9) .... at. Why don't we see if there's a nice bed and breakfast nearby?

A: Did you leave the door open?
B: I don't think so. Hazel was the last person (10) .... the house – it must have been her that left it open.

A: I'm lonely. I need someone (11) ....
B: Have you considered getting yourself a puppy?

A: I must have been crazy (12) .... to this.
B: Don't worry. Everything will be all right – you'll see.

43b Join the sentences. Use the *to*-infinitive.

0 We're going to do our best. We're ready.
   We *'re ready to do our best* .

1 He's going to move to Italy next year. He's keen.
   He ....

2 Don't interrupt people all the time. It's rude.
   It's ....

3 She's starting up her own business. That's her intention.
   Her ....

4 I want to take part in the Olympic Games one day. That's my ambition.
   It's ....

5 He bought a DVD. He'll watch it this evening.
   He bought ....

6 I disagreed with him. I was the only person.
   I was ....

Grammar: -ing forms and infinitives

43c Complete the e-mail. Use the correct form of the words in the box.

> aim / save   complicated / work out   easy / work   great / have
> important / get   place / stay   someone / replace   sure / be
> time / apply   welcome / share   ~~wonderful / hear~~

New Message

Hi Tasha,

Thanks for your letter. It was (0) *wonderful to hear* from you. Sorry I haven't been in touch for a while – the new job is keeping me busy. I thought it would be (1) .... as a hotel receptionist but the job is more demanding than I expected. Some of the bills are quite (2) .... and of course it's (3) .... for me .... them right. Having said that, it's (4) .... a job. My (5) .... is .... £500 by the end of the holidays – that will go a long way towards paying my tuition fees next year.

What are your plans? Why don't you come here to work? It's a good (6) .... for work in the restaurant. One of the waitresses left last week and they're looking for (7) .... her. Don't worry about finding a(n) (8) .... – you're (9) .... my flat with me. They keep you busy here but there's (10) .... time for us to enjoy ourselves too. Think about it.

Erica

43d Re-write the sentences. Use the *to*-infinitive.

0   Nobody left the party before him.
    He was the first person *to leave the party* .

1   I received your letter and I was delighted.
    I was delighted ....

2   Heating this house is very expensive.
    It's very expensive ....

3   Having interests outside work is important.
    It's important ....

4   That child learns very quickly.
    That child is ....

5   How do you think I should cook this fish?
    What's the best way .... ?

6   There was nobody who saw him after we did.
    We were the last people ....

101

Grammar: -ing forms and infinitives

44 Other uses of -ing forms

We can use *-ing* forms:

- as the subject of a sentence, sometimes after an adjective: **Smoking** is bad for you. Regular **swimming** is good for you.
- as the complement of *be*: His favourite activity **is watching** television and mine **is going** to the gym.
- as uncountable nouns, often after a determiner (e.g. *a, the, this, a lot of*) + adjective. The *-ing* form may be followed by *of*: I was woken up by **the ringing of** the doorbell. **This constant arguing** has got to stop!
- after *go* to mean that we do an activity, often a sport: We **went swimming** yesterday. She **goes skiing** every winter.   They've **gone shopping**.
- after expressions with *can't*: can't bear, can't face, can't help, can't stand, can't stop: I **can't face doing** the washing up – let's leave it until the morning. They **couldn't stand not knowing** the truth.
- after *for* to describe purpose: It's a knife **for cutting** bread.
- after some adjectives to talk about an activity in progress: We're **busy decorating** the flat.   It's **nice not being** at work.
- after some nouns: Sometimes she has **difficulty saying** 'no' to people.   I'm having **trouble checking** my e-mails.
- after *spend/waste* + period of time: We **spent many weeks studying**.
- in some expressions: *it's no good/use, there's no point (in), it's worth, it's a waste of time*: **It's no good/use complaining** – you have to take the test again.   **There's no point (in) trying** to change his mind.   The film **is worth seeing**.

PRACTICE

44a Complete the conversations. Use the correct form of the verbs in the box.

argue	be	do	eat	feel	find	get
give	measure	shop	sit	~~ski~~	work	

0   **A:** What are you doing during the holidays?
   B: We're going ......*skiing*...... in the French Alps – if there's enough snow, that is.

1 **A:** What's wrong?
   B: It's awful .... here. I can't stand .... at a desk all day in an office – I'm used to being outdoors.

2 **A:** What's that?
   B: It's an instrument for .... the amount of moisture in the air.

3 **A:** I can't help .... there's been a mistake.
   B: Yes, I agree with you.

Grammar: *-ing forms and infinitives*

4 **A:** I'm afraid .... isn't allowed in the library.
   B: I'm sorry. I'll have my sandwich outside.

5 **A:** It's a waste of time .... her advice – she won't listen to you.
   B: Perhaps, but I have to try.

6 **A:** Are we lost?
   B: Not really, but I'm having trouble .... the address.

7 **A:** You look sad. What's wrong?
   B: I miss .... with my family. I've never been away from home before.

8 **A:** I'm sorry we can't agree but it's no use ....
   B: You're right. There's no point in .... angry with one another just because we have different points of view.

9 **A:** Where on earth are Arthur and Olivia?
   B: They're in town. I think they've gone .... for some curtain material.

10 **A:** I phoned you last night but you weren't at home.
   B: I'm sorry. I was busy .... some research at the library and I must have left my mobile switched off.

44b Complete the e-mail. Use the correct form of the words in brackets.

Hi, Nigel!

Just to say I've moved into my new university accommodation. I (0) *spent a few days packing* (spend / a few days / pack) everything into boxes but I paid someone to move the stuff. In the end, I decided it (1) .... (be / worth / pay) professionals to do the job – I've got a lot of expensive electronic equipment and I (2) .... (can't face / the thought of it / get) damaged. Right now I (3) .... (be / busy / take) everything out of boxes and putting it away. They say that (4) .... (move) house is really stressful – and they're right!

Now I'm here, though, I think I'll like my new place. It's right next to the fitness centre so I'm able to (5) .... (go / swim) every day – they have an Olympic-size pool there. Unfortunately, some nights I have (6) .... (trouble / study) because of the people next door. They're so noisy! It's probably (7) .... (a waste of time / ask) them to be quieter but I might go and speak to them.

Anyway, it (8) .... (be / always / great / hear) from you so keep in touch.

Alistair

103

Grammar: -ing forms and infinitives

45 *doing, (to) do, being done, (to) be done,* etc.

-*ing* form	doing	I hate **asking** people their age.
passive -*ing* form	being done	I hate **being asked** my age.
perfect -*ing* form	having done	I'm proud of **having completed** the race.
perfect passive -*ing* form	having been done	I disliked **having been ignored**. (= I was ignored and I disliked it.)
infinitive	(to) do	I want **to invite** them to the party.
passive infinitive	(to) be done	I want **to be invited** to the party.
perfect infinitive	(to) have done	I'd like **to have invited** all of my friends to the party but I couldn't.
perfect passive infinitive	(to) have been done	I'd love **to have been invited** to the party but I wasn't.
continuous infinitive	(to) be doing	Beth's health seems **to be improving**.

The perfect -*ing* form and the perfect passive -*ing* form are very formal and we avoid them. We use the -*ing* form and passive -*ing* form instead: *I regret* **telling/having told** *him the truth.*   *They enjoyed* **being taken/having been taken** *to the park.*

PRACTICE

45a Circle the correct answer.

"I look young for my age and I hate (0) *asking* / *(being asked)* for identification when I go out with my friends. When we go to a club, they ask me (1) *to show / to be shown* proof that I'm eighteen. We went out last night and I resented (2) *having asked / being asked* for identification at the club door. Still, once I got inside, it was so good (3) *to be relaxing / to have relaxed* with friends that I forgot all about (4) *to be annoyed / being annoyed*. If it's still happening in a few years' time, though, I'm sure I'll be flattered (5) *to ask / to be asked* to prove my age!"

45b Complete the sentences. Use the correct form of the verbs in brackets.

0   I think we should postpone ....*going*............ on holiday. (go)
1   I don't like .... what to do. I'll make up my own mind. (tell)
2   He denied .... anything to me but I can prove he did. (say)
3   She was a difficult child, probably due to .... by different foster parents. (look after)
4   Karin decided .... to Rome for her holidays. (go)
5   I'd love .... a blank cheque and told to spend the money on anything I like. (give)
6   He seems .... a lot of weight since I last saw him. (lose)
7   I saw Amy last night. She seems .... better, slowly but surely. (get)

Check 8 -ing forms and infinitives

1 **Circle the correct answer.**
   1 Although it was many years ago, Connie clearly remembers *cry / crying* when her cat died.
   2 I like *to do / doing* the unpleasant jobs before I do the gardening.
   3 Judy and Gordon like their new home but they miss *to live / living* by the sea.
   4 The airline allows passengers *carry / to carry* one item of hand luggage.
   5 The cost of borrowing has forced many companies *to close / closing*.

   / 5

2 **Complete the conversation. Use one word in each gap.**
   A: What's that?
   B: It's a jack (6) .... lifting a car. I need to change a flat tyre.
   A: Will you be long? I want to (7) .... shopping and I'd prefer not (8) .... walk.
   B: It'll take me about half an hour but there's no point (9) .... waiting: I'll be using the car this afternoon.
   A: And I suppose it's a (10) .... of time trying to convince you to (11) .... me to have the car instead.
   B: I'm afraid so. I'll give you a lift to the bus stop, though.
   A: Thanks, but I can't (12) .... the thought of taking the bus today – it's too hot.
   B: Fine, so if you're staying in, will you (13) .... me change this tyre?

   / 8

3 **Complete the sentences. Use the correct form of the verbs in brackets.**
   14 The weather is unlikely .... in the next few days. (improve)
   15 Melanie is busy .... for her exams. (study)
   16 Ramon thought he saw someone .... him. (follow)
   17 Our plan is .... the house into a luxury hotel. (turn)
   18 We had no trouble .... your address – your directions were perfectly clear. (find)
   19 It's impossible .... an exact measurement but we can give an estimate. (give)
   20 Dirk has no job and nowhere .... (live)

   / 7

4 Circle the correct answer.

I always wanted (21) *to be / being / to have been* a photographer. When I was a child, my father (22) *allowed to use / allowed me use / allowed me to use* his camera and I'll never forget (23) *to take / taking / being taken* hundreds of pictures. I studied photography at college and went on (24) *to get / getting / having got* a job as a crime photographer with the police. I don't work regular hours and it can be difficult (25) *to get / get / to getting* out of bed to photograph a crime scene in the middle of the night. Fortunately, I love (26) *do / doing / being done* my job and (27) *to work / working / to be working* with people who feel the same way.

I didn't intend (28) *me to become / me becoming / to become* a private investigator – it just happened! Fortunately, you don't need (29) *to have / having / to be having* any special qualifications. Many people come into the profession from a police or military background but now it's possible (30) *to do / doing / to be doing* a work placement course. In fact, (31) *to train / training / having trained* on the job is essential. I love my work but the hours are not sociable. I often find myself (32) *to sit / sitting / to be sitting* on my own in a car for ten to fifteen hours when I'm on a case.

/ 12

5 Complete the second sentence so that it means the same as the first, using the word in bold. Use between two and five words.

33 I want them to offer me the job. **offered**
I want .... the job.

34 I don't like it when people ask me to do things like that. **being**
I hate .... things like that.

35 It seems that Leo has left the party. **to**
Leo seems .... the party.

36 I think Myra is studying for her exams. **be**
Myra seems .... for her exams.

37 They think he lied in order to get the job. **having**
He is suspected of .... in order to get the job.

38 When I heard they had got married, I was surprised. **hear**
I was .... that they had got married.

39 She has tried twice to sail round the world. **attempts**
She has made two .... round the world.

40 Let's find a place where we can have breakfast. **somewhere**
Let's find .... breakfast.

/ 8

Total: / 40

Self-check

Wrong answers	Look again at	Try CD-ROM
1, 2, 3, 8, 21, 23, 24, 26, 28, 29	Unit 41	Exercise 41
4, 5, 11, 13, 16, 22, 32	Unit 42	Exercise 42
14, 17, 19, 20, 25, 30, 38, 39, 40	Unit 43	Exercise 43
6, 7, 9, 10, 12, 15, 18, 27, 31	Unit 44	Exercise 44
33, 34, 35, 36, 37	Unit 45	Exercise 45

Now do **Check 8**

Reported speech

46 Reported statements: tense changes

- Punctuation is important in direct speech. The comma, full stop, question mark or exclamation mark come before the closing quotation mark: *'I'm leaving,' said Lottie. 'I'm tired,' she said, 'and I'm going home. Are you coming?'*
- When we report someone's words, we can use a past tense reporting verb like *said* and *told*:
  - *say* (+ *to someone*) (+ *that*): She **said** (**to me**) (**that**) she had seen the film.
  - *tell someone* (+ *that*): I **told them** (**that**) I was pleased.
- After a reporting verb in the past there are usually changes to:
  - pronouns and possessive adjectives: *'I'm going out with **my** friends,' said Bob.* → *Bob said (that) **he** was going out with **his** friends.*
  - verb tenses: present simple → past simple, present continuous → past continuous, past simple → past perfect simple, present perfect simple → past perfect simple, present perfect continuous → past perfect continuous, *am/is/are going to* → *was/were going to*: *'I **haven't seen** Yolanda,' said Claude.* → *Claude said (that) he **hadn't seen** Yolanda.*
  - modal verbs: *will* → *would*, *can* → *could*, *may* → *might*, *shall* → *should*, *must/have to* → *had to*: *'I'**ll help** you,' she said.* → *She said (that) she'**d help** me.*
  - some adverbs/adverbial phrases of time: *now* → *then*, *today* → *that day*, *tonight* → *that night*, *this morning* → *that morning*, *yesterday* → *the day before/the previous day*, *tomorrow* → *the day after/the following day*, *last week* → *the week before/the previous week*, *next month* → *the month after/the following month*, *(three) days ago* → *(three) days before*: *'We did it **yesterday**,' they said.* → *They said (that) they had done it **the day before**.*
  - *here* → *there*: *'We're staying **here** for a week,' she told him.* → *She told him (that) they were staying **there** for a week.*
  - *this* → *that*, *this/that* + noun → *the* + noun: *'**This bag** is expensive,' he said.* → *He said (that) **the bag** was expensive.*

▶▶ For reporting verbs, see Unit 49.

PRACTICE

46a Circle the correct answer.

A: Have you heard the weather forecast?
B: Yes, they said it (0) *is /* (*was*) going to rain.
———————

A: Have you had your meeting with Mr Lewis?
B: I'm afraid not. His secretary told me he (1) *couldn't / can't* see me because he (2) *is / was* too busy.
———————

A: Excuse me. I'm here to collect the book I ordered last week. The sales assistant told me it (3) *will / would* be ready for collection today.
B: I'm sorry, but it hasn't been ordered yet. I'll have to order it today.
———————

Grammar: *reported speech*

A: Can I help you?
B: I'm here to collect a book I ordered two weeks ago. I came to collect it last week and your assistant said it (4) *hadn't / hasn't* been ordered yet. He (5) *said / told* he was sorry and (6) *said / told* me he would order the book (7) *that / this* day.

A: Have you been to the doctor yet?
B: Yes. She told me I (8) *have to / had to* go on a diet. She also said I (9) *must / had to* get more exercise.

A: Have you seen Sandy today?
B: No, and Louis told me he (10) *hadn't / hasn't* seen her either.

46b Re-write the direct speech as reported speech and the reported speech as direct speech.

0 'The taxi has arrived!' Dinah told us.
   Dinah told us that the taxi had arrived.

00 Katya told her husband that she might be late for dinner that evening.
   'I may be late for dinner this evening,' Katya told her husband.

1 'You can leave your things in this wardrobe if you like,' Derek said.
   ....
   ....

2 Beth said that they were leaving the following day.
   ....

3 'It isn't far from here to my office, Ted,' said Bea.
   ....

4 Evan told the police officer that he'd seen the bank robbery that morning.
   ....

5 Hannah said, 'We must be patient.'
   ....

6 'I've been to this restaurant once before,' said Nanette to Ian.
   ....

7 Miguel told Gloria that he hadn't liked the film but he'd enjoyed the book.
   ....

8 'I may have left my bag on the bus this morning,' Eva said.
   ....

9 Alan said that we ought to get some flowers for Penny's birthday.
   ....

10 'I won't be gone long,' Lydia told her mother.
   ....

47 Reported statements: no tense changes

In reported speech, if the reporting verb is in a present tense, there is no tense change: 'They **left** last night.' → He **tells** me they **left** last night.   'We**'re having** dinner.' → She **says** they**'re having** dinner.

The present
- If a present situation is still true when we are reporting it, we don't need to change the tense after a past tense reporting verb: '*Alison **lives** with her parents,*' said Nick. → *Nick said that Alison **lives/lived** with her parents.*   '*Yann **has been working** on the project for months,*' they told us. → *They told us that Yann **has been working/had been working** on the project for months.*

The past
- If a past situation is still true when we are reporting it, we don't need to change the tense after a past tense reporting verb: '*We didn't stay in the hotel because it **was** too expensive.*' → *She said that they hadn't stayed in the hotel because it **was** too expensive.* (The hotel is still expensive.)
- When the past simple is used in a time clause, we don't usually change it: '*As soon as I **got** home, I went upstairs.*' → *She said that as soon as she **got** home, she **went/had gone** upstairs.*
- We don't usually change the past continuous: '*I **was working** until midnight.*' → *She said that she **was working** until midnight.*
- When the past continuous refers to an activity that was completed before an activity in the past simple, we usually change it to the past perfect continuous: '*We **were planning** to go out but then Thomas got ill.*' → *She said that they **had been planning** to go out but then Thomas **got/had got** ill.*
- We don't change the past perfect: '*I **hadn't realised** how angry he was,*' said Carol. → *Carol said she **hadn't realised** how angry he was.*

The future
- If an event is still in the future when we report it, we don't need to change the future form: '*We**'ll be** at the station in thirty minutes.*' → *She said that they**'ll be/'d be** at the station in thirty minutes.* (They aren't at the station yet.)   *She said that they**'d be** at the station in thirty minutes.* (They are at the station.)

PRACTICE

47a Report the statements. Don't change the tense unless it is necessary to do so.

   0 'I'm planning to set up my own business.'
      Paul says that *he's planning to set up his own business* .

   1 'When the project started, there was a lot of interest in it.'
      Joan said that ....

   2 'I was living in France when I met Nora.'
      Josh said that ....

   3 'It's pouring with rain here.'
      Ali tells me that ....

Grammar: *reported speech*

4 'I was hoping to meet you for lunch but my car broke down.'
Natalie said that ....

5 'The taxi had already arrived when I rang you.'
Maria told me that ....

47b Read the monologue. Then complete the article.

> I've been with the circus since I was eighteen years old. I do a trapeze act and every night I hang by my toes from a bar twelve metres above the ground. I've been hanging off the bar for two years and I spent six years in the circus before that.
> I trained in dance and performing arts when I was younger and then I went to circus school. I wanted to join the circus because it combined all the skills I'd learnt up till then. I also wanted to do something a little crazy. I went to my first circus when I was fourteen and I loved it. I took up circus work as a hobby and now I do it professionally.
> I've done about 2,300 shows with the Cirque du Soleil. Next year the show moves to Brazil but I won't be going with them. The trapeze is always challenging but I want to do other things. I want to have a baby in two or three years. I'm also planning to learn how to sing, which wouldn't be as hard on my body.

Every night trapeze artist Pauliina Rasanen hangs by her toes from a bar twelve metres above the ground. She says she (0) ..*has been hanging*.. off the bar for two years and she (1) .... six years in the circus before that.
  Pauliina trained in dance and performing arts before she went to circus school. She told me that she (2) .... to join the circus because it combined all the skills she (3) .... up till then. She also wanted to do something a little crazy. She said she (4) .... to her first circus when she was fourteen. She (5) .... it so much that she (6) .... circus work as a hobby before working in the circus professionally.
  Pauliina says that so far she (7) .... about 2,300 shows with the Cirque du Soleil. She told me that when the show (8) .... to Brazil next year, she (9) .... with them. Her reason? She said that she (10) .... to learn how to sing and she (11) .... to have a baby in two or three years' time.

48 Reported questions, commands and requests

Reported questions
- Reported questions have the same tense and word changes as reported statements. When we report a question, we use a reporting verb (e.g. *ask, enquire, want to know, wonder*). We don't use a question mark (?).
- To report a *yes/no* question, we use *if/whether* after the reporting verb: **'Have I seen** you before?' → She asked (me) **if/whether** she **had seen** me before.
- To report a *wh-* question, we use the question word: **'Where did** you **go?'** → He wanted to know **where** I **had gone**.
- The word order in reported questions is the same as in statements and there is no *do/does/did* auxiliary: **'Where are you going?'** → He asked (me) where **I was going**. **'Do you like** swimming?' → She enquired if **I liked** swimming.
- When we report questions with *shall/should*, we can use the *to*-infinitive after the question word: **'What should I buy** for Peter?' → She asked **what to buy** for Peter.
- We can report indirect questions in the same way as direct questions. Compare:
'Where is the bank?' → She asked me **where the bank was**.
'Could you tell me where the bank is?' → She asked me **where the bank was**.

Reported commands and requests
- To report commands, we can use *tell* or *order* + *to*-infinitive: **'Be quiet!'** → He **told** us **to be** quiet. **'Put your hands up!'** → The police officer **ordered** them **to put** their hands up.
- To report requests, we can use *ask* + *to*-infinitive: **'Please help us.'** → They **asked** us **to help** them. **'Would you shut the door, please?'** → I **asked** him **to shut** the door.
- To report negative commands and requests, we use *not* before the *to*-infinitive: **'Don't stay** out too late.' → She told me **not to stay** out too late.

PRACTICE

48a Report the questions, commands and requests.

0 'Where did you buy your hat?'
   He wanted to know *where I had bought my hat* .

1 'Would you see who is at the door, please?'
   She asked her husband ....

2 'Please don't make so much noise!'
   He asked them ....

3 'E-mail me if you need any help.'
   She told me ....

4 'Do you know how many people are coming tonight?' Janet asked her assistant.
   Janet wanted to know ....

5 'Did you enjoy yourselves at the concert?' Daryl asked them.
   Daryl asked them ....

6 'Have you been eating properly?' the doctor asked me.
   The doctor enquired ....

111

Grammar: reported speech

7 'Why didn't you go to the meeting?' Logan asked them.
Logan asked them ....

8 'Check this information for me, would you?' Brenda asked.
Brenda asked me ....

9 'Will you be travelling far?' Hasan asked us.
Hasan asked us ....

10 'Don't leave your bag on the floor,' Martin said to Joanna.
Martin told Joanna ....

48b Read the interview with a journalist. Then complete the article.

A: What mistakes do people make when they write e-mails?

B: Often they're too vague.

A: Are there any other common mistakes?

B: Yes, they ask for information they don't need – this wastes everyone's time.

A: So how can we make a good first impression in an e-mail?

B: Be specific about the subject – and for goodness' sake, don't use words like 'hello' on the subject line!

A: How formal should we be?

B: Be as formal or casual as the person who sent you the e-mail.

A: Do people send too many e-mails?

B: Yes. E-mails are for giving and confirming information. Don't use them for negotiations.

A: Could you tell me why companies monitor their employees' e-mails?

B: Many reasons. Sometimes they want to be sure that employees aren't giving secrets away to competitors.

I asked Hamish Elphinstone (0) *what mistakes people made* when they wrote e-mails and he replied that people were often unclear about what they wanted. I asked him (1) .... any other common mistakes and he said that people wasted time by asking for information they didn't need. Next, I asked him (2) .... a good first impression in an e-mail. Hamish told me (3) .... specific about the subject and (4) .... words like 'hello' on the subject line.

On the subject of style, I asked Hamish (5) .... in an e-mail. His suggestion was that we should be as formal as the sender of the original e-mail.

Then we discussed how to use e-mail most effectively. I enquired (6) .... too many e-mails and not surprisingly, he said that, yes, they did. He went on to say that e-mails were for giving and confirming information and he told me (7) .... them for negotiations.

Finally, I asked him (8) .... their employees' e-mails. Apparently, some businesses are concerned that employees might be selling secrets to competitors.

49 Reporting verbs

- We often use reporting verbs to summarise what someone said: *'Would you like to come and stay for the weekend?'* → He **invited us to stay** for the weekend.
'I'm sorry I'm late.' → She **apologised for being** late.
- We use the following structures with these reporting verbs. The verbs marked with an asterisk (*) can be followed by more than one structure:

verb + *to*-infinitive agree*, decide*, offer, promise*, propose*, refuse, threaten*	*'I won't answer any questions.'* → He **refused to answer** any questions.
verb + object + *to*-infinitive advise, beg, encourage, invite, persuade*, remind*, warn*	*'Don't walk home alone. It's dangerous.'* → She **warned me not to walk** home alone. *'It's a good idea to walk home with a friend.'* → She **advised me to walk** home with a friend.
verb + *-ing* form/noun admit*, deny*, recommend*, suggest*	*'Yes, I broke the window.'* → He **admitted breaking** the window. *'Let's have a party.'* → I **suggested having** a party.
verb (+ object) + preposition + *-ing* form/noun accuse someone of, advise* someone against, agree* (with someone) on/about, apologise (to someone) for, complain* (to someone) about, congratulate someone on, insist* on, warn* (someone) against/about	*'I'm sorry I was late.'* → He **apologised** (**to us**) **for being** late. *'I'll pay for the meal!'* → She **insisted on paying** for the meal. *'You passed your driving test! Well done!'* → We **congratulated him on passing** his driving test.
verb + *that* clause admit*, agree*, announce, boast, complain*, decide*, deny*, explain, promise*, suggest*, threaten*	*'We'll be on time.'* → They **promised** (**that**) they **would be** on time.
verb + object + *that* clause inform, persuade*, promise*, remind*, warn*	*'Don't forget – we have a meeting this afternoon.'* → She **reminded me** (**that**) we had a meeting that afternoon.
verb + *that* clause with *should* insist*, propose*, recommend*, suggest*	*'Why don't we ask Cindy to help us?'* → I **suggested that we should ask** Cindy to help us.

⚠️ *Insist, propose, recommend* and *suggest* are followed by different structures, depending on the subject of the sentence in direct speech. Compare:
'Why don't we stay longer?' → I **suggested staying** longer. (I suggested; we (including myself) stay)   *'Why don't they stay longer?'* → I **suggested that they should stay** longer. (I suggested; they stay)

Grammar: *reported speech*

PRACTICE

49a Report the statements.

Laura wants to quit university and look for a job. Read what she said and how other people responded.

0 'I want to leave university and find a job,' said Laura.
Laura announced *that she wanted to leave university and find a job*.

1 'You should finish your degree first,' said her tutor.
Her tutor advised ....

2 'Please think carefully before you take such a big step,' said her mother.
Her mother begged ....

3 'You'll never find a good job if you drop out,' her father said.
Her father warned ....

4 'I'll stop paying your rent if you leave university,' he said.
He threatened ....

5 'I'll let you stay at my flat until you find a place to live,' said her best friend.
Her best friend offered ....

6 'I think you should ask your tutor for advice,' said her sister.
Her sister suggested ....

7 'I'll buy you a car when you graduate,' said her grandmother.
Her grandmother promised ....

49b Report the statements. Use the verbs in the box.

| accused   advised   apologised   complained |
| ~~offered~~   refused   reminded   warned |

0 'I can see you're busy. I'll help you prepare that report if you like,' she said.
She offered to help me prepare the report.

1 'I'm not going to discuss the problem with you. It's a waste of time,' he said.
....

2 'I want you to know I'm upset that I wasn't invited to the meeting,' she said.
....

3 'You mustn't do it again or we'll fine you,' said the police officer.
....

4 'I know someone's been reading my e-mails. It was you, wasn't it?' she said.
....

5 'You've got to apply for a new passport. Yours is out of date,' he said.
....

6 'I'm sorry about the trouble I caused. I didn't mean to do anything wrong,' she said.
....

7 'You've been very ill. You should stay home for a few days,' said the doctor.
....

Check 9 Reported speech

1 **Circle the correct answer.**
   A: Did you see Roy yesterday?
   B: No, he rang and said he (1) *can't* / *couldn't* meet me.

   A: Where's Dylan?
   B: I don't know. He (2) *said* / *told* he (3) *'ll* / *'d* help me yesterday but he must have forgotten.

   A: Have you heard from Yvette?
   B: She called yesterday. She says they (4) *'re having* / *were having* a great time (5) *here* / *there*.

   A: I saw you talking to Rajiv.
   B: Yes. He asked if I (6) *went* / *'d gone* to the meeting last night.

   A: I spoke to Naomi and she (7) *asked* / *told* me why (8) *hadn't you called* / *you hadn't called* her last week.
   B: I hope you told (9) *to her* / *her* the reason. How is she?
   A: She says she (10) *'s feeling* / *was feeling* much better.

   / 10

2 **Report the statements and questions.**
   11 'I was watching television when they arrived.'
      Malcolm said that ....
   12 'I'll be there in an hour.'
      Amy says that ....
   13 'Niels hadn't left when I rang an hour ago.'
      Ulrich said that ....
   14 'Where have you left the newspaper?'
      Astrid asked me ....
   15 'Please don't say anything to Beatrice.'
      Leslie asked me ....
   16 'Shall I ask Sophie out for a meal?'
      Jack wondered ....
   17 'Do we have to stay here all evening?'
      Milos asked ....
   18 'Are you going out this evening?'
      Dieter asked Eve ....
   19 'I've been living in Cardiff for ten years.'
      Sian says that ....
      ....
   20 'I'll love you for ever.'
      Rodney told Winnie that ....
      ....

   / 10

3 **Complete the second sentence so that it means the same as the first, using the word in bold. Use between two and five words.**
   21 'I think you should rest for a few days,' the doctor told me. **advised**
      The doctor .... for a few days.
   22 'Remember you have to book your holiday,' Aaron told him. **reminded**
      Aaron .... his holiday.
   23 'I don't think you should go there,' Edith told her daughter. **not**
      Edith warned her daughter
      .... there.
   24 'Would you like to have dinner with me?' Brian asked me. **invited**
      Brian .... dinner with him.
   25 'You've passed all your exams! Well done!' said my father. **congratulated**
      My father .... all my exams.
   26 'Would you clear the table?' Vivian asked her son. **to**
      Vivian .... the table.
   27 'Don't move!' said the police officer to the man. **told**
      The police officer .... move.
   28 'It was me who took the car,' Robin said. **admitted**
      Robin .... the car.

   / 8

115

4 Choose the correct answer A, B, C or D.

Dear Sir/Madam,

I am writing to complain about a television set which I bought in the sale last week. When I asked the assistant why (29) ...... the only set of that make and model on sale, he (30) ...... me that it (31) ...... used for demonstrations on the shop floor. I also asked him (32) ...... it was in good working order and he assured me that it (33) ...... perfectly. He also promised (34) ...... I could return the set within fourteen days for any reason and receive a full refund.

Unfortunately, when I took the television home, I discovered that the sound and picture quality were poor. I called the shop and asked someone (35) ...... me through to the manager. The manager explained (36) ...... I could not get a refund as the television was a sale item. She (37) ...... to have the television repaired but said that the repairs (38) ...... at my expense. I would also like to add that the assistant who sold me the television (39) ...... promising me a refund if there was a problem with the set.

The manager suggested (40) ...... Head Office, which is why I am writing to you. I would like a full refund on the television as soon as possible.

Yours faithfully,

29	A was this		B it was
	C this had been		D it had been
30	A said		B says
	C told		D told to
31	A is		B is being
	C has been		D had been
32	A if		B why
	C how		D that
33	A works		B is working
	C worked		D would be working
34	A me that		B me if
	C if		D to me
35	A put		B to put
	C putting		D that I put
36	A me		B me that
	C that		D me how
37	A said		B told
	C informed		D offered
38	A are		B were
	C has been		D would be
39	A denied		B refused
	C informed		D decided
40	A to contact		B me to contact
	C that contacting		D that I should contact

/ 12

Total: / 40

Self-check

Wrong answers	Look again at	Try CD-ROM
1, 2, 3, 6, 9, 20, 30, 31, 33, 38	Unit 46	Exercise 46
4, 5, 10, 11, 12, 13, 19	Unit 47	Exercise 47
7, 8, 14, 15, 16, 17, 18, 26, 27, 29, 32, 35	Unit 48	Exercise 48
21, 22, 23, 24, 25, 28, 34, 36, 37, 39, 40	Unit 49	Exercise 49

Now do **Check 9**

Noun clauses

50 Noun clauses as object

- We can use a noun clause after verbs that express thoughts and feelings: *agree, assume, believe, doubt, expect, forget, hope, imagine, know, predict, presume, realise, regret, remember, suppose, think, understand, wonder.*
- A noun clause can be introduced by *that*. In informal speech *that* is often omitted: *I **imagine** (**that**) you're feeling homesick.   I **presume** (**that**) we'll be there by six o'clock.*
- After a past tense verb, the verb in the noun clause is often also in a past tense. Compare: *I **think** that you**'re being** unfair.   I **thought** that you **were being** unfair.*
- A noun clause can also be introduced by a question word or *if/whether*, indicating an indirect question: *I don't understand **what** you are saying.*
*She wondered **where** he had gone.   I doubt **if** they're going to come to the party. Can you remember **whether** he eats meat?*
- A noun clause introduced by a question word has the same word order as a statement. It doesn't require a question mark unless the first part of the sentence is a question. Compare: ***I know*** *where he lives.   **Do you know** where he lives?*
- We use question word + *to*-infinitive after verbs for mental processes and verbs of reporting and communicating: *decide, describe, discuss, explain, find out, forget, know, learn, remember, see, suggest, think, understand, wonder: The leaflet **explains what to do** to protect yourself.   You never **forget how to ride** a bicycle.*
- The verbs *ask, show, teach* and *tell* must be followed by an object: *My English teacher **showed me how to write** an essay.*

PRACTICE

50a Complete the letter. Use one word in each gap.

By now you've arrived at school and I hope (0) ......*that*...... you're feeling comfortable in your new surroundings. I remember (1) .... excited I was when I went abroad for the first time. I don't know (2) .... your experience will be like mine but I did think that you (3) .... being a little optimistic when you predicted that you (4) ....n't be homesick at all. I imagine (5) .... you may start to feel a little lonely in the next few weeks. Just in case, I'm attaching a leaflet on 'culture shock'. It explains (6) .... you might have certain feelings and tells you (7) .... to do about them.

Anyway, I'm sure that you'll have a great time in England – but always remember (8) .... you can rely on me if you need anything.

Grammar: *noun clauses*

50b Join the sentences. Use noun clauses beginning with *that*.

0   You're going with him. At least, I presume so.
    I presume that you're going with him.

1   He expected us to work on Sunday! I couldn't believe it.
    ....

2   Anja's coming round tonight. Have you forgotten?
    ....

3   The car will be fixed by Friday. At least, I'm hoping so.
    ....

4   Football is boring. I used to think so, anyway.
    ....

5   You're an hour late! Do you realise?
    ....

6   It's too late to apply for the job. At least, I suppose it is.
    ....

7   The treatment may not work. I understood that.
    ....

8   It's my father's birthday on Sunday. I suddenly remembered it.
    ....

50c Re-write the questions.

0   How did we get here? I don't know *how we got here* .
1   Where did I leave my bag? I've forgotten ....
2   Has he left his contact details? I can't remember ....
3   Will we get there on time? I wonder ....
4   Why don't you listen to me? I don't understand ....
5   When did she arrive? I don't know ....
6   What time does the class start? Can you remember .... ?
7   Will he recognise us after all these years? I wonder ....
8   Have many people turned up? I don't know ....

50d Complete the conversations. Use the correct form of the verbs in the box and a question word.

assemble   catch   ~~change~~   complete   put   send

0   A: I've got a flat tyre!
    B: Don't worry. I'll show you *how to change* it.

1   A: Will you teach me .... a group e-mail?
    B: Of course. It's easy.

2   A: Could we discuss .... these forms, please?
    B: Sure. They're a little confusing but I can help you.

3 A: I want to take the bus but I need to find out .... it.
B: You need the number 50. It stops outside the chemist's on Brooke Street.

4 A: The instruction manual explains .... the parts.
B: Will it look like the model in the picture when I've put it together?

5 A: Would you tell me .... these papers?
B: On the shelf there, please.

51 Other uses of noun clauses

- We can use a noun clause introduced by *that* as the subject of a sentence: ***That you don't love him*** *is obvious.* ***That he won the game*** *didn't surprise me.*
  However, it is more usual to use *it* + *that* clause: ***It is obvious*** (***that***) *you don't love him.* ***It didn't surprise me that*** *he won the game.*

- Noun clauses introduced by a question word or *whether or not* can also be the subject of a sentence: ***What happened between us*** *is a secret.* ***Why she ran away*** *is a mystery.* ***Whether or not he's coming tonight*** *is uncertain.* / ***Whether he's coming tonight or not*** *is uncertain.*

  ⚠️ Only *whether* is possible in the expression *whether or not*: *We need to know **if/whether** you agree or **not**.* *We need to know **whether or not** you agree.* (Not *We need to know if or not you agree*.)

- We can use *that* clauses after adjectives describing how we feel: *angry, annoyed, glad, grateful, happy, interested, pleased, sad, sorry, surprised, upset, worried*:
  *I'm **grateful** (**that**) so many people offered their help.* *I was **worried** (**that**) we wouldn't have enough money.*

- We can use *that* clauses after adjectives describing how certain we are: *certain, confident, convinced, doubtful, positive, sure*: *We're **confident** (**that**) he can do the job well.* *I'm **positive** (**that**) the work will be finished on time.*

- We can also use a *wh-* clause or question word/*whether* + *to*-infinitive after some of these adjectives: *He isn't **certain** why they did this.* *I hope we don't get lost. I'm not **sure** how to get there.* *I'm not **sure** whether to ring them or not.*

- We can use clauses beginning with *if/whether* after *doubtful*: *It's doubtful **if/whether** we'll arrive on time.*

- We can use a *that* clause after a noun as the subject or object of a sentence. Such nouns include *belief, fact, idea, hope, news, promise, suggestion, thought*:
  The thought that I upset her *is awful.* (subject) *I like **the suggestion that we should work together**.* (object)

- We cannot omit *that* when it comes at the beginning of a sentence or after an abstract noun: ***That he spoke to the police*** *is surprising.* *The papers carried the **news that a senior politician was about to resign**.*

- We can use *that* clauses, *wh-* clauses and question word + *to*-infinitive after *be*:
  *My feeling **is that we will lose the election**.* *The puzzling thing **is how he managed to escape**.* *The problem **is which one to choose**.*

119

Grammar: *noun clauses*

PRACTICE

51a Join the sentences. Use noun clauses.

0 They're getting married. I'm delighted.
I'm delighted that they're getting married.

00 They didn't lie to you. The suggestion is ridiculous.
The suggestion that they lied to you is ridiculous.

1 She hasn't made a complaint. We should be grateful.
....

2 He didn't tell her the truth. She seems very angry about that.
....

3 She'll write to us. She promised.
....

4 He's lying to you. I'm sure about that.
....

5 We might not get a pay rise. I don't like the thought.
....

6 I don't know where to go on holiday. This is my problem.
....

7 We were going to meet outside the club. It was my understanding.
....

8 They won't have enough money to pay their bills this month. They're concerned.
....

51b Correct the mistakes. Add, delete or change only one word in each sentence.

0 The thought I might not have a job next year is troubling.
The thought that I might not have a job next year is troubling.

1 That you're not happy about the decision it's clear.
....

2 The idea all people are equal is important in many societies.
....

3 If you give me the information now or later is not important.
....

4 The result gave me hope our team could win the championship.
....

5 I'm surprising that no one was there to meet us.
....

6 I have a promise the job will be mine if I apply for it.
....

7 I didn't pass all of my exams is disappointing.
....

8 That we didn't notice anything it was not surprising in the circumstances.
....

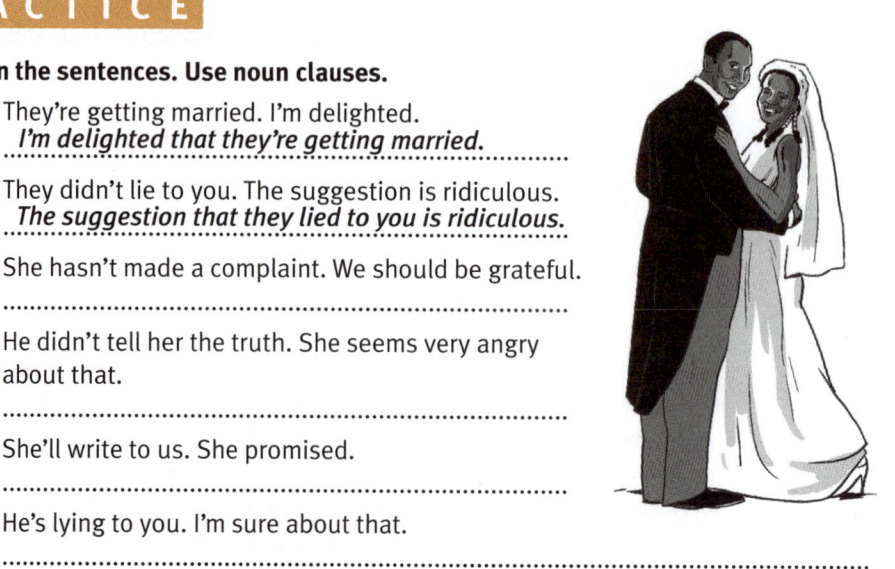

120

Grammar: *noun clauses*

51c Complete the conversations. Use the words in brackets.

0 A: How well do you think you did in the Maths test?
   B: It was easy so I'm .... *sure that I passed* .... it. (sure / pass)

1 A: Have you spoken to Linda recently?
   B: No, and I'm .... (worried / she / be / ill)

2 A: Have you heard yet whether you got the job?
   B: Not yet. Of course, there's always .... in the post. (a possibility / the letter / get / lost)

3 A: Have you decided which university you're going to?
   B: I'd love to go to Oxford. It's a top university but it's .... me a place. My results weren't that brilliant. (doubtful / they / offer)

4 A: Ivor is coming with us, isn't he?
   B: Yes, but .... here on time is another matter. (whether or not / he / be)

5 A: What do you think of .... on other planets? (the theory / there / be / life)
   B: Oh, I'm convinced of it.

6 A: What is your daughter going to do when she leaves school?
   B: Well, ... a vet so I guess she'll try to get a place at a good university. (her ambition / be / become)

51d Complete the second sentence so that it means the same as the first, using the word in bold. Use between two and five words.

0 Why the ancient city fell into ruins is a mystery. **is**
   It .... *is a mystery why* .... the ancient city fell into ruins.

1 It isn't clear if they broke the law or not. **or**
   Whether .... the law isn't clear.

2 No one knows his reason for lying about his whereabouts. **lied**
   Why .... isn't known.

3 I am surprised that they decided to cancel the event. **is**
   That they decided .... surprising.

4 Perhaps I shouldn't accept the job. **whether**
   I am not sure .... the job.

5 It is embarrassing to think that I made such a mistake. **thought**
   The .... such a mistake is embarrassing.

6 I believe that we will find a cure for cancer. **belief**
   It is .... find a cure for cancer.

7 Anyone can see that he has emotional problems. **is**
   That .... obvious.

8 How to solve the problem isn't clear. **certain**
   I am .... the problem.

Check 10 Noun clauses

1 Join the sentences. Use noun clauses.

1 She may have passed her exams. I don't know.
   I don't know ....

2 Tursun's coming round this evening. Have you forgotten?
   Have you forgotten .... ?

3 How's Hannah? Do you know?
   Do you know .... ?

4 Some people are coming to the meeting. I don't know how many.
   I don't know ....

5 He isn't dead. She still holds on to that belief.
   She still ....

6 She didn't lie to you. That suggestion is ridiculous.
   The suggestion ....

/ 6

2 Complete the conversation. Use one word in each gap.

A: Do you know yet (7) .... or not you've got the position?
B: Yes. They rang this morning and offered it to me!
A: Congratulations! You deserve it.
B: Thanks. My only worry is (8) .... I'm much younger than the people I'll be managing.
A: Oh, I wouldn't worry about that. I doubt (9) .... any of them will even think about the age difference. Besides, they'll soon get used to the idea (10) .... you're the boss.
B: I'm sure you're right. And if there is a problem, I'll decide (11) .... to deal with it at the time.
A: Absolutely. I know you weren't (12) .... that it was the right job for you – but I know you'll be great.

/ 6

3 Complete the second sentence so that it means the same as the first, using the word in bold. Use between two and five words.

13 What you want me to do isn't clear. **understand**
    I .... you want me to do.

14 I can't remember the solution to the problem. **solve**
    I can't remember .... the problem.

15 He learnt how to write an essay from Chloe. **taught**
    Chloe .... an essay.

16 She may not be telling the truth. **or**
    I don't know .... she is telling the truth.

17 It is sad to think we may never see them again. **thought**
    The .... may never see them again is sad.

18 No one knows for certain why the accident happened. **not**
    Why .... clear.

19 That they are getting married is not surprising. **surprise**
    It is no .... married.

20 I don't think he will accept the job. **doubtful**
    It is .... the job.

/ 8

Total: / 20

Self-check

Wrong answers	Look again at	Try CD-ROM
1, 2, 3, 4, 9, 11, 13, 14, 15	Unit 50	Exercise 50
5, 6, 7, 8, 10, 12, 16, 17, 18, 19, 20	Unit 51	Exercise 51

Now do **Check 10**

Relative clauses

52 Defining relative clauses

- We use defining relative clauses to give essential information about a person, thing, place, time or reason and to make it clear which one we are talking about: *She's the woman **who was driving the car at the time of the accident**.*
- We don't use commas to separate a defining relative clause from the main clause: *How well do you know the people **who live next door**?*

Subject relative pronouns

- A relative pronoun (*who, which, that*) can be the subject of a defining relative clause. We use *who* or *that* for people and *which* or *that* for things. *Who* and *which* are more common: *The talk was given by a man **who/that** used to live in Russia.* (The subject of *used to live* is *who/that*.)   *Did you see the letter **which/that came today**?* (The subject of *came* is *which/that*.)

Object relative pronouns

- A relative pronoun (*who(m), which, that*) can be the object of a defining relative clause: *There are a few things **which/that** I need to buy before we leave.* (The object of *buy* is *which/that*.) (Not *There are a few things **which/that** I need to buy **them** before we leave.*)
- *Whom* is more formal than *who*: *The woman **who/whom** we elected as chairperson has a great deal of experience.*
- We often omit the relative pronoun when it is the object: *There are a few things (**which/that**) I need to buy before we leave.*
- When the verb has a preposition, the preposition usually comes at the end of the relative clause: *That's the hotel (**which/that**) we were **looking for**.*
- In formal English the preposition can come before the relative pronouns *whom* or *which*, but not before *who* or *that*: *They're the people **to whom** we gave the money.* (Not *They're the people **to who** we gave the money.*)   *That's the information **for which** they were looking.* (Not *That's the information **for that** they were looking.*)

whose, when, where, why

- We use *whose* to show possession: *That's the man **whose car was stolen**.*
- We use *where*, *when/that* and *why/that* to refer to place, time and reason:
  - place: *That's the town **where my grandmother was born**.*
  - time: *2001 was the year **when/that we moved here**.*
  - reason: *Its location is the reason **why/that we chose this flat**.*

⚠ Compare:
*That's the hotel. We spent our holiday **there**.* → *That's the hotel **where** we spent our holiday.*
*That's the hotel. We spent our honeymoon **in it**.* → *That's the hotel (**which**) we spent our honeymoon **in**. / That's the hotel **in which** we spent our honeymoon.*

Grammar: *relative clauses*

PRACTICE

52a Complete the article. Use relative pronouns.

Britain's largest cave was discovered in the Peak District by a group of people (0) ......*who*........ followed the clues in a 200-year old book. The cave, called Titan, is about 140 metres from floor to ceiling. It also has a huge waterfall (1) .... falls far below the level of the ground.

Dave Nixon read about the cave in a paper (2) .... was written in 1793. The writer, James Plumtree, was an academic about (3) .... we know very little and (4) .... paper was found by Mr Nixon in a university library. In this paper, Plumtree described a cave system (5) .... went far beyond what anyone had explored in the area.

Mr Nixon and a group of friends spent three more years removing the rocks (6) .... concealed the entrance to the cave. He pointed out that it was research and hard work (7) .... helped him and his collaborators find the cave, not luck. The cave is now an important tourist attraction in the area (8) .... it was discovered.

52b Join the sentences. Use the underlined sentences to form defining relative clauses. Omit the relative pronoun where possible.

0   She's the one. <u>I told you about her</u>.
    She's the one I told you about.

1   The family moved here from Ireland. <u>They live next door</u>.
    ....

2   The woman is coming back to work soon. <u>I'm doing her job</u>.
    ....

3   This is the job. <u>I've always wanted it</u>.
    ....

4   It was during my first year of university. <u>I first met Bernard then</u>.
    ....

5   The hotel is the most expensive in the area. <u>It overlooks the sea</u>.
    ....

6   That's the house. <u>We lived there when we were university students</u>.
    ....

53 Non-defining relative clauses

- Non-defining relative clauses add extra information to the main clause and are not essential to identify what we are talking about. They are separated from the main clause by a comma or commas. Compare:
  Defining relative clause: *The couple **who bought that house** have three children*. The clause *who bought that house* tells us which couple we are talking about.
  Non-defining relative clause: *The Andersons, **who bought that house**, have three children*. The clause *who bought that house* gives us extra information about the Andersons. The main clause makes sense without the relative clause: *The Andersons have three children*.

- The relative pronouns *who* and *which* can be the subject of a non-defining relative clause: *This is my friend Ali, **who has just returned from Thailand**. Their country house, **which was built in 1856**, was famous for its staircase*.

- The relative pronouns *who*, *whom* and *which* can be the object of a non-defining relative clause: *Liz Barnes, **who/whom I know well**, has worked with me for years. Her latest book, **which I finished last week**, is fascinating*.

- We can use *whom* in formal English but it is more usual to use *who*: *Philip mentioned the problem to his new manager, **who/whom** he had only just met*.

- When the verb has a preposition, the preposition usually comes at the end of the relative clause. In formal English it can also come before *whom* and *which*: *Anna, **who/whom** I was speaking **to**, is a good friend of mine. Anna, **to whom** I was speaking, is a good friend of mine*. (Not *Anna, to who I was speaking, is a good friend of mine*.)

- We cannot use *that* or omit the object pronoun in non-defining relative clauses: *That old car, **which** my parents bought for me, has never given me any trouble*.

- We use *whose* for possession, *where* for place and *when* for time: *Inez, **whose** family I know well, lives in Majorca. Canada, **where** I grew up, is a multicultural country. They moved here last summer, **when** their first child was born*.

PRACTICE

53a Join the sentences. Use the underlined sentences to form non-defining relative clauses.

0   My parents are coming to visit me in England. <u>They live in Australia</u>.
    My parents, who live in Australia, are coming to visit me in England.

1   Their e-mail says they'll be staying for a week. <u>I received it yesterday</u>.
    ....

2   My fiancé is looking forward to their visit. <u>They haven't met him</u>.
    ....

3   Naturally, my parents want to meet my fiancé. <u>His parents want to meet mine</u>.
    ....

4   My mother is also planning to visit Scotland. <u>She was born there</u>.
    ....

5   She wants to go in August. <u>The heather blooms then</u>.
    ....

Grammar: *relative clauses*

53b Complete the article. Use relative pronouns.

Lacrosse, (0) ......*which*...... was invented by the Native North Americans, is widely considered to be the first real American sport. However, the game has changed drastically since the fifteenth century, (1) .... it was first played.

In early versions of the game, each team could have 100 to 1000 players, (2) .... played on an enormous field. Players threw balls, (3) .... could be made from deerskin, clay, stone or wood, at a tree or rock to gain points. Lacrosse games, (4) .... could last for days, were used to settle arguments between tribes and to prepare young men for war. Players sometimes killed or injured members of the other team, (5) .... they would attack in order to score a goal more easily.

In the nineteenth century, (6) .... lacrosse had become less violent, French Canadians started to play the game. Today lacrosse is the fastest growing sport in the United States and is popular throughout Canada, (7) .... it is the official summer sport. Balls are now made of rubber and there are ten players in a team, not hundreds. But lacrosse is still dangerous and players have to wear special protective clothing.

53c Join the sentences. Use the words in brackets.

0   J.K. Rowling is the creator of Harry Potter. She worked as an English teacher. (who)
   J.K. Rowling, who worked as an English teacher, is the creator of Harry Potter.

1   Pablo Picasso suffered from dyslexia. His paintings are some of the most famous in the world. (whose)
   ....

2   William Shakespeare is considered to be one of the greatest playwrights of all time. He wrote about thirty-seven plays. (who)
   ....

3   Muhammed Ali won the world heavyweight boxing title in 1964. He defeated Sonny Liston that year. (when)
   ....

4   In the 1980s Brad Pitt moved to Los Angeles. He took acting classes and worked as a chauffeur there. (where)
   ....

5   Cleopatra is one of the most famous rulers in history. She married two of her brothers. (who)
   ....

6   Bill Clinton was the forty-second President of the United States. His father died three months before he was born. (whose)
   ....

7   Although he was born in Bonn, Ludwig van Beethoven moved to Vienna in 1792. He soon established a reputation there as a piano virtuoso. (where)
   ....

Grammar: *relative clauses*

54 *which* referring to a whole clause

- In a coordinating relative clause, *which* refers to the whole main clause. Compare: *He decided to see a doctor about the problem **which** had been bothering him.* (*Which* refers to *the problem* and *which had been bothering him* is a defining relative clause.) *He decided to see a doctor about the problem, **which** was a good idea.* (*Which* refers to the fact that he decided to see a doctor about the problem.)
- Coordinating relative clauses come at the end of the main clause and are separated from it by a comma: *She spent the day resting in bed, **which was unusual**.* (= The fact that she spent the day resting in bed was unusual.)

PRACTICE

54 Write sentences with coordinate relative clauses. Use the sentences in the box.

> It made them ill.
> It was a sign that he was getting angry.
> It was a surprise for everyone.
> It was frightening for my sister and her husband.
> It will give her the rest she needs.
> This is impressive for a woman of her age.
> ~~This is making her very unhappy.~~
> This means you should pack lots of warm clothing.
> This was an expensive mistake.

0 She's going to have to sell the business.
   She's going to have to sell the business, which is making her very unhappy.

1 My grandmother runs five miles every day.
   ....

2 She's going to take a month off work.
   ....

3 He spent a lot of money on a car he couldn't afford.
   ....

4 The weather there is very cold at this time of year.
   ....

5 She arrived a day earlier than we expected.
   ....

6 My nephew had to go into hospital suddenly.
   ....

7 He suddenly got very red in the face.
   ....

8 The children ate too much cake at the party.
   ....

127

Grammar: *relative clauses*

55 Other ways to identify people and things

We can add information about a person or thing in a number of ways:

- We can use a prepositional phrase instead of a relative clause: *They live in a flat (**which is**) **in the city centre**.   Only people **with plenty of money** can afford to shop here.* (= who have plenty of money)   *Suzanne is the woman **in the black silk dress**.* (= who is wearing the black silk dress)

- We can use a present participle clause to replace:
  - a relative pronoun + present/past continuous verb: *The train **which is arriving at Platform 1** is the 14.35 for London.* → *The train **arriving at Platform 1** is the 14.35 for London.*   *The man **who was leaving** by the back door was acting suspiciously.* → *The man **leaving by the back door** was acting suspiciously.*
  - a relative pronoun + present/past simple verb to describe a permanent state: *The woman **who works at Reception** is good at her job.* → *The woman **working at Reception** is good at her job.*   *The old man **who lived next door** had an accident.* → *The old man **living next door** had an accident.*

- ⚠ We cannot use a present participle clause to talk about a single past action: *The people **who stopped me in the street** were tourists.* (Not ~~The people stopping me in the street were tourists~~.)

- We can use a past participle clause instead of a passive relative clause: *The identity of the man **who was known as 'Jack the Ripper'** remains unknown.* → *The identity of the man **known as 'Jack the Ripper'** remains unknown.*

- If the participle clause replaces a non-defining relative clause, it is separated from the main clause by commas: *Buckingham Palace, (**which was**) **built** in 1703, is the official residence of the monarchs of Britain.*

PRACTICE

55a Re-write the sentences. Use the underlined words to form prepositional phrases.

0   Manfred's the boy who's wearing the white jumper.
    Manfred's the boy in the white jumper.

1   We have already watered the flowers <u>which are at the front of the house</u>.
    ....

2   Clara is the girl <u>who's got blond hair and green eyes</u>.
    ....

3   Hester brought us some vegetables <u>which came from her garden</u>.
    ....

4   Alan is the tall man <u>who's wearing the uniform</u>.
    ....

5   We play tennis at the courts <u>which are opposite the park</u>.
    ....

6   Our players are the ones <u>who have the red and white shirts</u>.
    ....

Grammar: *relative clauses*

55b Re-write the numbered sentences in the articles. Use participle clauses or prepositional phrases.

(0) A dog which was looking for food for her puppies found a baby in a forest in Kenya. (1) The dog took the baby, which was wrapped in a dirty cloth, and put it next to her puppies.

(2) A witness said he heard a baby which was crying. (3) Another witness said she saw a dog that was carrying a baby across a road. Eventually, the baby was found and taken to hospital.

(4) A homesick Chinese cat that was given away by its owner walked forty days and a hundred miles to return home. (5) The cat's owner is a woman who has a small flat in Beijing. (6) She gave the cat to a friend who was living in the country. The cat's owner has promised not to give it away again.

0   *A dog looking for food for her puppies found a baby in a forest in Kenya.*
1   ....
2   ....
3   ....
4   ....
5   ....
6   ....

55c Re-write the relative clauses that can be shortened. Tick the ones that cannot be shortened.

New photographs (0) <u>which were taken from an orbiting spacecraft</u> suggest there may have been water on Mars until relatively recently. The photographs were taken by NASA's Mars Global Surveyor, (1) <u>which has been photographing the planet since 1996</u>.

The evidence, (2) <u>which suggests that there may be water</u> (3) <u>which is on the planet</u>, raises an interesting question. The photographs show marks (4) <u>which could be riverbeds</u>. Many scientists claim this is evidence of life on a planet (5) <u>which was once thought to be lifeless</u>.

0   *taken from an orbiting spacecraft*   1   ....
2   3   ....
4   5   ....

Check 11 Relative clauses

1 **Complete the sentences. Use relative pronouns.**
   1 Is she the manager .... 's taking over our department?
   2 Jody made the best suggestion, ... was unusual.
   3 The shop on the corner, ... I used to buy most of my food, closed last year.
   4 The case .... was stolen had some valuable papers in it.
   5 Ian Fleming, ... books have been made into successful films, was a prolific writer.
   6 Philip Pullman, ... wrote *His Dark Materials*, is a fine author.
   7 Oksana's flat, ... she bought last year, is near the park.
   8 Autumn is the season .... I feel most restless.
   9 Marcella's decided to teach abroad, ... will be a great experience for her.
   10 This is a picture of the place .... we're spending our holidays.

   / 10

2 **Join the sentences. Use the underlined sentences to form relative clauses.**
   11 I discussed the problem with my cousin. She is a lawyer.
   ....
   12 This is Will. I've known his sister since we were children.
   ....
   13 Last year we moved back to the town. I was born there.
   ....
   14 The Richardsons are the people. We met them on holiday last year.
   ....
   15 The children refused to eat the food. Their mother had prepared it.
   ....
   16 Elli called her brother. She hadn't spoken to him for weeks.
   ....
   17 We walked to the top of the hill. We had a picnic there.
   ....
   18 Do you know the people? They live next door.
   ....
   19 They moved in 1997. Their first child was born then.
   ....
   20 I put my contact details on the Internet. This was a mistake.
   ....

   / 10

3 Complete the article. Use the clauses in the box.

> conducted on two groups of people
> controlling appetite
> he or she can help you with
> in which one group slept
> that shows
> they had seen
> which is not enough
> which is the recommended average
> which we can then access
> who get less than eight hours a night
> who had had a good night's sleep
> who had not slept

DO YOU GET ENOUGH SLEEP?
Despite evidence (21) .... how sleep can affect our health, a large number of people suffer from a lack of it. Many adults get less than six hours of sleep a night, (22) .... In fact, most of us need seven to eight hours, (23) ....

CAN SLEEP AFFECT YOUR WEIGHT?
Apparently, it can. Sleep affects the hormones (24) .... According to one study, people (25) .... are more likely to be overweight.

WILL SLEEP MAKE ME MORE INTELLIGENT?
No, but sleeping on a problem can help solve it. When we sleep, the brain puts the day's memories into 'files', (26) .... In tests (27) .... , researchers showed each group a list of related words. Both groups were asked to remember the words (28) .... after a period of time (29) .... and the other was awake. The people (30) .... remembered more words. When they were asked to remember the ideas linking the words, the group (31) .... forgot 25% more than the group who had.

WHAT SHOULD I DO IF I CAN'T SLEEP WELL?
See your doctor. Your difficulties may result from a problem (32) ....

/ 12

4 Complete the article. Use prepositional phrases or participle clauses formed from the relative clauses in brackets.

In the opening scene of *Titanic*, Brock Lovett is a treasure hunter (33) .... (who is searching for a diamond necklace) (34) .... (which is believed to have sunk with the famous ship). He finds a safe (35) .... (which has a photograph of a woman) (36) .... (who is wearing the necklace). He shows the photo on television and an old woman (37) .... (who is called Rose Dawson Calvert) comes forward and claims that she is the person (38) .... (who is in the photograph).
   Rose, (39) .... (who is played by Kate Winslett), boards the *Titanic* when she is just seventeen years old. She is unhappily engaged to an American (40) .... (who has a lot of money). Rose falls in love with Jack Dawson (Leonardo DiCaprio), a third-class passenger on the ship. The historic events that follow change their lives forever.

/ 8

Total: / 40

✓ Self-check

Wrong answers	Look again at	Try CD-ROM
1, 4, 8, 10, 13, 14, 15, 18, 21, 25, 28, 29, 30, 31, 32	Unit 52	Exercise 52
3, 5, 6, 7, 11, 12, 16, 17, 19, 22, 23, 26	Unit 53	Exercise 53
2, 9, 20	Unit 54	Exercise 54
24, 27, 33, 34, 35, 36, 37, 38, 39, 40	Unit 55	Exercise 55

Now do **Check 11**

Linking words and structures

56 Compound and complex sentences

Compound sentences
- We can link simple sentences consisting of subject + verb to form compound sentences of two or more clauses. In a compound sentence, the clauses are of equal importance.
- We use the coordinating conjunctions *and* (addition), *but* (contrast), *so* (result) and *or* (alternative) to link the clauses. Usually there is no comma before the conjunction: *It's an old car **but** it's very reliable.   Hurry up **or** we'll be late.*
- We can also link sentences with linking adverbs like *moreover/furthermore* (addition), *however* (contrast) and *therefore* (result). Notice the use of the semi-colon and the comma: *She was unhappy; **therefore**, it came as no surprise when she left.*

Complex sentences
- Complex sentences have a main clause and a subordinate clause. The subordinate clause depends on the main clause for its meaning.
- We use subordinating conjunctions before the subordinate clause, e.g. *although/ even though/though* (concession), *because* (reason), *if/unless* (condition). If the subordinate clause comes before the main clause, we use a comma: ***Even though** the car is old, it runs well. / The car runs well **even though** it is old.   **Because** I lost my job, I had to move. / I had to move **because** I lost my job.*

▶▶ See Appendix 1: Punctuation rules, page 199.

PRACTICE

56 Complete the sentences. Use the conjunctions in the box. Add commas where necessary.

although   and   because   but   however   if   moreover   or   so

0 ....*If*......... you don't hurry up and get ready, we'll be late.
1 He was busy working .... he couldn't come with us.
2 Shall we go to the cinema .... should we stay at home?
3 You should try to eat less .... you should get more exercise.
4 .... a Rolls Royce is a beautiful car it's expensive to maintain.
5 They installed a new security system; .... they hired extra guards.
6 We've cut costs and increased production; .... we're still not making a profit.
7 .... he wasn't feeling well I offered to do the shopping for him.
8 Carla was supposed to drive us to the station .... her husband needed the car.

57 Adding and listing

- *Also*, *too* and *as well* (*as*) have a similar meaning to *and*. We can use them to add or join ideas in a sentence. *Also* is the most formal and *as well* is the least formal. Notice their positions in the sentence: *He speaks perfect French **and** German. He speaks English **too/as well**. He **also** speaks Italian. / **Also**, he speaks Italian.*
- We use *as well as* before a noun or -*ing* form: ***As well as speaking** several languages, she is a talented sportsperson.*
- We use *both ... and*, *either ... or* and *neither ... nor* for emphasis when we link ideas in a sentence.
  - *Both ... and* link two similar ideas: ***Both** Gina **and** her husband enjoy tennis. They can speak **both** English **and** Japanese.*
  - *Either ... or* link alternatives: *You can have **either** French fries **or** mashed potatoes with your steak.   You can **either** leave now **or** apologise.*
  - *Neither ... nor* link two similar negative ideas: ***Neither** his mother **nor** his father came to the wedding.   The equipment was **neither** safe **nor** accurate.*
- We use expressions like *in addition*, *moreover* and *furthermore* to add information or arguments. These expressions are quite formal and we use them mainly in writing. They are usually followed by a comma: *The rent is reasonable. **Moreover**, the location is perfect.*
- We can also use these expressions for listing ideas or arguments: *first of all/firstly/ first, secondly/second, thirdly/third, then, next, finally/lastly: The project was not practical. **Firstly**, it was too expensive. **Secondly**, the local people did not support it. **Lastly**, it would take too long to complete.*
- ⚠ We don't use *too* at the beginning of a clause. We don't usually use *also* at the end of a clause.

PRACTICE

57a Circle the correct answers. There may be more than one correct answer.

0 It's a more efficient system and (also) / as well / too, it's quite cheap.
1 She's a valued colleague and a great friend *as well / as well as / too*.
2 Smoking makes you ill. *Also / As well / Too*, it costs a lot.
3 He lived in *both / either / neither* Britain and the States for several years.
4 *First / First of all / Furthermore*, mix the flour and sugar. *Next / Then / In addition*, add the eggs.
5 Neither Piet *and / nor / or* his wife ate any meat dishes – they're vegetarians.
6 The food was terrible and the weather was awful *as well / either / too*.
7 *Both / Either / Neither* she leaves *and / or / nor* I will. It's your choice.
8 *Also / As well / As well as* being bad for your teeth, sugar can contribute to heart disease.
9 He's a successful actor. *Also / In addition / Too*, he's a talented singer.
10 Pamela should retire. Her health is poor; *as well / furthermore / moreover*, she's lost interest in the job.

Grammar: *linking words and structures*

57b Complete the essay. Use one word in each gap.

> Today 20% of the world's population consumes 80% of the world's natural resources. That same 20% (0) .....*also*..... creates half of the world's fossil fuel pollution. Unfortunately, our lifestyle (1) .... increases our well-being (2) .... makes the world a better place for our children.
>
> Let's start by looking at our attachment to the car. As well (3) .... being a status symbol, the car is convenient but how else does it affect us? (4) .... of all, we spend hours every week inside a car and this isolates us from nature. (5) ...., driving has replaced walking and other forms of exercise. And finally, gas emissions from cars are threatening to destroy the planet. (6) .... we face the problems now (7) .... we will have to deal with the consequences.
>
> So what can we do to take better care of our planet? To begin with, we can leave our car at home and start walking, running or cycling to work. We can spend more time outdoors (8) .... In (9) ...., we can encourage others to do the same and teach our children a sense of responsibility for their environment.

58   Contrast and concession

> These words and phrases have a similar meaning to *but* and link contrasting ideas.
> - *Although, though, even though, while* and *whereas* introduce a subordinate clause. If the subordinate clause comes before the main clause, we use a comma.
>   – We use *although* and *though* to introduce an idea that makes the idea in the main clause seem surprising. *Even though* is more emphatic than *although/though*: **Although** *her health was poor, she continued to work.*   *He went ahead with the experiment* **even though** *he knew it was dangerous.*
>   – *Though* can come at the end of a sentence in informal English: *I think she's Swiss. I'm not sure,* **though**.
>   – *While* and *whereas* are quite formal. We use them to highlight a difference: *The old system was complicated* **while/whereas** *the new one is simple.*
> - We use *in spite of/despite* to link ideas in these ways:
>   – *in spite of/despite* + noun/pronoun/*-ing* form: *He seemed unhappy* **in spite of his wealth**.   *He seemed unhappy* **despite being** *wealthy*.
>   – *in spite of/despite* + *the fact that* + clause: **In spite of the fact that he was wealthy**, *he seemed unhappy*.
> - We use *however* to contrast ideas across sentences or paragraphs. It usually comes at the beginning of a sentence but a middle or end position is also possible: *We can provide breakfast.* **However**, *there is an extra charge for this.* / *There is,* **however**, *an extra charge for this.* / *There is an extra charge for this,* **however**.
> - We use *on the one hand ... on the other hand* to introduce two contrasting facts or opinions: **On the one hand**, *nuclear power is cheap.* **On the other hand**, *you could argue it's not safe.*

PRACTICE

58a Circle the correct answer.

In 2006 more than 25% of holiday makers booked their holiday less than four weeks before leaving (0) *although* / (*whereas*) last year fewer than 5% made arrangements in the month before they went away. In 2005 35% of holiday makers booked a trip six months or more in advance (1) *however* / *while* only 13% do so now, said a travel industry researcher.

Another trend is that travellers are now more likely to research and book their own holidays. (2) *On the one hand* / *Whereas* previously they would rely on a travel agent, travellers are now obtaining their information through the Internet. Budget airlines are also having an effect on the travel industry. (3) *Despite* / *Although* the fact that these airlines offer only a basic service, they are a popular choice with many travellers.

The types of holidays people take are also changing. They are going away more frequently (4) *and* / *however* short breaks have replaced the traditional two-week summer holiday. (5) *Even though* / *In spite of* all of these changes, the number of people booking traditional package holidays is expected to remain the same over the next five years. (6) *But* / *However*, the number of people who take adventure or sporting holidays is expected to increase by 200%.

(7) *On the one hand* / *However*, these changes could be disastrous for tour operators and travel agents. (8) *Despite* / *On the other hand*, the changes are an opportunity for the travel industry to adapt and enter new markets, the report concludes.

58b Re-write the sentences. Use the words in brackets.

0 I'm not sure if my answers are right but you can copy them. (although)
   Although I'm not sure if my answers are right, you can copy them.

1 Despite the fact that her doctor told her to rest, she went to Spain. (even though)
   ....

2 She joined the company only a year ago but she's been promoted already. (in spite of)
   ....

3 He hasn't got any experience but he's keen to learn. (however)
   ....

4 I'd like to eat out but I should be saving money. (while)
   ....

5 I thought he looked ill; however, I wasn't completely sure. (but)
   ....

6 Even though it was raining, we went out for the day. (despite)
   ....

7 The government spent money on weapons but it neglected education. (whereas)
   ....

Grammar: *linking words and structures*

59 Cause, reason, purpose and result

- To introduce a cause or reason, we use *because/since/as* + clause: *He couldn't come **because** he had to work.   **As** it was dark, we took a torch with us.*
- We can also introduce a cause or reason with *because of/due to/owing to* + noun. *Due to* and *owing to* are more formal: ***Because of the bad weather**, the flight was cancelled.*
- We can also use *because of/due to/owing to* + *the fact that* + clause: ***Due to the fact that** the weather was bad, the flight was cancelled.*
- To talk about purpose, we can use *so* (*that*) + clause: *They'll take a map **so** (**that**) they don't/won't get lost.   We left early **so** (**that**) we wouldn't be late.*
- We can also use *so as* (*not*) *to/in order* (*not*) *to/to* + infinitive to talk about purpose. *So as to* and *in order to* are more formal than *to*: *He trained hard **in order to** improve his performance.   We whispered **so as not to** disturb anyone.*
- To talk about a result, we use *so* + clause: *I was tired **so** I went to bed.*
- *Therefore, as a result* and *for this reason* have a similar meaning to *so*. They usually come at the beginning of a sentence but a middle position is also possible for *therefore*: *Airline pilots are on strike. **Therefore/As a result/For this reason**, flights have been cancelled. / Flights have **therefore** been cancelled.*

PRACTICE

59a Circle the correct answers. There may be more than one correct answer.

Youngest children often feel frustrated (0) *because / since / (due to)* the fact that everyone in the family wants to take care of them. They (1) *for this reason / therefore / as a result* need to prove to others that they can make their own decisions (2) *so that / in order to / so as to* others will take them seriously.

    Middle children, on the other hand, can feel left out (3) *because / because of / owing to* they don't get the advantages that come with being the eldest or youngest child. However, there is a positive side to being a middle child. They are usually loyal and sociable and they are most likely to develop their talents fully (4) *due to / so / as* this is a way of getting attention.

    (5) *Therefore/ Since / As* their parents want the best for them, eldest children get lots of attention. They often take their responsibilities seriously and (6) *so as to / so that / as a result*, they work hard (7) *so / so that / in order to* prove they deserve the attention they get.

59b Complete the second sentence so that it means the same as the first, using the word in bold. Use between two and five words.

0   All my clothes got wet because of the storm. **there**
    All my clothes got wet ....*because there was*........... a storm.

1   The car crashed because the driver was careless. **of**
    The car crashed .... carelessness.

2   I studied for many years so that I could become a doctor. **order**
    I studied for many years .... a doctor.

3   I lied to him because I didn't want to hurt his feelings. **in**
    I lied to him .... his feelings.

4   She is studying because she has a test tomorrow. **so**
    She .... she is studying.

5   He had to leave his job owing to poor health. **since**
    He had to leave his job .... poor.

6   Let's leave early to avoid the rush hour. **that**
    Let's leave early .... the rush hour.

60 Time clauses

The future
- We use the present simple to refer to the future in time clauses with *after, before, when, as soon as, until* and *once*: *I'll wait here **until** you **get** back.*
- We use the present perfect to emphasise that an action will be complete before the action in the main clause: ***Once** you'**ve had** a good night's sleep, you'll feel better.*
- Often the meaning is the same if we use the present simple or the present perfect but sometimes it is different. Compare: *I'll give you the report **when** I **finish/have finished** it.* (= First I'll finish the report and then I'll give it to you.) *When I speak to her, I'll mention the subject.* (= I'll mention the subject at the same time I am speaking to her.) *When I've spoken to her, I'll ring you.* (= First I'll speak to her and then I'll ring you.)
- We use the present continuous with *when* and *while* to refer to an action that will be in progress in the future: *I'm going to talk to him about the problem **when/while** we'**re having** lunch.*

The present
We use present tenses in both clauses to talk about the present. *When* can mean 'every time': ***When** I **see** them, I **remember** all the good times we had together.*

The past
We can use *after, before, when, while, as soon as, until* and *once* to refer to actions in the past: ***When** they **arrived**, we **were eating**.* *They **arrived while** we **were having** dinner.* *I **saw** them a few days **before** they **left**.* ***After** they **left/had left**, we stayed in contact for some time.*

137

Grammar: *linking words and structures*

PRACTICE

60a Join the sentences. Use the words in brackets.

0   The children will finish their homework. We'll go out then. (when)
    When the children have finished their homework, we'll go out.

1   He'll be working. She'll be lying on the beach. (while)
    ....

2   You'll tell me what really happened. Only then will I help you. (once)
    ....

3   Jake will finish the report he's writing. He'll come over to my place. (as soon as)
    ....

4   Petra and Otto will go swimming. They'll do the washing up first. (after)
    ....

5   I'll see Helen. I'll give her your regards. (when)
    ....

6   Gareth will keep looking for his wallet. He'll find it. (until)
    ....

7   First you have to pass a driving test. Then you can get a driving licence. (before)
    ....

8   She'll add some herbs to the dish. It will taste better. (when)
    ....

60b Complete the interview. Use the correct form of the verbs in brackets.

A: So what are you going to do after you (0) ......*graduate*...... (graduate)?
B: Well, some of my friends are planning to see the world before they (1) .... (start) work. But I travelled quite a lot after I (2) .... (finish) school. As soon as I (3) .... (leave) university, I want to get a job and start paying off my student loan.
A: That sounds very practical. Do you think it will be easy to find work?
B: Well, when I (4) .... (choose) to study Physics, I knew there was a shortage of people with science degrees. In fact, before I (5) .... (come) to university, I did a lot of research – I wanted to be sure I wouldn't be wasting my time and money here!
A: Do you think you made the right decision?
B: I think so. After I (6) .... (give) my options a lot of thought, I decided to do a 'sandwich course'. That means I work for a year as part of my studies. So when prospective employers (7) .... (look) at my CV, they (8) .... (see) that I've had work experience – and that will make a difference to my job prospects.
A: And are you enjoying your course?
B: Most of the time. Sometimes, when I (9) .... (have) a paper to write, I (10) .... (think) I should be lying on a beach somewhere instead! But once I (11) .... (get) my degree, I don't think I'll have any regrets.

Grammar: *linking words and structures*

61 Common linking expressions in speech

- To give information a second time for emphasis or to explain what we mean, we can use *in other words*: *The new tax only affects people with large incomes,* or **in other words**, *the rich.*
- To emphasise or support something we have just said, we can use *after all*: *I don't know why you're so worried. **After all**, it's not your problem.*
- To add emphasis, to fill a pause or to show surprise or anger in a conversation, we can use *well*: **Well**, *I think it's a good idea.*   **Well**, *let me think.*   **Well**, *you could have phoned to say you'd be late.*
- To emphasise that something is true or to disagree politely, we can use *actually*: *I'm not disappointed. **Actually**, I'm rather glad I didn't get the job.*
- To add information or to correct what we have just said, we can use *I mean* or *or rather*: *You're better at writing reports than I am. **I mean**, you've had all that experience.*   *We all went in Sonia's car, **or rather**, her father's car.*
- To say that something is not important or to end a conversation, we can use *anyway* or *anyhow* (less formal): *They didn't have trainers in my size and **anyway**, I don't need another pair.*   ***Anyhow**, I must be going now.*
- To change the subject in a conversation, we can use *anyway/anyhow* or *by the way*: ***Anyway**, how have you been?*   ***By the way**, have you seen my keys?*

⚠ We can use *on the contrary* to show that we disagree but this is more common in writing: *It wasn't a good idea. **On the contrary**, it was a huge mistake.*

PRACTICE

61 **Circle the correct answer.**

A: (0)(By the way)/ On the contrary, I've just remembered. Have we got a birthday card for Ingrid yet?
B: No, I thought you were getting one.
A: We must buy one today. (1) *After all / Anyway*, it's her eighteenth birthday.

A: That was an interesting lecture.
B: (2) *Anyhow / Actually*, I thought it was dull, (3) *in other words / or rather*, the subject is dull. I don't like accounting.

A: Have you got the tickets for the concert tonight?
B: (4) *Well / I mean*, I haven't got them yet.
A: (5) *After all / In other words*, you've forgotten to buy them.

A: It was an exciting film, don't you think?
B: (6) *By the way / On the contrary*, I had trouble staying awake.
A: (7) *Well / I mean*, if you didn't want to see it, you should have said so.

139

Grammar: *linking words and structures*

62 Participle clauses: contrast, reason, result

- Participle clauses have the same subject as the verb in the main clause. They are quite formal and we use them more often in writing. We can use present participle clauses:
  - to replace clauses of contrast or concession. We use *while*, *in spite of* or *despite* to introduce the participle clause: *Although I understand your problem, I can't allow you to break the rules.* → **While/In spite of/Despite understanding your problem,** *I can't allow you to break the rules.*
  - to replace clauses of result: *He told her about the party they'd planned and so he ruined the surprise for her.* → *He told her about the party they'd planned,* **ruining the surprise for her.**
  - to replace clauses of reason: *We left early because we wanted to catch the last train.* → **Wanting to catch the last train,** *we left early.* *Because I'm a quiet sort of person, I didn't want to get involved in the argument.* → **Being a quiet sort of person,** *I didn't want to get involved in the argument.*
- We can use a perfect participle (*having* + past participle) to replace a clause of reason in the present perfect or past perfect: *As he's **lived** here all his life, he knows a lot about the town.* → **Having lived** *here all his life, he knows a lot about the town.*

▶▶ For reduced relative clauses, see Unit 55. For participle clauses of time, see Unit 63.

PRACTICE

62a Re-write the sentences. Use participle clauses.

0 I went round to see her as I was hoping I could apologise.
   Hoping I could apologise , I went round to see her.

1 While he hated the job, he carried on doing it for many years.
   ……………………………… , he carried on doing it for many years.

2 I had plenty of time to spare so I had a good look round the town.
   ……………………………… , I had a good look round the town.

3 I had been out all day so I was quite happy to stay in for the evening.
   ……………………………… , I was quite happy to stay in for the evening.

4 Since I had failed one of my exams, I couldn't get into university.
   ……………………………… , I couldn't get into university.

5 They managed to settle their disagreement because they were good friends.
   ……………………………… , they managed to settle their disagreement.

6 As I was happy with my exam results, I decided to go out and celebrate.
   ……………………………… , I decided to go out and celebrate.

7 Although I want them to like me, I can't be dishonest about who I am.
   ……………………………… , I can't be dishonest about who I am.

8 Because she was scared of spiders, she refused to go down to the cellar.
   ……………………………… , she refused to go down to the cellar.

Grammar: *linking words and structures*

62b Read the book review. Then re-write the numbered sentences. Use the words in brackets to form participle clauses.

(0) Charles Frazier got an idea for a story from a real-life journey made by his great-great-uncle and he decided to write a novel. (having) *Cold Mountain* is set in the American Civil War and tells the story of a soldier called Inman. (1) Inman has been wounded so he deserts the army. (having) (2) He journeys through the Appalachian Mountains because he wants to return home to the woman he loves. (wanting) (3) He struggles to stay alive because he faces many dangers. (facing)

(4) *Cold Mountain* is a deeply moving novel because it looks at war and its effect on people. (looking at) (5) It is also a powerful love story so it appeals to a wide readership. (being) (6) I have read the book and seen the film and I would strongly recommend either. (having)

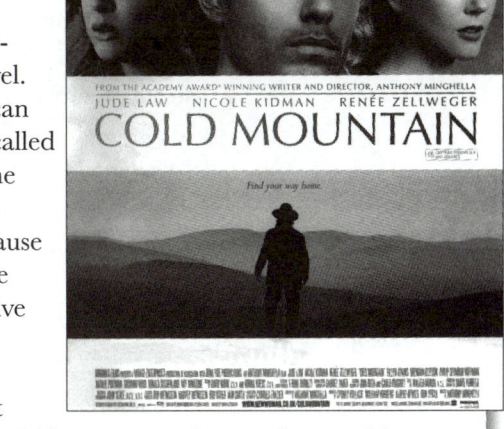

0 *Having got an idea for a story from a real-life journey made by his great-great-uncle, Charles Frazier decided to write a novel.*

1 ....
2 ....
3 ....
4 ....
5 ....
6 ....

63 Participle clauses: time

- We can use a participle clause to replace *and* + coordinate clause. The two actions in the sentence happen at the same time or at different times. When one action follows another, the action which takes place first comes first in the sentence:
  I stood in the garden and watched the children. → *I stood in the garden **watching the children**.* (same time)   *I switched off the light and tried to get some sleep.* → ***Switching off the light**, I tried to get some sleep.* (different times)

- We can use a participle clause after *after, before, since, while, on*, etc. The two actions happen at the same time or at different times: *When I met him, I didn't like him.* → ***On meeting him**, I didn't like him.* (same time)   *I spoke to him and then I felt better.* → *I felt better **after speaking to him**.* (different times)

- When we want to emphasise that one action happened before another, we use a perfect participle (*having* + past participle). The clause with *having* comes first:
  I'd made a decision and I was anxious to act on it. → ***Having made a decision**, I was anxious to act on it.*

141

Grammar: *linking words and structures*

PRACTICE

63a Re-write the sentences. Use participle clauses.

0   She came in and she looked furious.
    She came in looking furious.

1   He set off on his journey and he carried only one small bag.

2   I've changed my job since I last wrote to you.

3   Before I give you an answer, I need to discuss the situation with my parents.

4   He left school and then he worked in a restaurant for a year. (Begin: *Having* ...)

5   She switched on her computer and started to work.

6   We turned the corner and we saw a huge traffic jam ahead of us.

7   After he bought the painting, he discovered that it was a fake. (Begin: *Having* ...)

8   We had an argument and never saw one another again. (Begin: *Having* ...)

63b Join the sentences. Use participle clauses and the words in brackets.

0   I'd forgotten to set my alarm. I woke up late the morning of the interview.
    Having forgotten to set my alarm, I woke up late the morning of the interview.

1   I threw back the bedcovers. I rushed downstairs to the kitchen.

2   I made some coffee. Then I went back upstairs to have a shower and get dressed.

3   I put on my best suit and tie. Then I noticed that my jacket had a coffee stain down the front. (before)

4   I changed my clothes quickly. I rushed to the station to catch the train.

5   I reached the train station. I saw my train pulling away from the platform. (on)

6   I reached for my mobile so that I could ring and say I'd be late for the interview. I noticed that someone had left a message.

7   I read the message. I laughed out loud with relief.

8   I bought myself some breakfast at the station. Then I sat down to plan how to get to the interview on time the following day. (after)

64 Past participle clauses

- We use a past participle clause in place of subject + passive verb.
- Past participle clauses can replace clauses of cause, reason or condition: *He was bored with his job so he decided to leave.* → **Bored with his job,** *he decided to leave.*   *If I were given the opportunity, I would go back to school.* → **Given the opportunity,** *I would go back to school.*
- We can use *being* + past participle after *after, before, since, while, on,* etc.: *After it was cleaned, the bike looked as good as new.* → **After being cleaned,** *the bike looked as good as new.*   *Since the government was elected, it has had a series of problems.* → **Since being elected,** *the government has had a series of problems.*   *When I was informed, I called them.* → **On being informed,** *I called them.*

PRACTICE

64 **Re-write the sentences. Use past participle clauses.**

0 I was exhausted by lack of sleep and dozed off at my desk.
   Exhausted by lack of sleep, I dozed off at my desk.

1 Peter was abandoned by his parents at an early age and took to stealing.

2 Since I was promoted, I've had no time to go out.

3 After Richard was released from prison, he couldn't find a job anywhere.

4 When she was caught, she confessed to the crime.

5 If I am allowed to do so, I would like to present my side of the argument.

6 The money was hidden in the cellar and it wasn't discovered for many years.

7 Unless he is treated with more respect, he will leave the company.

8 If I am given the opportunity, I know I can make a success of the project.

9 Linda was saddened by the death of her father and needed to spend time alone.

10 Although it was written many years ago, the book is still relevant today.

11 Before you are allowed to enter the building, you will be searched.

12 She was scared of the dark so she switched on all the lights.

Check 12 Linking words and structures

1 **Circle the correct answer.**

1 I'm sorry I wasn't here earlier but I came *before / as soon as* I could.

2 I won't believe it *until / as soon as* I've seen it for myself.

3 *Finished / Having finished* work for the day, I got ready to go home.

4 *Leaving / Since leaving* school, Jasper has done a number of jobs.

5 We've invited the Kerrs *but / however* they may decide not to come.

/ 5

2 **Complete the conversations. Use the words in the box. You do not need all of them.**

| actually   after all   anyway |
| by the way   or rather   too   well |

6 A: Do you get on with your new flatmate?
B: I'm not sure. .... , she's only just moved in and I haven't had a chance to get to know her yet.

7 A: I thought you were going to get a new mobile phone?
B: I was, but this one works fine and .... , I can't afford the one I want.

8 A: Wasn't the Maths exam difficult?
B: .... , I didn't think it was too bad.

9 A: Rodrigo doesn't want to come to the game with us.
B: .... , he should have told us. I've already bought a ticket for him.

10 A: Are you going out with Pauline this evening?
B: We're going to a club. Why don't you come along .... ?

/ 5

3 **Complete the essay. Use one word in each gap.**

(11) .... the damaging effects of the motor car are well known, the number of vehicles on the road is growing rapidly. In 1950 there were fewer than 50 million cars in use round the world (12) .... in 2006 there were almost 33 million cars in the UK alone. Let's examine some problems associated with the car and a possible solution.

(13) .... of all, more people are killed in accidents involving cars than any other form of transport. (14) .... , road accidents receive less attention from the media than other less common but more spectacular accidents.

In (15) .... , the car is a major cause of pollution and petrol emissions are damaging to our health and to the environment (16) .... well. (17) .... spite of this, car sales continue to grow. Unfortunately, it seems that (18) .... concern for ourselves (19) .... concern for the planet will convince us to change our habits.

An obvious answer to the problem is better public transport. (20) .... public transport were cheaper, more comfortable and more reliable, we would be less inclined to use the car. But we need to act (21) .... it is too late. We must change our attitudes and priorities (22) .... that future generations can live in a better world.

/ 12

144

4 Circle the correct answer.

Vincent Van Gogh is one of the world's most famous painters. Sadly, his talent was not widely recognised during his life. It was, (23) *but / however / although*, much appreciated after his death.

(24) *Because failed / Having failed / Being failed* in every career he attempted, Van Gogh turned to art (25) *in order to / so that / for* express his strong religious feelings. (26) *On / When / Until* he decided to start painting around 1880, he used quite dark colours to create pictures of peasants and miners.

Then in 1886 Van Gogh visited his brother Theo in Paris. (27) *Attracted / Attracting / Since being attracted* by the work of the Impressionists that he saw there, Van Gogh decided to stay in Paris. He met Picasso (28) *and / as well / also* was encouraged by him to use more colour in his painting.

(29) *In addition / However / As a result*, Van Gogh's later work was brighter and more colourful.

In 1888 Van Gogh moved to the south of France. (30) *Inspired / Inspiring / Having inspired* by the wonderful landscape, he began to work frantically. This activity was interrupted by periods of depression but it (31) *too / as well / also* produced many of his most famous paintings. One of these is a self-portrait which Van Gogh painted (32) *since / after / as soon as* cutting off his own ear. A year later he committed suicide.

A lot is known about Van Gogh's life (33) *because / because of / since* the letters written to him by his brother Theo. Theo believed in his brother's genius (34) *whereas / although / so* he always encouraged him in his work. He was the person closest to Van Gogh.

/ 12

5 Re-write the sentences. Use the words in brackets to form participle clauses.

35 I decided to go into town because I had nothing better to do. (having) ....
....

36 We moved quietly so as not to disturb anyone. (wanting) ....
....

37 I wish I could help you but I can do very little. (while) ....
....

38 Because Hal is so conscientious, he rarely leaves the office early. (being) ....
....

39 Bettina heard a suspicious noise so she called the police. (hearing) ....
....

40 All patients are examined when they are admitted to hospital. (on) ....
....

/ 6

Total: / 40

Self-check

Wrong answers	Look again at	Try CD-ROM
5, 20, 28	Unit 56	Exercise 56
10, 13, 15, 16, 18, 19, 31	Unit 57	Exercise 57
11, 12, 14, 17, 22, 23	Unit 58	Exercise 58
25, 29, 33, 34	Unit 59	Exercise 59
1, 2, 21, 26, 32	Unit 60	Exercise 60
6, 7, 8, 9	Unit 61	Exercise 61
24, 35, 36, 37, 38, 39	Unit 62	Exercise 62
3, 4	Unit 63	Exercise 63
27, 30, 40	Unit 64	Exercise 64

Now do **Check 12**

Conditionals

65 The zero and first conditionals

The zero conditional
- We use the zero conditional to talk about things that are always or generally true as a result of an action or situation. We form zero conditional sentences with *if/when* + present simple + present simple: *If/When I **get** ill, I **rest** in bed.*
- When the *if* clause comes at the beginning of the sentence, we put a comma after it: *If I don't use sun cream, I get burnt.   I get burnt if I don't use sun cream.*

The first conditional
- We use the first conditional to talk about something that is likely to happen in the future as a result of an action or situation. We usually form first conditional sentences with *if* + present simple + *will*: *If she **does** well in her exams, she'**ll go** to college.*
- In the *if* clause we can also use the present continuous, present perfect simple, present perfect continuous, *can* and *should*: *If he's still **waiting** for you, he'**ll be** angry.   If she's **been listening** to the news, she'**ll be** worried.   If I **can finish** work early, I'**ll come** and help you.   If I **should hear** from them, I'**ll let** you know.* (should = it's not very likely I'll hear from them)
- In the main clause we can also use *be going to*, the future continuous, future perfect, imperative, *can, could, may, might, should, ought to* and *must*: *If she **passes** her exams, we'**re going to buy** her a car.   If you **arrive** late, **use** your key to get in.   If you **phone** me after eleven, I **might be** in bed.*
- When the *if* clause comes at the beginning of the sentence, we put a comma after it: *If you fix my computer, I'll give you twenty pounds.   I'll give you twenty pounds if you fix my computer.*

PRACTICE

65a Complete the sentences. Use the correct form of the verbs in brackets.

0 If you ......*don't tell*...... him the truth, I'm sure you ......*'ll regret*...... it one day. (not tell, regret)

1 She .... disappointed if she .... the job. (be, not get)

2 If we .... this holiday today, we .... on a warm beach in two weeks' time. (book, lie)

3 Please .... me if you .... any help. (call, need)

4 If he .... your e-mail yet, you .... from him today. (not read, not hear)

5 If I .... cheese, I .... in a terrible rash. (eat, break out)

6 If it .... all night, I .... the grass today like I'd planned. (rain, not cut)

65b Complete the article. Use the words in the box.

are	be	can	does	feel	if	leaning
~~learn~~	should	stand up	try	will		

Body language can make a bigger impression on people than you might think. If you (0) ...*learn*... how to use it correctly, body language (1) .... help you to make and keep friends. For example, if you (2) .... straight, you (3) .... look confident and attractive, while arms crossed over your chest say 'stay away'.

Mirroring is another way of sending out the right signals. (4) .... you want someone to like you, you (5) .... copy their body language. Why? If someone (6) .... what we do, we (7) .... that we have a lot in common with them. So if you (8) .... having a drink with someone, (9) .... taking a sip of your drink a few seconds after they do. Look at their posture. If they are (10) .... forwards, you should (11) .... doing the same. Of course, you have to be careful. You don't want to look as if you're making fun of them!

66 The second conditional

- We use the second conditional to talk about:
  - unlikely future events or situations: *If she **changed** her job, she**'d be** much happier.*
  - imaginary or improbable situations in the present: *If they **were** here, they**'d tell** us what to do.* (They aren't here so they can't tell us what to do.)
- We usually form second conditional sentences with *if* + past simple + *would* + infinitive without *to*: *If I **knew** the answer, I**'d tell** you.*
- We can use *was* or *were* in the *if* clause after *I/he/she/it*: *If I **was/were** rich, I'd leave my job and travel with you.*
- We use *if I were you* to give advice: *I **wouldn't worry** about it **if I were you**.*
- In the *if* clause we can also use the past continuous and *could*: *If you **were stopping** for lunch, I**'d join** you.*   *If I **could understand** his lectures, I'm sure I'd learn a lot from him.*
- In the main clause we can also use *could/might* + infinitive without *to* and *would/could/might* + *be* + *-ing* form: *If we **had** more free time, we **could go** out more often. If you **asked** for a pay rise, you **might get** one.   If we **had** more money, we **wouldn't be living** here.*
- In formal English we can use *if* + *were* + *to*-infinitive: *If you **asked** him, he **would come** with you.* → *If you **were to ask** him, he **would come** with you.*
- We can also omit *if* and use *were* + subject + *to*-infinitive: ***Were you to ask** him, he **would come** with you.*

147

Grammar: *conditionals*

PRACTICE

66a Circle the correct answer.

0 He wouldn't come here so often if he *doesn't* / *(didn't)* like it.
1 I'd work a lot harder if I *was* / *were* you.
2 I wouldn't be telling you this if I *thought* / *would think* you were going to repeat it.
3 If I were in your position, I *'ll* / *'d* get legal advice.
4 If she *lived* / *could live* anywhere she wanted to, she'd live in Brazil.
5 If I *were* / *would be* ten years younger, I'd go out with him.
6 If they had enough money, they *'d buy* / *bought* this house tomorrow.
7 If they were *asked* / *to ask* me for my opinion, I'd advise them to reconsider their decision.
8 She *might win* / *won* first prize if she entered the competition.
9 *Was* / *Were* they to offer you the job, would you accept it?
10 If I *wasn't working* / *didn't work* this weekend, I'd spend the time with you.

66b Complete the conversations. Use the correct form of the verbs in brackets.

A: How's Eli?
B: Not that well. Imagine how you (0) ......*'d feel*...... (feel) if you (1) .... (discover) that you'd failed nearly all of your exams!
A: I'd feel terrible but if it were me, I (2) .... (keep) trying. She can re-sit the exams she's failed in September.

A: Have you decided what you're doing this weekend?
B: If I (3) .... (can / borrow) some money, I (4) .... (definitely / go) away with you but I don't think there's anyone who can lend it to me.
A: Couldn't Nigel lend you the money?
B: Not really. You see, he's broke. He (5) .... (can / earn) lots of money if he (6) .... (want) to but money's not that important to him.

A: My car's broken down. Can you help me?
B: If I (7) .... (know) anything about cars, I (8) .... (try) to fix it but I know less than you do. If I (9) .... (be) you, I (10) .... (call) a garage.

A: Sven has everything he wants but he's always complaining. I'm sure if I (11) .... (have) so much money, I (12) .... (not complain) all the time.
B: Maybe not, but money isn't everything.

148

67 The third conditional

- We use the third conditional to talk about possible events in the past that didn't happen. We also use it to talk about regrets or to make criticisms: **If I had worked harder, I would have passed** my exams. (But I didn't work hard so I didn't pass.) **If you had set** the alarm, **we wouldn't have missed** the train. (But you didn't set the alarm so we missed it.)
- We usually form third conditional sentences with *if* + past perfect + *would have* + past participle: **If you had told** me it was dangerous, **I would have stayed** home.
- In the *if* clause we can also use the past perfect continuous or *could have* + past participle: **If we had been travelling** in that car, **we would have been** injured. **If we could have got** a taxi, **we would have come** to see you.
- In the main clause we can also use *could/might have* + past participle: **If I hadn't gone** skiing, **I wouldn't have broken** my leg. (certainty) **If you had told** me about your plans earlier, **I could have arranged** to meet you. (possibility) **If** the police **had arrived** sooner, they **might have caught** the burglars. (possibility)
- In formal English we can omit *if* and use *had* + subject + past participle: **If I had known** you needed help, **I would have been** there. → **Had I known** you needed help, **I would have been** there.

⚠ We don't use *would have* in the *if* clause: **If he had married** Laura, he **wouldn't have been** happy. (Not ~~If he would have married Laura, he wouldn't have been happy.~~)

PRACTICE

67a Complete the articles. Use the correct form of the verbs in brackets.

Five Indonesian fishermen found themselves in deep trouble when a storm blew up suddenly off the coast of Australia and wrecked their boat. They were almost out of food when they were spotted by a rescue plane. In a way, they were unlucky: if they (0) ...**hadn't gone**... (not go) out fishing, their boat (1) .... (not be) destroyed. But in another way, they were extremely fortunate: if the plane (2) .... (not see) them, they (3) .... (probably / die).

An English couple had a narrow escape when a large tree fell on their home. They were parking their car at the time of the accident. If the couple (4) .... (arrive) home a few minutes earlier, they (5) .... (be) in the house when the tree came crashing down and they (6) .... (might / be) killed.

Grammar: *conditionals*

An Australian diver who found himself in the mouth of a great white shark survived to tell the tale. The diver managed to stab the shark in the mouth with his knife and the great fish released him. If the diver (7) .... (not have) a knife with him, the shark (8) .... (not open) its mouth and the diver (9) .... (might not / survive).

A woman in Australia was bitten on the foot by a dangerous snake which miraculously left no poison in the bite. If the snake (10) .... (inject) poison into her foot, the woman (11) .... (could / die).

67b Re-write the sentences.

0   The weather was terrible so we didn't go out yesterday.
    If *the weather hadn't been terrible, we would have gone out yesterday* .

1   You didn't phone us so we didn't get there in time.
    We ....

2   I wasn't able to help you because you didn't explain the problem to me.
    I might ....

3   They weren't listening carefully so they didn't understand what she was saying.
    They might ....

4   He couldn't phone her so he couldn't tell her what was happening.
    If ....

5   You didn't see him because you didn't come round earlier.
    If ....

6   You took me to your friend's party and I met Kazuko.
    If ....

7   When she married him, she didn't know how selfish he was.
    She might not ....

8   The management wouldn't agree to a pay rise so there was a strike.
    Had ....

68 unless, provided (that), in case, etc.

- We can use *unless*, *provided/providing* (*that*) and *as/so long as* in first conditional sentences.
    - *Unless* means 'if not': **Unless** *the rain stops, we'll cancel the game.*
    - *Provided/providing* (*that*) and *so/as long as* mean 'on condition that': *You can come with us* **as long as** *you pay for your own ticket.*
- We can also use the following linking words and expressions:
    - *even if*: **Even if** *we hurry, we'll be late.* (= Hurrying will not change the situation.)
    - *or else*: *Hurry up* **or else** *we'll miss the train.* (= If you don't hurry, we'll miss the train.)
    - *otherwise*: *We were delayed at the airport;* **otherwise,** *we'd have been there by noon.* (= If we hadn't been delayed, we'd have been there by noon.)
    - *assuming* (*that*): **Assuming** (**that**) *you get a university place, how will you pay for your studies?* (= if you get a university place)
    - *suppose/supposing/imagine* (*that*) (= what if ... ?): **Suppose** *you lose your job, what will you do?* **Supposing** *they had lied to us, what would we have done?* **Imagine** *you've won a million pounds. Would you carry on working?*
- We use *in case* to talk about something we do to avoid difficulty in the future. Compare: *I'll buy an umbrella* **if** *it rains.* (= I'll buy an umbrella if it starts to rain.) *I'll buy an umbrella* **in case** *it rains.* (= I'll buy an umbrella because it might rain.)

PRACTICE

68 Re-write the sentences. Use the words in brackets.

0   You can start training a few weeks before the marathon providing you've been running regularly for at least a year before that. (on condition that)
    You can start training a few weeks before the marathon on condition that you've been running regularly for at least a year before that.

1   Don't consider running a marathon if you aren't in good physical condition. (unless) ....

2   Don't leave training until just before the marathon because you might injure yourself. (in case) ....

3   Take time off from running every week or else your body will not have a chance to rest. (otherwise) ....

4   Provided that you train carefully, you can avoid injury. (as long as) ....

5   If you are sensible, you should run a marathon safely and successfully. (assuming) ....

Grammar: conditionals

69 Mixed conditionals

- In mixed conditional sentences the *if* clause and the main clause refer to different times.
- The most common mixed conditional is one where a past event has an effect on the present. The *if* clause refers to the past (third conditional) and the main clause refers to the present or future (second conditional): *if* + past perfect + *would/could/might*: **If I had gone** to university, I **might have** a better job now.   **If she had remembered** to buy a ticket, she **would be coming** with us to the game tonight.
- The *if* clause can also refer to the present or future (second conditional) and the main clause to the past (third conditional): *if* + past simple + *would/could/might have* + past participle: **If she were** sensible, she **wouldn't have left** her job. (= She isn't sensible so she left her job.)   **If you had** a car, I **would have asked** you to give me a lift. (= You don't have a car so I didn't ask you to give me a lift.)

PRACTICE

69a Circle the correct answer.

0 If you *told* / *(had told)* me about the problem earlier, everything *(would be)* / *would have been* all right now.

1 If she *didn't die* / *hadn't died* so young, she *would be* / *would have been* a famous musician now.

2 You should relax. If you *didn't work* / *hadn't worked* so hard all the time, you *wouldn't be* / *wouldn't have been* ill last year.

3 If he *didn't waste* / *hadn't wasted* so much money in his youth, he *could be* / *could have been* a wealthy man now.

4 If I *have been* / *were* a more sensitive person, I *wouldn't upset* / *wouldn't have upset* her in the way that I did.

5 If they really *want* / *wanted* to emigrate, they *would move* / *would have moved* to another country by now.

6 If he *worked* / *had worked* harder last month, he *wouldn't be* / *wouldn't have been* so busy now.

7 I *wouldn't be doing* / *wouldn't have been doing* this job today if I *knew* / *had known* how boring it would be.

8 If the train *wasn't delayed* / *hadn't been delayed*, we *will be* / *would be* there now.

9 If the passenger *didn't forget* / *hadn't forgotten* her passport, she *would be boarding* / *would have been boarding* the plane now.

10 If you *followed* / *had followed* the diet your doctor gave you, you *might not be* / *might not have been* ill now.

Grammar: conditionals

69b Complete the conversations. Use the correct form of the verbs in the box.

| be (x3)   begin   not have (x2)   not sit   ~~not spend~~ |
| not weigh   set   set off   take out   tell |

A: What's wrong? You look worried.
B: I am, but I've only got myself to blame. If I (0) ...**hadn't spent**... so much money, I (1) .... such a big credit card bill to pay next month.

A: Is Lars a careful driver?
B: No, he isn't. If he (2) .... , he (3) .... that nasty accident last month. And if he (4) .... better insurance, his car (5) .... in the garage at this moment. As it is, he can't afford to have it repaired.

A: Are we nearly at Lan and Jinhai's house?
B: No, we've still got a long way to go. But if we (6) .... an hour earlier, we (7) .... nearly there now.
A: I'm sorry, but if you (8) .... me yesterday that you wanted to leave at eight, I (9) .... my alarm for seven.
B: How was I to know that you get up so late in the mornings?

A: How are things?
B: They've been better. I'm on a diet and I joined a fitness centre last week. If I (10) .... the diet and joined the centre six months ago, I (11) .... so much now and I (12) .... also .... a lot fitter.

70   I wish, if only

- To express dissatisfaction with a present situation, we use *I wish* + past simple: ***I wish I was/were*** *rich.* (But I'm not.)   ***I wish I didn't have to*** *go to work.* (But I have to.)

- To express regret about the past, we use *I wish* + past perfect: ***I wish I had known*** *you were coming.* (But I didn't know.)

- To express dissatisfaction and annoyance about something that we would like to be different but that probably won't happen or that we can't control, we use *I wish + would* + infinitive without *to*: ***I wish*** *my parents* ***wouldn't treat*** *me like a child.* (But they do and I can't change them.)

- To talk about something we are unable to do, we use *I wish + could* + infinitive without *to*: ***I wish I could remember*** *his name.* (But I can't.)

- *If only* can replace *I wish*. It is usually more emphatic: ***If only*** *you* ***had told*** *me the truth!*   ***If only*** *they* ***would turn*** *the music down, we could get some sleep.*

⚠ We use *hope* to talk about events that are possible and *wish* to talk about events that are unlikely or impossible: ***I hope*** *you* ***enjoyed*** *the film.* (It's possible you enjoyed it.)   ***I wish*** *you* ***had enjoyed*** *the film.* (But I know you didn't.)   ***I hope*** *he'll attend* *the meeting.* (He may attend.)   ***I wish*** *he* ***would attend*** *the meeting.* (I don't think he will attend.)

Grammar: *conditionals*

PRACTICE

70a Complete the messages from a message board on the Internet. Use the correct form of the verbs in the box.

| be   can / learn   can / study   live   not do   start   stop |

Jocool — I really admire people who can draw and paint but I can't draw even the simplest things. If only I (0) ....*could learn*.... to draw!

Alexis — I'd gained weight, my clothes didn't fit and I didn't like myself. But since I started running every morning, I feel a lot better about myself. I wish I (1) .... taking regular exercise a long time ago!

Li — I come from a family of lawyers and my parents expect me to carry on the tradition, so even though I really wish I (2) .... information technology next year, I'll get a law degree first.

Melanie — My alarm went off at six this morning. I must have switched it off and gone back to sleep so I was late for an exam. I wish I (3) .... such a stupid thing!

timfromnowhere — Nothing exciting ever happens in my town and I get so bored! If only I (4) .... in a city like London or Brighton, I'd be so much happier.

Scott — I wish my parents (5) .... complaining about the way I dress. I wish I (6) .... more patient with them too.

70b Complete the second sentence so that it means the same as the first, using the word in bold. Use between two and five words.

0 It is a pity I have to go to school today.   **wish**
   I ....*wish I didn't*............ have to go to school today.

1 I am disappointed that he didn't call me.   **only**
   If .... me.

2 I regret leaving my last job.   **had**
   I wish .... my last job.

3 Please stop criticising me all the time!   **would**
   I wish .... me all the time.

4 I am sorry we can't afford a new car.   **could**
   If only .... a new car.

5 It is a shame we haven't got more time together.   **had**
   If .... more time together.

6 I regret not finishing my university degree.   **I**
   I wish .... my university degree.

154

71 Other ways to express hypothetical meaning

- We use *it's time* (+ *for someone*) + *to*-infinitive to say that we think an action should happen. We can also use *it's time* + past simple/continuous: *It's ten o'clock. **It's time for us to leave.** / **It's time** we **left.** / **It's time** we **were leaving.***
- We use *it's high time* + past simple/continuous to say that we think it is urgent that an action should happen: ***It's high time** they **started** studying harder.*
- We use *would rather* + subject + past simple/continuous to say what someone would like someone else to do in the present or future: ***I'd rather you didn't go** out alone.*
- We use *would rather* + subject + past perfect to express dissatisfaction with what someone did in the past: ***I'd rather you hadn't gone** without me.*
- We use *as if/though* + present tense for something we think is true: *She's looking at him **as though** she **knows** him.* (Perhaps she does know him.)
- We use *as if/though* + past simple/past perfect when we think something is not likely to be true: *She's looking at him **as if** she **knew** him.* (She doesn't know him.) *She looked **as though** she'**d seen** a ghost!* (But she hadn't.)

PRACTICE

71 Complete the sentences. Use the correct form of the verbs in the box.

be (x2) book go grow learn
not go not leave not say ~~ring~~ tell win

0 It's time you ......*rang*...... your parents. You haven't spoken to them for ages!
1 Sometimes you speak to me as if I .... a child and it annoys me!
2 I'd rather we .... out tonight. I'm not feeling well.
3 It sounds as though she .... ill. I hope she gets better soon.
4 I'd rather you .... anything to my parents about my exam results – I wanted to tell them myself.
5 Isn't it time they .... their parents they're planning to get married?
6 You're talking as if you .... the game when I know you lost it.
7 How can I tell my housemate I'd rather he .... all of the cooking to me? It's high time he .... how to cook for himself!
8 Sometimes Maribel acts as if money .... on trees!
9 It's July already and it's high time we .... our holiday. I'm afraid we may have left it too late.
10 They don't want to go by themselves. They'd rather we .... with them to show them the way.

155

Check 13 Conditionals

1 **Circle the correct answer.**

1 *If / Unless / In case* you had a lot of money, would you give up work?
2 *Provided / Even if / If only* I could get a job! Then life here would be perfect.
3 *Provided / As long as / Unless* he asks me politely, I won't help him.
4 *If only / I hope / I wish* you've enjoyed the evening.
5 *What if / Assuming that / When* the train arrives on time, we'll see them in a few minutes.

/ 5

2 **Choose the correct answer, A, B, C or D.**

Dear Irene,

It was nice to hear from you, and yes, I'd love to come and visit you in Spain! (6) ..... I can save enough money before the summer holidays start, I (7) ..... at the end of July. (8) ..... , I'll see you in the autumn because I'm sure I (9) ..... enough money by October – if I (10) ..... my job by then! Unfortunately, lots of people in our company are being made redundant. If I (11) ..... any sense, I (12) ..... this job ages ago. By the way, congratulations on your promotion. If you keep on like this, you (13) ..... the school soon!

It sounds (14) ..... the weather's been really good over there. It's been terrible here. If it (15) ..... at the weekend, I (16) ..... soon be emigrating to somewhere with a better climate! Seriously, I'm wondering if it's time (17) ..... about going abroad again.

Look forward to seeing you soon. Say hello to your family for me.

Love, Violetta

6 A If only	B In case	C Unless	D Provided
7 A come	B 'll come	C 'd come	D came
8 A If	B When	C Unless	D Otherwise
9 A 'll save	B 'll be saving	C might save	D 'll have saved
10 A didn't lose	B don't lose	C haven't lost	D won't lose
11 A have	B had	C 've had	D 'll have
12 A 'll leave	B 'd leave	C 'd be leaving	D 'd have left
13 A 'll run	B 'll be running	C 'll have run	D should run
14 A as if	B as	C if	D only
15 A still rains	B rains still	C 's still raining	D still rained
16 A should	B can	C could	D have
17 A for me to think	B I'm thinking	C I've thought	D I think

/ 12

156

3 Re-write the sentences.

18 The authorities didn't issue a warning because they didn't know there was a threat.
Had ....

19 My car broke down so I was late for work.
If ....

20 The event was cancelled because it was raining.
If ....

21 I didn't meet you at the station because I didn't know you were coming.
If ....

22 He missed his flight because the taxi didn't arrive on time.
If ....

/ 5

4 Complete the conversations. Use the correct form of the verbs in brackets.

A: I'm having a tough time with my essay. Would you help me with it, please?
B: I'm sorry. I (23) .... (help) you with it if I (24) .... (have) more time but I'm so busy right now. Could you come back this evening?
A: Of course. Are you sure you don't mind?
B: I (25) .... (not help) you if I (26) .... (not want) to. But you do realise that if you (27) .... (work) harder during these past few weeks, you (28) .... (not have) these problems now.

A: I wish I (29) .... (not agree) to take on the job. It's too much work and I really wish I (30) .... (have) more free time.
B: Yes, but if you (31) .... (not take) it on, you (32) .... (not have) so much money to spend when you do have free time.

/ 10

5 Complete the second sentence so that it means the same as the first, using the word in bold. Use between two and five words.

33 It is a pity he didn't accept our offer. **wish**
I .... our offer.

34 You should keep the papers in a safe place. **were**
If I .... the papers in a safe place.

35 She will bring her camera because she might want to take a photo. **case**
She will bring her camera .... to take a photo.

36 The farmers will be facing disaster unless it rains soon. **if**
The farmers will be facing disaster .... soon.

37 I think you should find a job. **time**
It is .... a job.

38 I would be happier if we stayed at home. **rather**
I .... at home.

39 I would like to lose some weight. **wish**
I .... some weight.

40 If they offered him the job, he would accept it. **to**
Were .... the job, he would accept it.

/ 8

Total: / 40

Self-check

Wrong answers	Look again at	Try CD-ROM
9, 10, 13, 15, 16	Unit 65	Exercise 65
23, 24, 25, 26, 34, 40	Unit 66	Exercise 66
18, 19, 20, 21, 22	Unit 67	Exercise 67
1, 3, 5, 6, 7, 8, 35, 36	Unit 68	Exercise 68
11, 12, 27, 28, 31, 32	Unit 69	Exercise 69
2, 4, 29, 30, 33, 39	Unit 70	Exercise 70
14, 17, 37, 38	Unit 71	Exercise 71

Now do **Check 13**

Changing sentence structure

72 Changing word order

- In English, we can change the normal word order of a sentence (subject – verb – object – complement) for emphasis.
- We can begin the sentence with the object or complement. This is more common in spoken English: *I enjoyed his first film. I didn't like **his second film** at all.* → *I enjoyed his first film. **His second film** I didn't like at all.*
- We can begin the sentence with an adverbial: *I've been doing this boring job **for a year**.* → ***For a year** I've been doing this boring job.*   *We **often** go to the cinema at the weekend.* → ***Often**, we go to the cinema at the weekend.*

▶▶ For position of words in a sentence, see Unit 36.

- We can also begin a sentence with a negative expression or adverb: *hardly ... when, little, never, no sooner ... than, not once/only/since, only after/then/later, rarely, seldom, under no circumstances*. We invert the subject and verb: *He had no sooner left than the phone rang.* → ***No sooner** had he left than the phone rang.*   *She was **rarely seen** in public.* → ***Rarely** was she seen in public.*   *I won't change my mind under any circumstances.* → ***Under no circumstances** will I change my mind.*

PRACTICE

72a Re-write the sentences.

0   The disease is hardly ever fatal.
    Hardly ever *is the disease fatal* .

1   I have not often heard such an inspiring speech.
    Seldom ....

2   Almost immediately after I had started my lunch, a client arrived to see me.
    No sooner ....

3   Her words didn't seem important at the time but they did seem important later.
    Only ....

4   I have never been so confused by a lecture before.
    Never ....

5   She didn't ask me once how I felt about the accident.
    Not once ....

6   You shouldn't sign those papers under any circumstances.
    Under no circumstances ....

7   I didn't know that I would be facing such big changes at work.
    Little ....

8   My parents hardly ever argue about anything.
    Rarely ....

72b Complete the conversations. Use the sentences in brackets and change the word order to make them more emphatic.

0   A: How old do you think Mr Roberts is? Thirty?
    B: He's at least forty. *Thirty he isn't.* (He isn't thirty.)
1   A: What kind of films do you like?
    B: Well, I don't like action films. .... (I do like comedies.)
2   A: Have you always driven a Ford?
    B: No, I used to drive a Fiat. .... (That was my first car.)
3   A: When did your parents arrive? Last night or this morning?
    B: .... (They arrived this morning.)
4   A: We'd better hurry. .... (It'll be dark soon.)
    B: Of course. I know you don't like travelling at night.
5   A: How long would you like the report to be?
    B: I don't care about the details. .... (But I do want the gist.)

73 The passive (1)

- In an active sentence the subject is the 'doer' and performs the action of the verb. In a passive sentence the object of the active verb becomes the subject:

Active	They	have delayed	our flight.
Passive	Our flight	has been delayed.	

- We use the passive:
  - to focus on the action rather than the doer (the agent) of the action: *President John F. Kennedy **was assassinated** in 1963.*
  - to avoid using a vague subject like *they* or *someone*: *My watch **has been stolen**!*
  - when the doer of the action is obvious: *He **was arrested** last night.* (It's clear who arrested him: the police.)
  - to avoid saying who was responsible for something: *Your parcel **has been lost**.*
  - in written reports, signs and notices, and to describe processes: *Shoplifters **will be prosecuted**.   The fruit **is treated** with wax and then **stored**.*

- If we want to mention the agent, we use *by*. We use *with* to mention the tool or instrument that was used: *St Paul's Cathedral was built **by Sir Christopher Wren**. He was killed **with a knife**.*

- We form the passive with an appropriate form of *be* + past participle:
  They **feed** the animals.   → The animals **are fed**.
  They **are feeding** the animals.   → The animals **are being fed**.
  They **fed** the animals.   → The animals **were fed**.
  They **should feed** the animals.   → The animals **should be fed**.

⚠ If the verb is followed by a preposition or particle, we don't omit it in the passive sentence: *They **closed** the cinema **down**.* → *The cinema **was closed down**.*

- We can use *get* in place of *be* in informal English: *We often **get asked** this question.* (= We are often asked this question.)

Grammar: *changing sentence structure*

PRACTICE

73a Re-write the sentences. Use the passive.

0 They should have finished the project ages ago.
   The project should have been finished ages ago.

1 No one has cleaned the windows for weeks.
   ....

2 His company made him redundant a year ago.
   ....

3 The pressures of work were affecting her health.
   ....

4 The fire fighters put out the fire before it did much damage.
   ....

5 If it hadn't rained so much, we would have finished the job on time.
   ....

6 The people at the garage are repairing our car.
   ....

7 Someone hit him on the head with a heavy instrument.
   ....

8 I hope they'll choose me for the basketball team.
   ....

73b Complete the article. Use the passive form of the verbs in the box.

| allow | call | can / understand | define |
| determine | fight | may / divide | rear | ~~write~~ |

Thousands of books (0) *have been written* about the territorial instinct of animals. Humans are territorial too and when we understand this, some kinds of aggressive behaviour (1) .... more easily.

Every country is a territory with boundaries which (2) .... usually clearly .... Within each country there are smaller territories: counties and cities. Throughout history wars (3) .... by people protecting the territory in which they live.

However, there are other kinds of territory as well. One such territory (4) .... 'personal space'. For animals, the size of this space depends on the conditions in which the animal (5) .... , whether in the wild or in a zoo. For humans, it depends on the density of the population in the place where they grew up. To some extent, the size of an individual's personal space (6) .... by their culture.

Personal space (7) .... into four zones: the intimate, personal, social and public zones. The intimate zone extends fifteen to forty-five centimetres from the body. Only close friends and relatives (8) .... to enter the intimate zone. If a stranger enters it, the individual becomes anxious and may feel threatened.

74 The passive (2)

- When an active verb has two objects, a direct object and an indirect object, it is more common for the indirect object to become the subject of the passive sentence:

Active	They have offered **me a job**. (*me* = indirect object; *a job* = direct object)
Passive	I **have been offered** a job. / **A job** has been offered to me.

- Some verbs (e.g. *hear, help, make, see*) are followed by the infinitive without *to* when they are active and by *to*-infinitive when they are passive: *I **heard** her **criticise** him.* → *She **was heard to criticise** him.*   *They **made** me **stay** at home.* → *I **was made to stay** at home.*
- We can't use *let* + infinitive without *to* in the passive; we use *allow* + *to*-infinitive instead: *They **didn't let** me **go** out.* → *I **wasn't allowed to go** out.*
- *Need doing* and *need to be done* have a passive meaning: *The house **needs painting**.* (= The house needs to be painted.)   *Does this shirt **need to be ironed**?*

PRACTICE

74a Re-write the underlined parts of the sentences. Use the passive. Do not include the agent unless it is necessary.

0   My new digital camera was faulty so <u>the shop gave me a full refund</u>.
    My new digital camera was faulty so ......*I was given a full refund*...... .

1   The children have to be in bed by ten and <u>their parents don't let them use the computer after eight</u>.
    The children have to be in bed by ten and ....

2   The car is very dirty and <u>we need to wash it</u>.
    The car is very dirty and ....

3   We're travelling by coach and <u>a local guide will show us the sights when we get there</u>.
    We're travelling by coach and ....

4   I felt so ill that I took a taxi to the hospital but <u>they made me wait for hours to see a doctor</u>.
    I felt so ill that I took a taxi to the hospital but ....

5   She attended the party but <u>they saw her leave shortly after her arrival</u>.
    She attended the party but ....

6   He's getting a pay rise and <u>the company has also promised him a bonus</u>.
    He's getting a pay rise and ....

7   My grandfather has difficulty walking but <u>a kind passer-by helped him cross the street</u>.
    My grandfather has difficulty walking but ....

8   This information is important and <u>you must hand it out to all employees</u>.
    This information is important and ....

Grammar: *changing sentence structure*

74b Re-write the sentences. Use the passive.

0   Britain's banks lent nearly £12 billion to successful applicants last year.
Nearly £12 billion *was lent to successful applicants* by Britain's banks last year.

1   Unfortunately, banks let many people borrow more money than they can repay.
Unfortunately, many people .... more money than they can repay.

2   Some banks lent people a sum that was more than their annual income.
People .... that was more than their annual income.

3   They gave other loans to people who had no source of income.
Other loans .... who had no source of income.

4   Consumer groups say that both banks and borrowers need to face the problem.
Consumer groups say that the problem .... by both banks and borrowers.

5   They argue that banks should not give loans to people who can't afford them.
They argue that loans .... who can't afford them.

75 The passive (3)

- We can use the passive with verbs such as *believe, claim, expect, know, report, say, think, understand,* etc. to report an event or to talk about an opinion held by some people/a lot of people/people in general/experts, etc. The following patterns can be used:
  - *it* + passive + *that* clause: **It is understood that** the Queen **approves** of the decision.
  - subject + passive + *to*-infinitive: **The Queen is understood to approve** of the decision.

- Note the form of the verbs:
  It is said that he **is** one of the richest men in the world.
  He is said to be one of the richest men in the world.

  It is expected that he **will hand** over the business to his daughter.
  He is expected to hand over the business to his daughter.

  It is reported that he **is buying** a private island.
  He is reported to be buying a private island.

  It is believed that he **has invested** much of his money in property.
  He is believed to have invested much of his money in property.

  It is thought that he **made** a billion pounds last year.
  He is thought to have made a billion pounds last year.

Grammar: *changing sentence structure*

PRACTICE

75a Complete the second sentence so that it means the same as the first, using the word in bold. Use between two and five words.

0 They believe that skin cancer will cause more deaths in the coming years. **believed**
   It *is believed that skin cancer* will cause more deaths in the coming years.

1 People think that he is living in South America. **be**
   He .... in South America.

2 They expect that the repairs will take three to five weeks. **that**
   It .... the repairs will take three to five weeks.

3 People say that she left the country months ago. **have**
   She .... the country months ago.

4 They think that the manager will resign. **is**
   It .... the manager will resign.

5 Experts believe that the house was built in 1735. **been**
   The house .... built in 1735.

6 The accident is reported to have been caused by human error. **that**
   It is reported .... by human error.

75b Re-write the sentences in two ways. Put the underlined parts in the passive.

0 They say that a fire has completely destroyed the Royal Hotel.
   It *is said that the Royal Hotel has been completely destroyed by a fire.*
   The Royal Hotel *is said to have been completely destroyed by a fire.*

1 They say that the fire is still burning.
   It ....
   The fire ....

2 They think that the fire started in the kitchen.
   It ....
   The fire ....

3 They believe that ambulances have taken fifteen people to hospital.
   It ....
   Fifteen people ....

4 They report that seven people are in a serious condition.
   It ....
   Seven people ....

5 They believe that a cigarette started the fire.
   It ....
   The fire ....

6 They expect that the police will investigate the cause of the blaze.
   It ....
   The cause of the blaze ....

76 The causative: *have/get something done*

- We use the causative form (subject + *have/get* + object + past participle) when we don't do something ourselves but arrange for someone else to do it for us: *We had the windows cleaned.* (= We arranged for someone to clean the windows.)
- *Have something done* and *get something done* are often interchangeable but there are some differences.
  - We use *have something done* to talk about something unpleasant: *I had my bag stolen last week.* (Not *I got my bag stolen last week*.)
  - We also use *have something done* when we are concerned with the process itself and not the preparatory arrangements: *I love having my hair done.*
  - We use *get something done* to emphasise that we have to make an effort in order for something to be done. Compare: *She has her car serviced every six months.* (= A mechanic services her car every six months.) *She gets her car serviced every six months.* (= She goes to the trouble of taking her car to the garage, where a mechanic services it.)
- All tenses and modal verbs are possible with *have something done*: *We're having our flat decorated. We should have our flat decorated.*
- We don't use *get something done* in the present perfect or past perfect: *You've had your hair cut!* (Not *You've got your hair cut*.)
- ⚠ We can use *get something done* to say that we do something ourselves. It suggests that there is a lot to be done or that it is difficult but that we manage to finish it: *I got the entire report written yesterday.*

PRACTICE

76 Complete the conversations. Use *have* or *get something done* and the words in brackets.

0   A: What shall we do to celebrate our anniversary?
    B: Why don't we *have our photograph taken* ? (our photograph / take)

1   A: What happened to Ash? He looks terrible.
    B: I think he .... in a fight. (his nose / break)

2   A: How does that feel?
    B: Wonderful. I love .... (my shoulders / massage)

3   A: What have you done so far today?
    B: Well, I've managed to .... (the invitations / send out)

4   A: What time is it?
    B: I don't know. My watch is broken and I .... yet. (it / not repair)

5   A: The car isn't running very well.
    B: I know. I .... last week but I didn't have time. (it / should / service)

6   A: That wasps' nest is dangerous. You must do something about it.
    B: I know. I .... as soon as possible. (it / remove)

77 there is/are or it is/they are?

- We can use *there/it* + *be* as a preparatory subject in a sentence. The real subject of the sentence comes after *there/it* + *be*.
- We use *there* + *be* + noun:
  - to say that something exists: **There is a lot of traffic** in the mornings.
    There weren't many people at the meeting.
  - to refer to something for the first time. We use *it* or *they* when we refer to it again:
    There will be a concert on Friday. **It** will be held in the town hall.
- We use *there* with:
  - all tenses of *be*: **There will be** a meeting tonight.   **Has there been** a mistake?
  - modal verbs: **There must be** something wrong.   **There could be** an explanation.
  - *seems/appears* + *to*-infinitive: **There seems to be** a problem.
- We can use *it* + *be* to avoid long and complex subjects:
  - *it* + *be* + adjective/noun + *to*-infinitive: **To take a day off work** (subject) **is a luxury.**
    → **It's a luxury to take** a day off work.
  - *it* + *be* + adjective/noun + *-ing* form: **Seeing you in person** (subject) **is nicer than writing to you.** → **It's nicer seeing** you in person than writing to you.
  - *it* + *be* + adjective/noun + clause: **That he didn't accept the job** (subject) **is a pity.**
    → **It's a pity that** he didn't accept the job.   **How he did it** (subject) **isn't clear.** →
    It isn't clear how he did it.

▶▶ For uses of *to*-infinitive, see Unit 44. For verb + *-ing* forms, see Unit 45.

- We use *it* + *be* to talk about the time, weather and distance: **It's** ten o'clock.
  Is it still raining?   **It's** ten miles from here to my place.
- We can also use *it* + *take* + time reference + *to*-infinitive to talk about a period of time: **It took hours to get** there by bus.

PRACTICE

77a Complete the conversation. Use *there* or *it*.

A: Hi. How are you? (0) ......*It*...... 's been ages since I saw you.
B: I know. (1) .... 's a shame we haven't kept in touch. Is (2) .... true that you're about to move overseas?
A: Yes, next month, in fact – to Istanbul. (3) .... are a lot of opportunities if you're prepared to travel. (4) .... 's likely that we'll be there for a couple of years. Listen, (5) .... are a few people coming round tomorrow evening. Are you free to join us?
B: I'd love to. Oh, is (6) .... an Underground station near your place? My car is in the garage.
A: Barking is the nearest. (7) .... takes ten minutes to walk from there to our place. I'll e-mail you a map with directions.

Grammar: *changing sentence structure*

77b Complete the sentences. Use *there*, *it* or *they* and the correct form of an appropriate verb.

0   *It took* .... me a day to fill in the forms but I finished them.
1   I think .... a nice day tomorrow.
2   .... any more bread? I'm still hungry!
3   How long .... to travel from here to London? .... far?
4   .... to be a lack of communication between them.
5   .... wonderful to see you all. Thank you so much for coming.
6   .... some stains on the tablecloth. I think .... coffee stains.

77c Re-write the sentences.

0   Concentrating in this heat is hard.
    It *'s hard concentrating in this heat* ....
1   Saying goodbye after all this time isn't easy.
    It ....
2   That we should be there when he arrives is important.
    It ....
3   When exactly they'll be sending us the papers to sign isn't clear.
    It ....
4   That you still remember me is amazing.
    It ....
5   Contacting her by phone was difficult so I sent an e-mail.
    It ....
6   How they committed the crime is not known.
    It ....

78 Emphasis: *It was ... that, What, All*

- To emphasise information, we can begin a sentence with *it*, *what* (= the thing that) or *all* (= the only thing).
- We can use:
  – a cleft sentence with *it*: *it* + *be* + emphasised word/phrase + clause:
    Kirsten told me the bad news last night. →
    It was Kirsten who/that told me the bad news last night. (not another person)
    It was last night that Kirsten told me the bad news. (not today)
    It was bad news that Kirsten told me last night. (not good news)
  – *what* + verb + *be* + emphasised word/phrase:
    His tone of voice surprised me. → **What surprised** me **was** his tone of voice.
  – *all* (+ *that*) + verb/clause + *be* + emphasised word/phrase:
    Your safety matters. → **All that matters is** your safety.
- We can use *what/all* with *do/did* to emphasise the actions or events in a sentence:
  What he **did** was **make a terrible mistake.**   All he **did** was **tell her the truth.**

166

Grammar: *changing sentence structure*

PRACTICE

78a Complete the article. Use one word in each gap.

007 Creator's Home was For His Eyes Only

Fans of James Bond will know that (0) ...*it*... was the Jamaican island retreat of Goldeneye (1) .... was the secret home of Bond's creator, writer Ian Fleming. (2) .... they may not know (3) .... that Fleming also owned another tropical paradise in the West Indies – Goat Island. (4) .... was while he was on Goat Island (5) .... Fleming wrote many of his books. In fact, it (6) .... while he was reading a book about West Indies birdlife written by a Terence James Bond (7) .... he got the name of his secret agent hero.

Local historian Edward Hernandez points out that very little is known about people who went to the island. (8) .... visitors wanted (9) .... privacy – and they found it.

78b Re-write the sentences. Use emphatic forms.

0   Jane paid for the meal last night, not me.
    It *was Jane who paid for the meal last night* .

1   Children need love and affection, not toys.
    What ....

2   The way he keeps changing his mind worries me.
    It ....

3   The only thing I'm asking for is a little respect.
    All ....

4   I really hate getting up when it's still dark.
    What ....

5   I need a hammer and some nails – nothing else.
    All ....

6   You should be talking to me, not them.
    It ....

7   We should ring someone for help.
    What ....

8   The thing they want more than anything is a less stressful life.
    It ....

Check 14 Changing sentence structure

1 Re-write the sentences. Use the passive.

1 They made me wait for hours at the hospital.
   ....

2 Rene's colleague helped him finish the report.
   ....

3 My boss never lets me leave work early.
   ....

4 They should have called the police when the accident happened.
   ....

5 Many people believe that he lied about the scandal. (Begin: *He* ...)
   ....

/ 5

2 Re-write the sentences.

6 As soon as she left, I realised she had taken my car keys by mistake.
   No ....

7 I've never felt so confused before.
   Never ....

8 They think that Gulay is selling the company.
   Gulay ....

9 The result of the match disappointed us.
   What ....

10 They say that the new plane is fuel-efficient.
   The new plane ....

11 Everyone believes that the butler inherited her money.
   The butler ....

12 Someone must be at the door.
   There ....

13 We'll leave them a note so they don't worry.
   What ....

14 We need twenty hours to fly to New Zealand.
   It ....

15 I heard the news report only a few minutes ago.
   It ....

/ 10

3 Complete the second sentence so that it means the same as the first, using the word in bold. Use between two and five words.

16 You should be talking to Franco. **is**
   It .... be talking to.

17 The windows are dirty and someone needs to clean them at once. **cleaned**
   The windows are dirty and .... at once.

18 Many people believe that the government has made a mess of things. **is**
   The government .... a mess of things.

19 They consider that Erin is the best musician in the group. **considered**
   Erin .... the best musician in the group.

20 Renata seldom eats at home. **eat**
   Seldom .... at home.

21 You are not to go out under any circumstances. **no**
   Under .... go out.

22 The only thing I care about is your safety. **matters**
   All .... your safety.

23 The dentist hasn't checked my teeth this year. **had**
   I .... checked this year.

/ 8

168

4 Complete the article. Use one word in each gap.

Animals on the Roads

The number of vehicles on our roads is going up every year so it is not surprising that the number of wild animals that are (24) .... killed is also increasing. Roads often cross the routes that (25) .... taken by animals when they are migrating, breeding or feeding. As a result, each year (26) .... are thousands of animals, including toads, badgers, hedgehogs and even birds, that fall victim to the motor vehicle. Can anything (27) .... done to protect them?

In 1969 a road tunnel for use by wildlife (28) .... built in Switzerland and was a great success. Since then, many other tunnels have (29) .... constructed across Europe. In Florida, where the rare Florida panther lives, authorities decided that steps needed to (30) .... taken to protect the animals. (31) .... only were tunnels built under the highway (32) .... fencing was put up to guide the animals safely into the underpasses.

Road signs warning drivers to look out for particular animals (33) .... often seen in the US and (34) .... is hoped that they will become a common sight on the roads of Europe. (35) .... is clear is that we can and should act to minimise the dangers we pose to wildlife.

/ 12

5 Complete the conversations. Use *have* or *get something done* and the words in brackets.

A: I haven't seen you for days. Have you been away?
B: No, but I've been busy writing an essay. I managed to (36) .... (it / finish) yesterday, just in time.

A: I thought you (37) .... (your hair / cut) this morning.
B: I was, but I've had to cancel the appointment. I (38) .... (just / my wallet / steal).
A: Oh, dear. Is there anything I can do?

A: The car isn't running very well, is it?
B: No. I (39) .... (a new engine / should / put in) but I can't afford it.

A: I've got a terrible headache.
B: (40) .... (you / your eyes / test) recently?

/ 5

Total: / 40

Self-check

Wrong answers	Look again at	Try CD-ROM
6, 7, 20, 21, 31, 32	Unit 72	Exercise 72
4, 17, 24, 25, 27, 28, 29, 30, 33	Unit 73	Exercise 73
1, 2, 3	Unit 74	Exercise 74
5, 8, 10, 11, 18, 19, 34	Unit 75	Exercise 75
23, 36, 37, 38, 39, 40	Unit 76	Exercise 76
12, 14, 26	Unit 77	Exercise 77
9, 13, 15, 16, 22, 35	Unit 78	Exercise 78

Now do **Check 14**

Prepositions

79 Prepositions of place and movement

at	We arrived **at** the station. Who's **at** the door?
from ... to	They drove **from** London **to** Edinburgh in a day.
in, into, out of	To talk about enclosed places: *I'll wait for you **in** the car.* (position) *Could you get **in/into/out of** the car?* (movement)
on, onto, off	To talk about a surface or line: *There were some lovely pictures **on** the wall.* (position) *She walked **on** the pavement.* (movement) *She stepped **onto** the grass.* (= movement: from the pavement onto the grass) *Shall we take that mirror **off** the wall?* (movement)
across, along	*We swam **across** the river.* (= from one side to the other) *They walked **along** the path towards the bridge.* (= They followed the path towards the bridge.)
among, between	*He disappeared **among** the crowd.* (= through a group of people) *We often fly **between** London, Paris and Rome.* (= from London to Paris, from Paris to Rome, from Rome to London) *I sat down **between** Jane and Sue.* (= in the space that separated Jane and Sue)
above, below	To talk about position when something is higher or lower than something else: *The mountains tower **above** the town. Water was dripping onto the floor **below**.*
over, under	To talk about something that is higher or lower than something else. *Over* and *under*, not *above* and *below,* are used to show position when there is contact between things or to show movement: *I'm wearing a coat **over** my jacket and a sweater **under** it.* (contact) *They flew **over** France.* (movement) *We sailed **under** the bridge.* (movement)
beneath, underneath	To talk about something that is higher or lower than something else. There may be contact between them or a distance: *I felt the warm sand **beneath/underneath** my feet.*
on top of, against	*There's a letter **on top of** the cupboard. The cat rubbed **against** my legs.*
opposite	*There's a car park **opposite** the hotel.*
by	*I stood **by** the window.* (= close to) *They walked **by** the river.* (= close to, along)
past	*She walked **past** me without saying 'hello'.* (= movement: up to and beyond)
beside, next to, inside, outside	To show position in relation to an object, container or enclosed space: *Put it on the table **beside/next to** the bed. I'll meet you **inside/outside** the theatre.*

Vocabulary: *prepositions*

PRACTICE

79a Circle the correct answers. There may be more than one correct answer.

0 A lamp hung *(above)* / *among* / *on top of* the table.
1 The actors walked *at* / *from* / *onto* the stage at the end of the performance and bowed.
2 The road that goes *above* / *over* / *against* the mountain *at* / *to* / *into* the village is steep and dangerous.
3 The ball rolled *along* / *among* / *between* his feet and *at* / *to* / *into* the garden shed, where it got lost *against* / *among* / *between* the tools on the floor.
4 There's an envelope *above* / *on top of* / *over* the fridge with some money *in* / *inside* / *into* it.
5 I could hear voices *in* / *at* / *inside* the garden *below* / *beneath* / *past* my window.
6 They could see something shining *below* / *from* / *in* the surface of the water.
7 If you're going *by* / *next to* / *past* my house, would you give me a lift?
8 We walked *from* / *opposite* / *along* our home *at* / *to* / *in* the centre of town and had lunch at a restaurant *against* / *beside* / *by* the river.
9 The supermarket is *along* / *across* / *next to* the cinema and *by* / *next to* / *opposite* the car park on the other side of the street.
10 The shout came from *at* / *inside* / *into* the house *across* / *among* / *past* the street.
11 We arrived *at* / *into* / *to* our destination and parked the car *out of* / *against* / *opposite* the entrance.
12 The child accidentally kicked the ball *above* / *over* / *on top of* the wall.
13 He leaned *against* / *next to* / *along* the wall and watched the people going by.
14 After walking *at* / *along* / *beside* the river for an hour, they stopped *at* / *into* / *past* a small inn for a bite to eat.

79b Complete the blog. Use prepositions.

We caught the ferry (0) ......*from*...... Dover and travelled (1) .... the English Channel to France. Within an hour we had arrived (2) .... the ferry terminal (3) .... Boulogne. We went to the market (4) .... the main square, where I bought some souvenirs to take back to my family in England. It was a beautiful day so we had lunch (5) .... the beach. It was very relaxing, with the sound of the waves and the seagulls flying (6) .... our heads.

After lunch we walked (7) .... the beach (8) .... the old part of town. We walked uphill (9) .... the narrow streets towards the castle but when we got there, they told us we had to pay an admission fee to get (10) .... the castle so we didn't bother. Instead, we explored the old town for an hour. By then it was time to go back to the ferry terminal. All in all, it was a good day out.

Vocabulary: *prepositions*

80 Prepositions of time

at	• with clock times or ages: **at** *nine o'clock* **at** *(the age of) fifteen* • with points or periods of time: **at** *the beginning/end* **at** *present* **at** *Ramadan* **at** *the weekend* **at** *lunch* **at** *night*
on	with days or dates: **on** *Monday* **on** *25th September* **on** *the morning of 4th June* **on** *a good day* **on** *Christmas Day*

in	• with parts of the day, months, years, seasons and centuries:
	  in *the morning/afternoon/evening* **in** *February* **in** *2006*
	  in *the autumn* **in** *the last century*
	• *I'll see you **in** an hour.* (= after an hour)
	• *I wrote my essay **in** a day.* (= It took me a day to write my essay.)

by	*They'll inform us of their decision **by** the end of the month.* (= not later than the end of the month)
before, after	*I never go to bed **before** midnight.* *I'll meet you **after** the class.*
since	with a point in time: *We've been here **since** Tuesday.*
for	with a period of time: *They lived in Poland **for** three years.*
during	with a period of time: *I worked **during** the summer.* (= all through the summer) *She was ill **during** the summer.* (= at some point/period of time in the summer)
until/till	*The ticket is valid **until/till** March.* (= It will not be valid after March.) *He slept from midnight **until/till** eight o'clock.* (Then he woke up.)
past	*We worked **past** midnight.* (= up to and beyond midnight)
through	*She worked **through** the night.* (= during and to the end of the night)

⚠ We use *for* to say how long something lasts. *During* means 'while something lasts/is happening': *We rented a cottage **for** a month.   We rented a cottage **during** the summer.* (Not *We rented a cottage during a month.*)

PRACTICE

80a Circle the correct answer.

0 It was *by* / (*past*) midnight when the party ended and everyone went home.
1 My husband often works *at / in* night. I see him *at / in* the morning.
2 My grandfather fought *during / for* the war. He was in the army *during / for* four years.
3 They've only had the Ford *for / since* two months. *By / Until* last year they didn't own a car.
4 She caught malaria *during / through* her holiday in Africa. *Before / By* then, she'd never been abroad.
5 The film should be over *until / by* nine o'clock. We'll be home *before / in* an hour.
6 We're leaving for Prague *on / at* 19th July and we'll be there *through / until* the end of the month.

Vocabulary: *prepositions*

80b Complete the conversation. Use prepositions.

A: Are you free to come round for a meal (0) ....**on**.... Saturday?
B: Do you mean (1) .... the evening?
A: That's right. Come round (2) .... eight o'clock, if that's OK.
B: Thanks, I'd love to but I'll have to leave (3) .... about midnight – I've got to get up early (4) .... Sunday morning.
A: That's all right. I don't like staying up much (5) .... midnight, anyway.
B: Neither do I. I stayed up (6) .... three o'clock last Saturday and I felt terrible (7) .... the morning.

80c Complete the article. Use the prepositions in the box.

| after   by   during (x2)   for (x2)   in (x2)   since (x2)   until |

Buckingham Palace has been the London home of Britain's royal family (0) ....**since**.... 1837.

(1) .... 1761 George III bought Buckingham House as a family home for his wife, Queen Charlotte. Then (2) .... 1826 George IV decided to turn Buckingham House into a palace. Workmen doubled the size of the house and built the Marble Arch in front of the palace. The work continued (3) .... four years and (4) .... 1829 half a million pounds had already been spent on it. George IV never lived in Buckingham Palace.

Queen Victoria was the first monarch to make Buckingham Palace her official home. (5) .... her marriage to Albert in 1840, she decided that the palace needed a nursery and more guest rooms. (The Marble Arch was moved to a park in central London so that workmen could add a fourth wing to the building.) The work continued (6) .... 1847 and today the palace has 775 rooms. The last major changes to the building were made (7) .... the early twentieth century, when the stone on the front of the building was replaced.

Today Buckingham Palace is a major tourist attraction. (8) .... 1993 the state rooms in the west wing have been opened to the public (9) .... two months (10) .... the summer and they are visited by about 300,000 people over this period.

173

Vocabulary: *prepositions*

81 Other prepositions

by, with, from
- We can use *by*:
  - before the agent in a passive sentence: *I was attacked **by** a dog.*
  - to say what means or method someone uses to do something: *You can reserve the tickets **by** phone.*
- We can use *with*:
  - to say what instrument or tool someone uses to do something: *Chop the vegetables **with** a sharp knife.*
  - to say what covers or fills something: *Her shoes were covered **with** mud.*
  - to indicate possession: *He was a tall man **with** a beard.*
  - to say that two or more people or things are together in the same place: *I saw him in town **with** his girlfriend.*
- We can use *from*:
  - to say what substance is used to make something: *Chocolate comes **from** the cocoa bean.*
  - to say that something happens as a result or consequence of something else: *Death rates **from** accidents are increasing.*
  - to say where something is before it is removed: *He took the knife **from** my hand.*
  - to say what is prevented or forbidden: *Cars will be banned **from** entering the city centre.*

about, on
- We usually use *about* to refer to a subject or topic in vague, general terms: *I'm looking for a book **about** birds.*   *They said something **about** leaving town.*
- We usually use *on* to refer to a subject or topic in a more specific way: *You can get information **on** local services by calling this number.*   *She's writing a book **on** the birds of central Africa.*

PRACTICE

81a Circle the correct answer.

0 Bread is made *by* / *(from)* / *about* flour, water and yeast.
1 Only people *by* / *from* / *with* plenty of money can afford to shop here.
2 I borrowed a book *from* / *on* / *with* nineteenth century music from the library.
3 She said something *about* / *from* / *on* leaving town. Is it true?
4 He went to hospital because he was suffering *by* / *from* / *with* stomach pains.
5 Some of our customers prefer to pay *by* / *from* / *with* cheque.
6 They attacked the old man *by* / *from* / *with* a knife.
7 Last night we watched a documentary *on* / *with* / *about* Egypt.
8 The house is made *by* / *from* / *on* bricks and timber.
9 All our furniture was made *from* / *with* / *by* local craftsmen.
10 I'd like to find some information *about* / *from* / *with* the subject.

Vocabulary: *prepositions*

81b Complete the article. Use *by*, *from*, *on* or *with*.

> All **BULLYING** involves attacks (0) ...**by**... an individual or group on a weaker person. Bullying can be an attack (1) .... a weapon or words, or it can be more subtle and involve spreading lies and rumours. It can affect your self-esteem and prevent you (2) .... succeeding at work or school. If you are being bullied, this is what you can do:
> - Get help or advice (3) .... an adult that you trust. Tell them what is happening. They can provide you (4) .... the support you need. You can also get advice (5) .... how to protect yourself (6) .... going online.
> - Act confident. You are less likely to be attacked.
> - Avoid being alone (7) .... bullies. Avoid areas that are isolated or unsupervised (8) .... adults.

82 Prepositional phrases

at	**at** breakfast/lunch/dinner **at** first **at** college/home/school/work/university **at** last **at** least **at** once **at** present **at** the beginning/end **at** the latest **at** the moment **at** the same time **at** times
by	**by** accident **by** air/land/sea **by** car/bus/plane/train **by** chance **by** cheque **by** credit card **by** far **by** hand **by** heart **by** mistake
for	**for** a change **for** a while **for** ages **for** breakfast/lunch/dinner **for** ever/good **for** sale/hire/rent
from	**from** bad to worse **from** memory **from** morning to night **from** now on **from** time to time
in	**in** a hurry **in** a mess **in** advance **in** aid of **in** bed/hospital **in** cash **in** conclusion **in** control **in** danger **in** favour of **in** future **in** general **in** other words **in** stock **in** the beginning/end **in** the way **in** time **in** use
on	**on** a diet **on** arrival **on** average **on** behalf of **on** business **on** duty **on** fire **on** foot **on** holiday **on** my own **on** no account **on** offer **on** purpose **on** the bus/train **on** the contrary **on** the phone **on** the way **on** the whole **on** time **on** television
out of	**out of** breath **out of** control **out of** danger **out of** date **out of** doors **out of** fashion **out of** luck/money/time **out of** order **out of** sight **out of** stock **out of** the way **out of** touch **out of** work
under	**under** age **under** control **under** discussion **under** pressure **under** way
to	**to** date **to** some extent/degree **to** my surprise

175

Vocabulary: *prepositions*

PRACTICE

82a Complete the sentences. Use the prepositional phrases in the box.

> at last   at least   at the end   at the latest   in the end
> in the way   in time   on the way   to date

0 This is her best performance ......*to date*...... .
1 I thought about the problem for a long time and .... I decided that the best thing to do was to ask for help.
2 He's probably .... to London by now.
3 .... fifty people were waiting in the queue to buy tickets for the concert.
4 If you have any questions, can you ask them .... of the lecture, please?
5 .... we can afford a holiday! We've been saving for months.
6 There's a car .... and I can't get out of the garage.
7 I won't be late. I should be back by eleven o'clock ....
8 Will the new stadium be finished .... for the match?

82b Complete the story. Use one word in each gap.

> My family wanted to do something different this summer and (0) ....*in*.... the end, we decided to go (1) .... a safari holiday in Tanzania. We booked our holiday (2) .... advance and because I'm studying zoology (3) .... college, I prepared myself by learning the scientific names of many animals (4) .... heart!
>
> (5) .... last our departure date arrived. We were met (6) .... our arrival in Tanzania and we travelled (7) .... car to our hotel in the safari park. We stopped (8) .... the way to the hotel and (9) .... my surprise, we saw a lion a few metres from the car!
>
> Every day at the park was different and we were busy (10) .... morning to night. We would set off early in a Land Rover as it was too hot to go far (11) .... foot and return to the hotel (12) .... time for lunch. Most evenings we ate out (13) .... doors.
>
> But it was the animals that were (14) .... far the best part of the holiday. Lying in bed at night, I could hear them and (15) .... times, they came very close to my window. But I never felt I was (16) .... danger. (17) .... the contrary, I felt closer to nature than I've ever been in my life.
>
> (18) .... the end of our stay there was a farewell party attended by everyone on the safari. We were all sad to be leaving but (19) .... the same time, we knew we'd had the experience of a lifetime.

Check 15 Prepositions

1 Complete the fact sheet. Use prepositions.

ANTARCTICA

HISTORY: (1) .... 1773 Captain James Cook crossed the Antarctic Circle in his ships, *HMS Resolution* and *HMS Adventure*. (2) .... 14th December 1911 Roald Amundsen led the first expedition to reach the geographic South Pole. Amundsen used skis and dog sleds to travel (3) .... the Bay of Whales to the South Pole.

GEOGRAPHY: About 98% of Antarctica is covered (4) .... the Antarctic ice sheet, which is (5) .... least 1.6 km thick.

CLIMATE: (6) .... the winter months the minimum temperature is –80°C to –90°C. Antarctica receives little precipitation; the South Pole receives less than 10 cm of rain or snow per year (7) .... average.

ECONOMY: Tourism exists on a small scale. In 2004–2005 fewer than 30,000 tourists visited Antarctica. This number is predicted to increase to over 80,000 (8) .... the year 2010.

RESEARCH: Meteorites discovered in Antarctica have allowed scientists to learn a great deal (9) .... our solar system. The meteorites are thought to come (10) .... asteroids or larger planets.

POLITICS: Antarctica has no government and belongs to no country. (11) .... 1959 countries have been banned (12) .... conducting any kind of military activity on the continent, including the testing of weapons.

/ 12

2 Complete the conversation. Use the prepositions in the box. You do not need all of them.

> across among by for in on
> opposite out of outside with

A: I'm not sure I can meet you tomorrow – my car has broken down.
B: Why don't you travel (13) .... train?
A: I suppose I could. Where shall I meet you?
B: When you arrive, leave the station and walk (14) .... the road to the coffee shop directly (15) .... the station. I'll meet you there.
A: What time?
B: About half past twelve. I'll try to be (16) .... time but I may be delayed by traffic. I'll stop (17) .... the coffee shop and wait for you (18) .... the car. Then we can drive somewhere nice (19) .... lunch.
A: I might bring Roberta (20) .... me. Is that all right?
B: Of course.

/ 8

Total: / 20

✓ Self-check

Wrong answers	Look again at	Try CD-ROM
3, 14, 15, 17, 18	Unit 79	Exercise 79
1, 2, 6, 8, 11	Unit 80	Exercise 80
4, 9, 10, 12, 20	Unit 81	Exercise 81
5, 7, 13, 16, 19	Unit 82	Exercise 82

Now do **Check 15**

Words that go together

83 Adjective + preposition

- Some adjectives are followed by a *to*-infinitive and some are followed by a preposition. Some adjectives can be followed by either form: *I'm **sorry to hear** you aren't well.   I'm **sorry for hurting** your feelings.*

- After a preposition, we use a noun, a pronoun or the *-ing* form of a verb: *He's **afraid of the dark**.   Their parents **are proud of them**.   She isn't **keen on going** there alone.*

- Sometimes more than one preposition is possible, depending on the meaning: *The floods were **responsible for** over a hundred deaths.* (= The floods caused them.)   *He's **responsible for** training new staff.* (= He's in charge of them.)   *She's **responsible to** the Personnel Manager.* (= The Personnel Manager is her boss.)

  *They're **involved in** an important project.* (= They're taking part in it.)   *She seems to be **involved with** some dangerous people who may be criminals.* (= She has a relationship with them.)   *My parents are **angry with** me **about** my grades.* (= They're angry with me. They're angry about my grades.)

▶▶ See Appendix 7: Adjective + preposition, page 201.

PRACTICE

83a Choose the correct answer A, B or C.

0 I'm tired ...... watching television. Let's go for a walk.
   A by   B from   **C** of

1 No matter how hard I try, I'm useless ...... Maths.
   A at   B for   C to

2 Odette wasn't amused ...... my joke. In fact, she was offended.
   A by   B from   C with

3 It's healthy for young people to be suspicious ...... strangers.
   A about   B at   C of

4 Put the cage over there, where the birds will be safe ...... the cat.
   A for   B from   C with

5 Many students are reliant ...... their parents for financial support.
   A from   B in   C on

6 People who become addicted ...... drugs must seek help from professionals.
   A by   B to   C with

7 Although they're twins, they're very different ...... each other.
   A at   B from   C to

8 He's seems very content ...... his job, home and family.
   A about   B from   C with

Vocabulary: *words that go together*

83b Complete the conversation. Use prepositions.

A: I'm really worried (0) ...*about*... Duncan.
B: Why's that?
A: He's been absent (1) .... quite a few classes lately and he's often late (2) .... the ones he does attend.
B: Yes, I've noticed. I also know he was confident (3) .... getting an A for his last exam and was really disappointed (4) .... not getting one.
A: Someone told me he's got involved (5) .... some strange people. I saw him the other day and he wasn't at all friendly (6) .... me – in fact, he was rude (7) .... me.
B: I'm surprised (8) .... that. That's not like him. And have you noticed that Ken's been acting strangely too?
A: I think he's keen (9) .... Mina but he's afraid (10) .... asking her out in case she says 'no'.
B: Well, they should both be more careful (11) .... how they behave. Some of their friends are getting fed up (12) .... them.

83c Complete the article. Use prepositions and the correct form of the verbs in brackets.

The Ferrari automobile company is famous (0) ...*for producing*... (produce) fast and beautiful cars. Scuderia Ferrari is the part of the company which is concerned (1) .... (race) cars competitively, while Ferrari S.p.A. is involved (2) .... (make) exceptional sports cars which even the wealthy and famous are proud (3) .... (own).

Ferrari's founder, Enzo Ferrari, was born in Italy in 1898. He had little formal education but he was interested (4) .... (drive) fast cars. After he left the army, he applied for work at Fiat but he wasn't successful (5) .... (get) a job there. In 1920 he started racing cars for Alfa Romeo. After demonstrating that he was skilful (6) .... (win) small local races, Enzo was asked to race in larger competitions. He finished his racing career in 1932.

In 1929 Enzo set up Scuderia Ferrari, where he was responsible (7) .... (build) up a racing team of over forty drivers. However, it was only in 1945 that he founded Ferrari S.p.A. Enzo thought that selling sports cars would make it possible to continue financing his racing activities at Scuderia Ferrari.

The famous Ferrari logo, a black horse on a yellow background, has been in existence since the 1930s. Interestingly, however, an Austrian company called Avanti has a logo which is so similar (8) .... Ferrari's that it is almost identical.

Vocabulary: *words that go together*

84 Verb + preposition

- We use a preposition after some verbs. The most usual pattern is: verb (+ object) + preposition + noun/pronoun/-*ing* form: *My mother **paid for** my driving lessons. He didn't **pay me for** it. I **paid him for washing** my car.*
- Sometimes more than one preposition is possible after a verb, depending on the meaning: *I've **heard of** him.* (= I know he exists.) *I've **heard from** him.* (= He contacted me.) *Did you **hear about** the accident?* (= Do you have information about it?)
- Some combinations of verb + preposition have an idiomatic meaning: *Please **look after** my cat while I'm on holiday.* (= take care of)
- With some verbs the pattern is: verb + noun + preposition: *We **made friends with** them. I **took care of** my younger sister. We **took part in** the school play.*
- Notice the pattern with these verbs:
  - explain (something) (to someone): *I **explained the problem to him**.*
  - describe something (to someone): *She **described the painting to me** in detail.*
  - listen/write/speak to someone: *I **wrote to my mother** last week. I **spoke to them** yesterday.*
  - telephone someone: *He **telephoned us**.*
  - send (someone) something/something to somebody: *I **sent him a card**. / I **sent a card to him**.*

▶▶ See Appendix 8: Verb + preposition, page 202.

PRACTICE

84a Circle the correct answer.

0 I'm suffering *for* / *(from)* a bad back so I need to stay in bed.
1 Not many people succeed *to* / *in* losing weight and keeping it off.
2 We can't seem to agree *on* / *with* anything these days. We're just not getting along.
3 They all laughed *about* / *at* her jokes. She was very funny.
4 He insisted *about* / *on* carrying my bags even though I told him not to bother.
5 We shouted *at* / *for* them to stay away but they couldn't hear us.
6 I'm sorry but I don't agree *about* / *with* you. I have a different opinion.
7 Would you help me look *for* / *after* my glasses? I can't find them anywhere.
8 The judge asked the witness to describe the incident *to* / *at* him.
9 I heard all *from* / *about* the party. Victor told me.
10 Who do you take *after* / *for*? Your mother or your father?
11 Her parents didn't approve *about* / *of* her new boyfriend.
12 Thieves broke *onto* / *into* the museum and stole some priceless objects.
13 Sharon prefers chess *to* / *from* any other game.
14 The meal consisted *for* / *of* a number of delicious Indian dishes.

Vocabulary: *words that go together*

84b Complete the e-mail. Use prepositions. If no preposition is necessary, write – in the gap.

New Message

Hi Ruth,

Have you heard (0) ...*from*... Brendan recently? I telephoned (1) .... him last week and also sent (2) .... him an e-mail but he hasn't got back to me. I want to apologise (3) .... him (4) .... forgetting to water his plants while he was away at half term. He left me the keys to his room but I completely forgot. I don't suppose he'll ever rely (5) .... me for anything after this!

Are you going to take part (6) .... the music concert at the end of term? I am. Rehearsals start this week and I'm going to sing a traditional song from my country. I think it's a great way to make friends (7) .... people I wouldn't meet otherwise.

By the way, I must congratulate you (8) .... your test results! I wish someone would explain (9) .... me how to get an A on a grammar test! Seriously, though, you worked hard and you deserve it.

Take care, Diego

84c Complete the blog. Use one word in each gap.

Opening a bank account is not difficult but if you are not sure where to start, consult the welfare officer at your school. He or she will advise you (0) ...*about*... what you need to do.

Once you have chosen a bank, you need to go there in person to open an account. Take your passport with you as identification. You should also ask your school (1) .... a letter saying that you are a student there and confirming your name and address. (The bank needs this confirmation to prevent criminals (2) .... opening bank accounts which they can use to deposit money from illegal activities.) If you have any difficulty providing these documents, ask the bank to refer you (3) .... the bank employee who is responsible for dealing (4) .... difficult or unusual cases. He or she will take care (5) .... you.

Once you have a bank account, you can deposit or withdraw money. You can also arrange to pay your bills by direct debit or standing order. This means that you can ask the bank to take money from your account to pay (6) .... things like gas and electricity. You should speak (7) .... your bank about how to set these up. The good news is that once you have an account, most services are free. However, you will not be able to borrow money (8) .... the bank unless you set up a special account.

181

Vocabulary: *words that go together*

85 Noun + preposition

- Some nouns can be followed by a *to*-infinitive and some can be followed by a preposition: *I have **a plan to work** abroad for a year.*   ***The advantage of living** in another country is that you learn about a different culture.*
- After a preposition we use a noun, a pronoun or the *-ing* form of a verb: *I have a lot of **respect for** her work.*   *There was **an argument about** it.*   *He has **a reputation for being** a brilliant actor.*
- We often use the same preposition after nouns and verbs that are related:
  *The football manager had **an argument with** the referee **about** his decision.*
  *He **argued with** the referee. They **argued about** the referee's decision.*
  *The mountaineer **failed in** his attempt to reach the summit.*   *There was **a failure in** the computer system.*
- Compare *connection/relationship/contact* + *with* or *between*:
  – A person/thing has a *connection/relationship/contact with* another person/thing:
    *I have **a good relationship with** my parents.*
  – There is a *connection/relationship/contact between* two people/things: *There is **a connection between** smoking and cancer.*

▶▶ See Appendix 9: Noun + preposition, page 204.

PRACTICE

85a Choose the correct answer A, B or C.

0 There seems to be a connection ...... pollution and the death of trees.
  (A) between   B from   C with

1 There are many differences ...... public and private schools.
  A between   B in   C with

2 He's an expert ...... ancient Egyptian art.
  A about   B in   C on

3 A good sun cream will give you protection ...... the harmful rays of the sun.
  A for   B from   C of

4 Officials are still looking into the cause ...... the crash.
  A for   B of   C to

5 She stays in contact ...... many of her ex-students.
  A between   B to   C with

6 There are several advantages ...... getting a good education.
  A for   B of   C to

7 He expressed his admiration ...... her exciting and innovative designs.
  A about   B for   C with

8 Recently there has been a great deal of interest ...... the subject.
  A in   B about   C of

9 I simply don't share your fascination ...... old coins.
  A in   B about   C for

10 What was their reaction ...... the news?
  A to   B for   C with

85b Complete the notes for a film review. Use prepositions.

A comparison (0) ...**between**... a book and a film usually favours the book. Naturally, we mustn't forget that there are differences (1) .... the two.

The director has a reputation (2) .... making powerful films as well as a talent (3) .... subtle psychological development. But by comparison (4) .... his other films, this one is disappointing.

The beginning (5) .... the film is promising but it fails to keep the audience interested. One of the reasons (6) .... the problem is the poor choice (7) .... leading actors. The relationship (8) .... the protagonists is simply not believable.

Another problem (9) .... the film is the script – there's a lack (10) .... attention to dialogue and the exchanges between characters sound forced. And of course, part of the blame (11) .... the result lies with the soundtrack, which is one of the worst I've ever heard.

85c Re-write the sentences. Use the nouns in the box and prepositions.

change   discussion   fall   increase   reason   ~~relationship~~   solution

0   Ruth: I get on well with my manager.
    Ruth has a good ..**relationship with**.. her manager.
1   Ruth: Last week I spoke to him about my salary.
    Last week she and her manager had a(n) .... her salary.
2   Ruth: I have a lot of responsibility but he won't give me a rise.
    Ruth's manager won't give Ruth a(n) .... her salary.
3   Ruth: He explained why he couldn't do it.
    He gave her a good .... not doing it.
4   Ruth: He's worried because sales have been dropping.
    He's worried because there has been a(n) .... sales.
5   Ruth: We said we'd talk again if the situation changes.
    They agreed to discuss the matter again if there is a(n) .... the situation.
6   Ruth: I'm sure we can solve the problem.
    Ruth is sure they can find a(n) .... the problem.

183

Vocabulary: *words that go together*

86 Phrasal verbs

- A phrasal verb is a combination of verb + adverb (e.g. *in, out, up*) The combination often has a new, idiomatic meaning: *To **find out** more, visit our website.* (= get information after trying to discover it, or by chance)   *I was **brought up** in a large family.* (= raise a child)
- Intransitive phrasal verbs have no object: *We must **set off** early tomorrow.*   *I **grew up** in London.*
- The object of a transitive phrasal verb comes:
  – after or before the adverb if the object is a noun: *She **made up** that story.* *She **made** that story **up**.*
  – before, not after, the adverb if the object is a pronoun: *That story's not true – she **made it up**.* (Not *she made up it*)
- Some phrasal verbs have more than one meaning. One meaning may be intransitive and the other transitive: *Business has been slow but it's **picking up** now.* (= intransitive: improve)   *I'll **pick** you **up** at eight.* (= transitive: let someone get into your car, boat, etc. and take them somewhere)   *The plane **took off** on time.* (= intransitive: if an aircraft takes off, it rises into the air from the ground)   *Please **take** your boots **off**.* (= transitive: remove a piece of clothing)
- A phrasal-prepositional verb is a combination of verb + adverb + preposition. The object of such a verb comes after the preposition: *She **came up with** some good ideas.*   *I don't **get on with** my cousins.*   *I'm **looking forward to** taking a holiday.*

PRACTICE

86a Complete the sentences. Use the adverbs in the box.

| away (x2)   down (x3)   in (x2)   on (x2)   out (x2)   up (x2) |

0 She turned ....*down*........ the job because she didn't want to travel.
1 You've got exams soon. You can't carry .... going out every night.
2 We'll never get this problem sorted .... if we don't talk about it.
3 They've been asked to come .... with some new ideas.
4 He gave .... most of his books when he finished college.
5 Why don't you put .... your new outfit and we'll go out for dinner to that new restaurant.
6 I'm trying to find .... about Japanese courses in the area.
7 He was tired and didn't feel like joining .... the game.
8 I drink too much coffee but I'm trying to cut ....
9 I'm glad the situation is improving. It's time things picked ....
10 They like to get .... from London as often as they can.
11 You shouldn't look .... on people just because they have less money or education than you.
12 It's very cold. Winter seems to have set .... early this year.

Vocabulary: *words that go together*

86b Re-write the sentences. Use the correct form of the phrasal verbs in brackets.

0 It was raining so hard that they had to cancel the match. (call off)
   It was raining so hard that they had to call off the match.

1 She continued to work even after she'd had a heart attack. (carry on)

2 They waited for him for over an hour before he finally arrived. (turn up)

3 We went to bed later than usual because we wanted to watch the film. (stay up)

4 After several tries I succeeded in reaching her on the telephone. (get through)

5 It will take them ages to complete all these forms. (fill in)

6 We can let you stay for the night in the spare room. (put up)

7 Please stop inventing excuses for why you won't go out with me. (make up)

8 If you don't know the meaning of a word, you can look for it in a dictionary. (look up)

9 The machine's stopped working so they'll have to call in someone to repair it. (break down)

10 She found a solution to the problem. (work out)

86c Complete the article. Use the correct form of the phrasal verbs in the box.

| back down | bring up | end up | give up | grow up |
| knock out | not get on with | ~~take after~~ | take up |

Laila Ali (0) ......*takes after*...... her father, the great boxer Muhammed Ali. She (1) .... boxing when she was twenty-one. Since then she has won five women's heavyweight boxing titles.

Laila's childhood wasn't always easy. She (2) .... in a famous family but her parents were divorced and she (3) .... by her mother. Unfortunately, she (4) .... her father, whom she only saw during the summers. Before long, Laila started getting into trouble and fighting with people. She says that she wouldn't start the fights but she wouldn't (5) .... from one either. Eventually, she (6) .... in trouble with the law; when she was sixteen, her boyfriend gave her a credit card but he didn't tell her it was stolen.

In 1999 Laila (7) .... her job in a salon, joined a gym and started boxing. She had her first fight on 8th October 1999. She (8) .... April Fowler in the first few minutes of the fight. Since then she has never been defeated.

185

87 Confusing words (1)

make, do
- We can use *make* to mean 'create' or 'produce'. We can use *do* to talk about work or activities in general. We can also use *make* and *do* in fixed expressions:
  - **make** an attempt **make** a decision **make** an effort **make** an excuse **make** friends **make** an impression **make** a mistake **make** money **make** a noise **make** an offer **make** progress **make** a speech **make** a success **make** sure
  - **do** badly/well **do** your best **do** business **do** exercise **do** a favour **do** damage **do** research **do** sport **do** work/a job

give, do
- We use *give*, not *do*, in these expressions: **give** a description **give** a party **give** a performance **give** an example **give** directions/instructions

take, bring, get
- We can use *take* to mean 'move something or go with someone from one place to another': **Take** a coat in case it rains. He's going to **take** us to the airport.
- We can use *bring* to mean 'take something/someone with you to the place where you are or to the place you are talking about': Please **bring** me my bag here.
- We can use *get* to mean 'receive' or 'become': I **got** a letter from them today. The weather is **getting** colder.
- We can also use *take* and *get* in fixed expressions:
  - **take** a breath **take** a bus/taxi/etc. **take** control **take** an exam **take** medicine **take** a seat **take** time/an hour/etc. **take** a walk
  - **get** the flu **get** ill/well **get** a mark/grade **get** married **get** a letter/e-mail **get** a shock

take, have
- We can use *have* in fixed expressions: **have** a bath/shower **have** fun **have** a good time **have** a meal/a drink **have** a rest **have** a swim **have** time

⚠ Compare: This job will **take time** to do well. (= This job will require time.) Fortunately, I **have** plenty of **time**.

come, go
We use *come* for movements toward the speaker and *go* for movements to other places: Would you **come** closer, please? I **go** to work by car.

get to know, know
We use *get to know* to describe the process of becoming familiar with someone. We use *know* to describe a state: I'm **getting to know** him. I've **known** him for years.

PRACTICE

87a Circle the correct answer.

0 Have you (known)/ got to know one another for very long?
1 Don't forget to *get / take* your passport with you when you go to the airport.
2 Is it all right if I *bring / take* some friends to your party?
3 The storm *did / made* a lot of damage to the buildings in the area.

Vocabulary: *words that go together*

4 I've finished *doing / making* my homework. I'm *doing / making* dinner now.
5 I don't understand – would you *do / give* me an example, please?
6 I'm *coming / going* round to Bettina's house to find out what's wrong.
7 I *knew / got to know* them quite well in the few months I lived with them.
8 Please *take / make* a seat and make yourself comfortable. I won't be long.
9 She *gets / does* really angry if you borrow her things without asking.
10 What time will you be *going / coming* home? I'll wait up for you.

87b Complete the advice. Use the correct form of the verbs in the box.

| do (x3)   get (x2)   get to know   go   know   make (x4)   take (x2) |

Are you planning to study abroad? Then read this useful advice!

✈ (0) **Make** sure you have the right clothes. If you're (1) .... somewhere with a cold climate, (2) .... plenty of warm clothes.

✈ If you have any special dietary requirements, the people who will be (3) .... your meals should (4) .... what these are before you arrive.

✈ If you (5) .... ill, you will (6) .... better faster and (7) .... your classmates a favour if you stay in bed until you've recovered.

✈ (8) .... your best and you'll almost certainly (9) .... progress.

✈ (10) .... friends. Be patient. It will (11) .... time to (12) .... the people you're living and studying with. Of course, it will help if you join a club or (13) .... a sport.

88 *as, like*

- We use *like*:
  - to mean 'similar to': *He looks more **like** his father every day.*
  - to mean 'for example': *Avoid fattening foods **like** cakes and biscuits.*
  - to ask for descriptions or information: *What's their house **like**?*
- We use *as*:
  - to describe someone's job, role or duty: *She works **as** a doctor.*
  - to describe how we use something: *They used a heavy stone **as** a hammer.*
  - to say that something happens in a certain way. The pattern is: *as* + subject + verb: *He repaid the money, **as he promised** he would.*

⚠ Compare: ***Like** a teacher, I want to educate people.* (= In a similar way to a teacher, I want to educate people – but I'm not a teacher.)   ***As** a teacher, I want to educate people.* (= In my role as a teacher, I want to educate people.)

Vocabulary: *words that go together*

PRACTICE

88 Circle the correct answer.

0 My sister's hair is dark brown, *as* / *(like)* mine.
1 He was employed *as* / *like* an engineer by a large construction company.
2 The election results were seen *as* / *like* a victory for the government.
3 *As* / *Like* many young people, she's finding it hard to make ends meet.
4 The children dressed up *as* / *like* ghosts and witches for the party.
5 My brother has a car just *as* / *like* yours. What do you think of it?
6 We use the spare room *as* / *like* a study most of the time.
7 Fruits *as* / *like* oranges and kiwis have lots of vitamin C.
8 *As* / *Like* we reported earlier, the fire was probably started by arsonists.
9 So you went to the concert last night. What was it *as* / *like*?
10 *As* / *Like* most people, they would love to have a home of their own.

89 Confusing words (2)

countryside, environment, nature
- The *countryside* is the land outside cities/towns: *We grew up on a farm in the **countryside**.*
- The *environment* is the air, water and land which can be harmed by humans: *Pollution caused by air travel is harming the **environment**.*
- *Nature* is everything in the world that is not controlled by humans, e.g. plants, animals and the weather: *Her poems are about **nature**, especially the sea and mountains.*

fun, funny
- *Fun* is what we enjoy doing: *The picnic was really **fun**.*
- Something *funny* makes us laugh: *He told them a **funny** story.*

nervous, irritable
- A *nervous* person is worried or frightened: *I was **nervous** about my exams and I couldn't sleep.*
- An *irritable* person gets annoyed quickly or easily: *Since she quit smoking, she's been really **irritable**.*

journey, travel, trip, way
- A *journey* is a period of time spent travelling from one place to another: *I read during the train **journey** to work.*
- *Travel* is the activity of moving from place to place: *We went by bus because it's the cheapest form of **travel**.*
- A *trip* is a journey for pleasure or a particular purpose: *How was your **trip** to Paris?*
- A *way* is a road, path or direction that you take to get to a place: *Can you tell me the **way** to the post office?*

Vocabulary: *words that go together*

PRACTICE

89a Circle the correct answer.

0   We must act now to save the (environment)/ *nature* for the next generation.
1   It's dark. Do you think you can find your *way / trip* back to the car park?
2   If this is your idea of a joke, I don't find it at all *fun / funny*.
3   We're going to take a *trip / journey* to the mountains. Would you like to come?
4   I've always been a *countryside / nature* lover. I enjoy spending time in the *countryside / nature*.
5   The *journey / travel* home from London takes six hours.
6   I'm feeling tired and *irritable / nervous* because I haven't had much sleep.

89b Complete the advertisement. Use the words in the box.

| countryside | environment | fun | nature | nervous | ~~travel~~ | trip |

A brief guide to volunteering abroad

Are you interested in (0) ...*travel*... ?
Would you like to go abroad and do something useful at the same time?
Then why not volunteer to work in another country?

What kind of work can I do?
There are many different types of work you can volunteer for. If you are interested in helping to save the (1) .... , you can guard endangered turtles in Panama or protect the precious rainforest in Madagascar. Either way, you will have the opportunity explore the (2) .... and experience the beauties of (3) .... at its best.

What if I haven't travelled before?
You don't have to be (4) .... about anything. The project organisers will assist you to make arrangements for your (5) .... and help you to settle in when you arrive at your destination.

How long will I be away?
You can volunteer for as little as one week or as long as a year. Find out for yourself how much (6) .... it can be to make a difference!

189

Check 16 Words that go together

1 **Circle the correct answer.**
   1 My teacher uses games to make our lessons *fun / funny*.
   2 Italy is famous not only for its cities but for its beautiful *nature / countryside*.
   3 The *journey / way* from my place to Gundula's house takes about three hours.
   4 It's expensive to live in capital cities *as / like* London.
   5 Many people hate speaking in public because it makes them *irritable / nervous*.
   6 Tom works *as / like* an assistant in a large department store.
   7 They *did / gave* a wonderful performance and the audience cheered wildly.
   8 We have a very good relationship *between / with* our neighbours.
   9 Do you think she has any hope *of / for* winning the competition?
   10 The country's economy depends heavily *on / for* tourism.

   / 10

2 **Complete the second sentence so that it means the same as the first, using the word in bold. Use between two and five words.**
   11 There is no resemblance between Stephen and his brother. **look**
      Stephen .... his brother.
   12 It is Martina's job to train new staff. **responsible**
      Martina .... new staff.
   13 I serve food and drink to customers in a restaurant but I want to be an actor. **waiter**
      I work .... but I want to be an actor.
   14 Alaric's parents take pride in his achievements. **proud**
      Alaric's parents .... his achievements.
   15 Have they solved the problem? **solution**
      Have they found .... the problem?
   16 Did you lend that book to Petra? **borrow**
      Did Petra .... you?
   17 I managed to convince them to come with me. **succeeded**
      I .... them to come with me.
   18 My father thinks it is a good idea. **approves**
      My father .... the idea.

   / 8

3 Choose the correct answer A, B, C or D.

J.K. Rowling is the author of a successful series (19) ..... books. She uses the initials J.K. because her publishers thought that a book by a woman might not appeal (20) ..... boys.

Rowling was born in 1965 and brought (21) ..... in England and South Wales. After she finished university, she got a job in London.

In 1990, while she was travelling from Manchester to London, her train was held (22) ..... and during the four-hour delay she got the idea of writing about a young wizard. In 1991 she (23) ..... to Portugal, where she had a job teaching English, and she (24) ..... the manuscript for the first Harry Potter book with her. She returned to Britain in 1993 and carried (25) ..... writing it.

Rowling completed *Harry Potter and the Philosopher's Stone* in 1995. Twelve publishers turned (26) ..... before Bloomsbury agreed to publish it. The decision was apparently (27) ..... by the young daughter of the company's chairman, who loved the first chapter of the book.

In 1995 Bloomsbury advised Rowling that she had little chance (28) ..... making money writing children's books. Today she has a fortune of around $US 1 billion. Rowling believes that people who have a lot of money should (29) ..... sure they use it responsibly. For this reason, she has given (30) ..... millions of dollars to charitable causes.

19	A in	B for	C of	D on
20	A for	B of	C on	D to
21	A down	B up	C through	D along
22	A up	B on	C in	D back
23	A arrived	B came	C brought	D went
24	A brought	B fetched	C came	D took
25	A off	B on	C over	D through
26	A it down	B down it	C it up	D up it
27	A had	B done	C given	D made
28	A to	B for	C of	D about
29	A do	B make	C have	D get
30	A away	B back	C in	D out

/ 12

4 Complete the conversation. Use one word in each gap.

A: I do apologise (31) .... forgetting about your birthday last week. Did you (32) .... a good time?

B: That's all right. Unfortunately, I (33) .... the flu a few days before. My parents had given me tickets to the music festival but I was too ill to go. I'm upset (34) .... missing it.

A: I'm not surprised. I hope you got some nice presents.

B: Well, my parents know I'm interested (35) .... buying a new mobile phone so they also gave me some money to help pay (36) .... it. And a lot of people came (37) .... to see me when I was better. I even heard (38) .... Ken! He's travelling in Thailand these days.

A: Is he? Anyway, would you like a lift to the match tomorrow? I can pick you (39) .... at eight.

B: Thanks. I'm looking (40) .... to it. Are you?

/ 10

Total: / 40

Self-check

Wrong answers	Look again at	Try CD-ROM
12, 14, 34, 35	Unit 83	Exercise 83
10, 11, 16, 17, 18, 20, 31, 36, 38	Unit 84	Exercise 84
8, 9, 15, 19, 28	Unit 85	Exercise 85
21, 22, 25, 26, 30, 37, 39, 40	Unit 86	Exercise 86
7, 23, 24, 27, 29, 32, 33	Unit 87	Exercise 87
4, 6, 13	Unit 88	Exercise 88
1, 2, 3, 5	Unit 89	Exercise 89

Now do **Check 16**

Word formation

90 Prefixes

We use these prefixes to make words negative:

un- + adjective/verb/noun	**un**fair, **un**pack, **un**employment
dis- + adjective/verb/noun	**dis**respectful, **dis**like, **dis**satisfaction
il- (+ -*l*) + adjective/noun	**il**logical, **il**legal, **il**legibility
im- (+ -*m*/-*p*) + adjective/noun	**im**moral, **im**perfect, **im**possibility
in- + adjective/noun	**in**direct, **in**competent, **in**convenience
ir- (+ -*r*) + adjective/noun	**ir**rational, **ir**regularity

These are prefixes with other meanings:

co- (= together with) + adjective/verb/noun	**co**-operative, **co**-exist, **co**-education
mis- (= bad/wrong) + adjective/verb/noun	**mis**guided, **mis**calculate, **mis**take
re- (= again) + adjective/verb/noun	**re**united, **re**create, **re**marriage
over- (= too much) + adjective/verb/noun	**over**cooked, **over**do, **over**-exposure
sub- (= under/less/lower) + adjective/noun	**sub**normal, **sub**marine
under- (= not enough) + adjective/verb/noun	**under**fed, **under**cook, **under**graduate

PRACTICE

90 Complete the conversations. Use the words in brackets and an appropriate prefix.

0 **A:** Haven't you ....*unpacked*.... your bags yet? (packed)
   B: No, but I'm about to.

1 **A:** Shall we watch *Casablanca* with Humphrey Bogart and Katharine Hepburn?
   B: Surely Bogart's .... in *Casablanca* was Lauren Bacall? (star)

2 **A:** How was the meeting?
   B: It got off to a bad start. We .... how long it would take to get there and we were twenty minutes late. (calculated)

3 **A:** Why aren't you wearing sun cream? .... to the sun can cause permanent damage to your skin. (exposure)
   B: You're right. I'll put some on now.

4 **A:** If we invite Ben, we'll have to invite Liz. They're .... (separable)
   B: Well, they've been friends since they were .... at Cambridge. (graduates)

5 **A:** I don't know what to do about Neville. His .... behaviour has made him unpopular with his teachers. (respectful)
   B: Have you tried talking to him?

192

91 Forming adjectives: suffixes

We often form adjectives from verbs and nouns with these suffixes:

-able/-ible	comfort – comfort**able** like – like**able** response – respons**ible**
-al	accident – accident**al** critic – critic**al** culture – cultur**al**
-ent/-ant	efficiency – effici**ent** arrogance – arrog**ant**
-ful	beauty – beauti**ful** harm – harm**ful** use – use**ful**
-less	care – care**less** harm – harm**less** worth – worth**less**
-ic/-ical	sympathy – sympathet**ic** analysis – analyt**ical**
-ish	baby – baby**ish** fool – fool**ish** style – styl**ish**
-ive	act – act**ive** expense – expens**ive** imagine – imaginat**ive**
-ous	courage – courage**ous** fury – furi**ous** humour – humor**ous**
-(l)y	guilt – guil**ty** salt – sal**ty** wealth – weal**thy** week – week**ly**

PRACTICE

91a Complete the sentences. Use adjectives formed from the words in the box.

> courage   guilt   imagine   ~~like~~   nation   truth

0 He's very ......*likeable*...... and has always had lots of friends.
1 I feel really .... about forgetting your birthday again.
2 Although he was wrong, he was .... enough to admit it.
3 She's a talented artist who makes .... use of colour.
4 I have a question and I want a(n) .... answer.
5 Before the match people stood up and sang the .... anthem.

91b Complete the article. Use the word at the end of some of the lines to form a word that fits in the gap on the same line.

The first *Big Issue Magazine* was sold as a (0) ......*monthly*......	MONTH
publication in London in 1991. (1) .... sister magazines	REGION
were later published in the UK. Today the *Big Issue* is sold as	
a (2) .... magazine in countries round the world.	WEEK
It is written by (3) .... writers and sold by people who	PROFESSION
are either (4) .... or in danger of losing their homes.	HOME
The magazine deals with (5) .... social issues. It also	IMPORTANCE
features interviews with many (6) .... figures,	FAME
including celebrities and politicians. It is (7) .... of	INDEPENDENCE
any (8) .... party. Over 722,000 copies are sold	POLITICS
each year in the UK.	

Vocabulary: *word formation*

92 Forming nouns: suffixes

We form nouns from adjectives with these suffixes:

-ness	bright – bright**ness** happy – happi**ness**	-ence	intelligent – intellig**ence** patient – pati**ence** violent – viol**ence**
-ity/-iety	active – activ**ity** various – var**iety**	-th	warm – warm**th** deep – dep**th** long – leng**th** strong – streng**th**

We form nouns from verbs with these suffixes:

-ion	invent – invent**ion** destroy – destruct**ion**	-er/-or	employ – employ**er** teach – teach**er** sail – sail**or**
-ance/-ence	disturb – disturb**ance** depend – depend**ence**	-ee	employ – employ**ee** refuge – refug**ee**
-ment	advertise – advertise**ment** agree – agree**ment**	-y	discover – discover**y** recover – recover**y**

We add suffixes to some nouns to change their meaning:

-ian	music – music**ian**	-ist	science – scient**ist**
-hood	mother – mother**hood**	-ship	friend – friend**ship**
-ism	terror – terror**ism** race – rac**ism**		

⚠️ Some nouns have the same form as the verb: *an attack – to attack*
a diet – to diet   transport – to transport

PRACTICE

92 Complete the essay. Use nouns formed from the words in brackets.

Human beings are characterised not only by their (0) ...*intelligence*... (intelligent) but by their (1) .... (able) to use technology to shape their environment. The (2) .... (discover) of how to use fire was one of the most important events in the history of our species and the (3) .... (invent) of the plough and the wheel were also significant (4) .... (develop).

  It is difficult to imagine what our (5) .... (civilise) would be like without technology. In our own time, computers and the Internet have speeded up (6) .... (communicate) and ordinary people now have access to (7) .... (inform) that was once available to only a privileged few.

  However, technology also has a negative aspect. Our planet is facing (8) .... (destroy) because of global warming, (9) .... (pollute) and over-population. We will all need to work together with the help of (10) .... (science) and (11) .... (politics) to save our planet and there is no doubt that new technologies will play a role in finding (12) .... (solve).

93 -ing and -ed adjectives

- Many present and past participles can be used as adjectives.
  - Present participles: *a **crying** child*   *an **exciting** trip*   ***melting** ice*
  - Past participles: ***broken** equipment*   *a **locked** door*   *a **torn** shirt*
- These adjectives often mean 'the thing/person that is ...': *a **crying** child* = a child that is crying   *a **broken** vase* = a vase that is broken
- Present participles can describe things which make us feel a certain way: *She told me a **surprising** story.*   *That's an **interesting** question.*
- Past participles can describe how we feel: *I'm **surprised** you remembered my birthday.*   *He's always been **interested** in music.*

PRACTICE

93a Circle the correct answer.

→ Are you young, enthusiastic and (0) *motivating* / (*motivated*) to succeed?

→ Are you (1) *interesting* / *interested* in making a career for yourself with a (2) *respecting* / *respected* computer software producer?

→ Are you looking for (3) *challenging* / *challenged* work with a rapidly (4) *expanding* / *expanded* company?

If your answer is 'yes' and you hold a degree in information technology or a (5) *relating* / *related* field, then we could have an (6) *exciting* / *excited* opening for you. Send us your CV and a (7) *completing* / *completed* application form now!

93b Complete the sentences. Use adjectives formed from the words in the box.

break   change   continue   dry   embarrass
love   park   ~~relax~~   steal

0 It was a restful holiday and I feel much more ......*relaxed*...... now.
1 I kept calling her by the wrong name – it was ....
2 Please get some .... fruit from the supermarket so that I can make a cake.
3 They've always been poor and shortage of money is a(n) .... problem.
4 The increase in the divorce rate reflects .... attitudes to marriage.
5 The police may charge them with receiving .... goods.
6 Children should not play near .... cars.
7 They say he died of a(n) .... heart but I don't know if that's true.
8 They're a(n) .... family who give one another a lot of support.

195

Vocabulary: *word formation*

94 Compound adjectives

- We can form compound adjectives in a number of ways:
  - adjective/adverb + past participle: a **badly-dressed** woman   a **newly-married** couple   an **old-fashioned** idea   a **good-looking** man   a **well-behaved** child
  - adjective/adverb + -ing form: a **best-selling** novel   a **fast-moving** story   a **long-running** argument   a **slow-moving** vehicle
  - adjective + noun: **cutting-edge** technology   a **fast-food** restaurant   a **free-time** activity   a **front-row** seat   a **full-time** job   **high-technology** equipment   a **low-fat** diet   a **modern-day** problem   a **single-storey** building
  - noun + adjective: a **brand-new** car   **duty-free** goods   **lead-free** petrol   a **worldwide** reputation   **handmade** shoes   **homegrown** vegetables

- Many compound adjectives describe people: bad-tempered, big-headed, broad-shouldered, good-natured, green-eyed, grey-haired, middle-aged, right/left-handed, short-sighted, clear-thinking, easy-going, good-looking, hard-working

PRACTICE

94a Complete the sentences. Use the correct form of the words in the box.

| age   build   go   hand   head   make   wide   work   ~~write~~ |

0 It was a well-...*written*........ play and the actors were also excellent.
1 Jenny's a hard-..................... person but she's also quite easy-..................... .
2 He's a useful person in an emergency – level-..................... and decisive.
3 Witnesses described the attacker as middle-..................... , tall and well-..................... .
4 All our goods are hand..................... and we use only natural materials.
5 It's possible to buy scissors which are made specially for left-..................... people.
6 The televised event attracted a world..................... audience of over a billion people.

94b Complete the advertisements. Form compound adjectives.

Missing. Ming Ming is a (0) short-...*haired*........ , (1) blue-..................... Siamese cat. Last seen on Saturday night. If you have any information, please ring 0208 465 3678.

Two Cities is the latest book by (2) ....-selling novelist Ewan Andrews. A (3) fast-..................... story of (4) modern-..................... problems and (5) ....-fashioned solutions. Out now.

Flats to let: These modern, (6) air-..................... apartments in a (7) ....-new, (8) high-..................... block are ideal for people working in the city centre. Ring Victoria Properties today on 0207 948 3678.

95 Compound nouns

We can form compound nouns in these ways:
- noun + noun: *a burglar alarm   a car park   current affairs   traffic lights*
- noun + -ing form: *air conditioning   food poisoning   power dressing*
- -ing form + noun: *a dining room   a driving licence   opening hours*
- other combinations of words: *mother-in-law   feedback   make-up   lateral thinking   passer-by   software   sunshine   upbringing*

⚠ We can write compound nouns as one word, two words or with a hyphen. Some compound nouns are written as one word or hyphenated, depending on the dictionary referred to: *dishwasher/dish-washer   eyewitness/eye-witness*

PRACTICE

95a Complete the definitions. Use one word from each box in each sentence.

| air   burglar   feed |
| job   soft   ~~sun~~ |

| alarm   back   conditioning |
| ~~glasses~~   sharing   ware |

0 *Sunglasses* are dark glasses that protect your eyes from the sun.
1 .... is a system that makes the air in a room cooler and drier.
2 .... is an arrangement by which two people both work part-time doing the same job.
3 .... is the set of programs that tell a computer how to do a particular job.
4 .... is advice or criticism about how successful or useful something is.
5 A(n) .... is a piece of equipment that makes a loud noise when someone tries to get into a building illegally.

95b Complete the conversations. Use the words in the box.

| ~~brother~~   computer   food   opening   pain   traffic |

0 **A:** Have you met my *brother*-in-law, Johann?
   B: Pleased to meet you, Johann.
1 **A:** I've got an awful headache.
   B: Would you like a(n) ....killer?
2 **A:** Turn left at the next .... light you come to.
   B: Here?
3 **A:** What are you doing this evening?
   B: I think I'll stay in and play my new .... game.
4 **A:** Put that in the fridge or you'll end up with .... poisoning.
   B: Yes, you're right.
5 **A:** What are the .... hours for shops in the UK?
   B: It depends where you are. London shops tend to have longer hours.

Check 17 Word formation

1 Complete the book extract. Use the word at the end of some of the lines to form a word that fits in the gap on the same line.

I have a natural (1) .... to find bad news. If it's out there, I want to know about it. The people who work for me realise this and keep me informed.	ABLE
A lot goes wrong in any (2) .... , even a good one.	ORGANISE
A product fails. You're (3) .... by a customer who suddenly switches to another company.	SUPRISE
A (4) .... brings out a product that appeals to a broad new market. Maybe a product is going to be late, or it's not going to do what you expect it to do, or you've been	COMPETE
(5) .... to hire enough of the right kinds of people to carry out your plans. An (6) .... manager wants to hear about what's going wrong before he or she hears about what's going right. You can't react appropriately to	ABLE
	EFFECT
(7) .... news if it doesn't reach you soon enough.	DISAPPOINT
You concentrate on bad news in order to get started on the (8) .... quickly. As soon as you're aware of a problem, everybody in your company must go into (9)	SOLVE
	ACT
An (10) .... measure of a company's digital nervous system is how quickly people in the company find out about bad news and respond to it. Digital technology speeds business response time in any emergency.	IMPORTANCE

/ 10

2 Complete the sentences. Use words formed from the words in brackets.

11 The workers face .... if the factory closes. (employment)

12 I must have .... you. Could you repeat it? (understood)

13 The couple were .... after a long separation. (united)

14 I prefer fresh vegetables to .... ones. (freeze)

15 He is .... He makes stupid mistakes. (competent)

/ 5

3 Complete the sentences. Use the words in the box.

power row running series thinking

16 Vicky dreams of becoming a film star one day. She might succeed – she's just got an important part in a television ....

17 It's a long-................. sitcom.

18 She invited me to watch the show and made sure that I got a front-................. seat.

19 She swears that in her early days of acting it was .... dressing that helped her to convince people to take her seriously.

20 Personally, I think she's a creative person who's used lateral .... to help her find the success she wants.

/ 5

Total: / 20

Self-check

Wrong answers	Look again at	Try CD-ROM
5, 11, 12, 13, 15	Unit 90	Exercise 90
6, 10	Unit 91	Exercise 91
1, 2, 4, 8, 9	Unit 92	Exercise 92
3, 7, 14	Unit 93	Exercise 93
17, 18	Unit 94	Exercise 94
16, 19, 20	Unit 95	Exercise 95

Now do **Check 17**

Appendices

1 Punctuation rules

Capital letter
We use a capital letter:
- at the beginning of a sentence: *They listened to the weather report before they set off.*
- for proper nouns. These include:
  - the names of people, places, nationalities and languages: *Richard   Ms Fiona Hamilton   the King of Spain   Turkey   Moscow   Florida   Lake Superior   Italian*
  - days and months: *Monday   April*
  - the titles of books, newspapers and magazines: *David Copperfield   The Daily Mail   Vogue*
  - films and plays: *The Lion King   Hamlet*
  - paintings: *The Shout*
  - religions and festivals: *Islam   Christmas Day*

Full stop
We use a full stop (.) at the end of a sentence: *It was a dark and stormy night.*

Question mark
We use a question mark (?):
- at the end of a direct question: *Have you seen the film?   Where does she live?*
- at the end of an indirect question if the first part is itself a question: *Do you know who painted that?*
- after a question tag: *Let's go, shall we?*

Exclamation mark
We use an exclamation mark (!) at the end of a sentence, phrase or word that expresses surprise, anger or excitement: *It was a wonderful surprise! What a terrible accident!   Great!*

Semicolon
We use a semi-colon (;) to separate closely related independent clauses in a compound sentence: *They weren't sure what to do; however, they knew they had to act quickly.*

Colon
We use a colon (:) after a statement in order to introduce a list: *Three languages are spoken in Switzerland: German, French and Italian.*

Comma
We use a comma or commas (,):
- after a sentence adverb: *Personally, I liked the book.*
- to set off a word or phrase that comes between the subject and verb in a sentence: *Everyone agrees that there are problems. The solutions, however, are not easy to find.*
- when a secondary clause comes before the main clause in a sentence: *Although I was angry, I tried not to show it.*
- to set off a non-defining relative clause from the main clause: *Last year we visited the Louvre, which is one of the most famous museums in the world.*
- when a participle clause comes before the main clause in a sentence: *Being a very tall man, he has difficulty finding clothes that fit him.*
- to set off a reduced non-defining relative clause: *The passengers, exhausted after their journey, waited for hours to collect their luggage.*
- between items in a list. There is no comma before the last item: *I'm going to the supermarket to buy some milk, cheese, eggs and spaghetti.*

Apostrophe
We use an apostrophe ('):
- to indicate possession: *Cora's baby   James'/James's home   Danny and Sophie's wedding   the dog's tail   my friends' parents   the children's shoes*
- to indicate omission: *I haven't got a brother. It's freezing today!   She'll be here on time.*

Dash
We use a dash or dashes (–) to set off a phrase or clause for dramatic effect in less formal writing: *Douglas arrived very late – in fact, he missed the first half of the play!*

Quotation marks and comma in direct speech
We use quotation marks ('...') around direct speech. A comma may be used to separate the direct speech from the reporting verb: *'Come here!' he shouted. 'What's your name?' she asked.   'Join us for dinner on Saturday,' she said kindly.   I said, 'I might not be able to come.'*

2 Spelling rules

Noun/Verb + -s

most nouns/verbs	add -s or -es	cat → cat**s** wash → wash**es**
nouns/verbs ending in consonant + -y	change -y to -i and add -es	berry → berr**ies** study → stud**ies**
nouns/verbs ending in vowel + -y	add -s	donkey → donkey**s** stay → stay**s**
nouns/verbs ending in -o	add -s or -es	radio → radio**s** hero → hero**es** do → do**es** go → go**es**
nouns ending in -f or -fe	add -s or change -f/-fe to -v and add -s or -es	roof → roof**s** wolf → wol**ves** wife → wi**ves**

Verb + -ed/-ing

most verbs	add -ed/-ing	hunt → hunt**ed** look → look**ing**
verbs ending in -e	add -d take away the -e and add -ing	live → live**d** live → liv**ing**
verbs ending in -ee	add -d/-ing	agree → agree**d** agree → agree**ing**
verbs ending in consonant + -y	change -y to -i and add -ed add -ing	carry → carr**ied** carrying → carry**ing**
verbs ending in vowel + -y	add -ed/-ing	enjoy → enjoy**ed** enjoy → enjoy**ing**
verbs ending in one vowel + one consonant	double the final consonant and add -ed/-ing if the last part of the word is stressed	hop → hop**ped** regret → regret**ted** hit → hit**ting** begin → begin**ning** But: open → open**ed** happen → happen**ing**
verbs ending in -ie	add -d change -ie to -y and add -ing	die → die**d** lie → l**ying**
verbs ending in one vowel + -w/-x	add -ed/-ing	snow → snow**ed** mix → mix**ing**
verbs ending in one vowel + -l	double the -l and add -ed/-ing	cancel → cancel**led** travel → travel**ling**

Adverbs formed from adjectives

most adjectives	add -ly	slow → slow**ly**
adjectives ending in -y	change -y to -i and add -ly	heavy → heav**ily**
adjectives ending in -le	take away the -e and add -y	simple → simp**ly**
adjectives ending in -ic	add -ly or -ally	public → public**ly** tragic → trag**ically**

Comparative and superlative adjectives

most adjectives	add -er/-est	cold → cold**er** → cold**est**
adjectives ending in -e	add -r/-st	large → large**r** → large**st**
adjectives ending in -y	change -y to -i and add -er/-est	easy → eas**ier** → eas**iest**
adjectives ending in one vowel + one consonant	double the final consonant and add -er/-est	slim → slim**mer** → slim**mest**

Appendices

3 Verbs followed by *-ing* form

admit	can't help	deny	fancy	hate	miss	recommend
adore	can't stand	detest	feel like	imagine	postpone	resent
avoid	carry on	dislike	finish	keep	practise	risk
can't bear	consider	dread	give up	mention	put off	suggest
can't face	delay	enjoy	go on	mind	recall	

4 Verbs followed by *to*-infinitive

agree	choose	help	mean	pretend	want
arrange	decide	hope	need	promise	would hate
ask	expect	intend	offer	refuse	would like
can't afford	fail	learn	plan	tend	would love
can't wait	forget	manage	prepare	try	would prefer

5 Verbs followed by *-ing* form or *to*-infinitive

(a) With no change in meaning

begin	continue	prefer
bother	love	start

(b) With a change in meaning

forget	like	regret	stop
go on	mean	remember	try

6 Verbs followed by object + *to*-infinitive

(a) Verbs that need an object before the *to*-infinitive

advise	cause	force	invite	persuade	teach	warn
allow	encourage	get	order	remind	tell	

(b) Verbs that can have an object before the *to*-infinitive

ask	help	want	would like	would prefer
expect	need	would hate	would love	

7 Adjective + preposition

absent from
acceptable to
accustomed to
addicted to
afraid of
amazed at/by
amused at/by
angry about (something)
angry with (someone)
annoyed about (something)
annoyed with (someone)

anxious about
ashamed of
aware of
bad at (something)
bad for (someone)
bored with
brilliant at
busy with
capable of
careful about/with
certain about/of

concerned about (someone/something)
concerned with (something)
confident about
confused about
content with
crazy about
critical of
crowded with
dependent on
delighted about/with

201

different from
disappointed at/about (something)
disappointed with (someone/something)
engaged to
enthusiastic about
envious of
excellent at
excited about
familiar to (someone)
familiar with (something)
famous for
fed up with
fond of
friendly to/with
frightened of
full of
furious about (something)
furious with (someone)
generous to
good at (something)
good for/to (someone)
guilty of
happy about/with (something)
hopeless at
impressed by/with
independent of

inferior to
interested in
involved with (someone)
involved in (something)
jealous of
keen on
kind to
late for
lucky for (someone)
lucky in (something)
married to
necessary for
nervous about
nice to
occupied with
patient with
patronising to
pleased about (something)
pleased with (someone/something)
polite to
proud of
ready for
related to
reliant on
responsible for/to
right about
rude to

safe from
satisfied with
scared of
sensitive to
serious about
shocked at/by
short of
similar to
skilful at
skilled at/in
sorry about (something)
sorry for (someone)
successful at/in
sure about/of
surprised at/by
suspicious of
sympathetic to
terrible at
terrified of
tired of
typical of
upset about/at/by (something)
upset with (someone)
useless at
worried about
wrong about

8 Verb + preposition

accuse (someone) of (something)
advise (someone) about/on (something)
agree with (someone)
agree about/on (something)
apologise for (something)
apologise to (someone)
apply for
approve of
argue with (someone)
argue about (something)
arrest (someone) for (something)
arrive at/in
ask (someone) about/for (something)
believe in
belong to
benefit from
bet on
blame (someone) for (something)
blame (something) on (someone)
borrow (something) from (someone)

break into
care about/for
change (something) into (something)
collide with
come from
communicate with
compare (someone/something) to/with (someone/something)
compete against/with
complain about
concentrate on
congratulate (someone) on (something)
connect (something) to/with (something)
consist of
cope with
count on
crash into
criticise (someone) for (something)
deal with
decide on

Appendices

depend on
describe (someone/something) to (someone)
die of
differ from
disagree about (something)
disagree with (someone)
disappear from
discuss (something) with (someone)
divide (something) into (something)
dream about/of
end in/with
escape from
explain (something) to (someone)
feel like
fight about (something)
fight with (someone)
fill (something) with (something)
forget about
forgive (someone) for (something)
happen to
hear about/from/of
hope for
improve on
insist on
introduce (someone) to (someone)
joke about (something)
joke with (someone)
know (something) about (someone/something)
laugh at
lead to
learn about
lend (something) to (someone)
listen to
live with
look after
look at
look for
look like
object to
pay for
persist in
point at/to
prefer (someone/something) to (someone something)
prepare for
prevent (someone/something) from (doing something)
protect (someone/something) from (something)

protest about/against
provide (someone) with (something)
provide (something) for (someone)
punish (someone) for (something)
quarrel about (something)
quarrel with (someone)
react to
recover from
refer to
rely on
remind (someone) about/of (something)
reply to
resign from
result in
return (something) to (someone)
save (someone) from (something)
say (something) to (someone)
search for
see to
share (something) with (someone)
shout at/to
smell of
smile at
speak about (someone/something)
speak to (someone)
spend (money/time) on (something)
stare at
steal (something) from (someone)
succeed at/in
suffer from
suspect (someone) of (something)
sympathise about (something)
sympathise with (someone)
take after
talk about (someone/something)
talk to (someone)
taste of
tell (someone) about (something)
thank (someone) for (something)
think about/of
translate (something) into (something)
turn into
wait for
warn (someone) about/against/of (something)
waste (money/time) on (something)
worry about
write about (someone/something)
write (something) to (someone)

9 Noun + preposition

admiration for
advantage of
advertisement for
advice about/on
agreement about (something)
agreement with (someone)
alternative to
answer to
apology for
application for
appointment with
approval of
argument about (something)
argument with (someone)
arrival at/in
attack on
attitude to
ban on
beginning of
belief in
bet on
blame for
cause of
change in/of
choice of
collection of
collision with
comment on
communication with
comparison between/with
competition between/for
complaint about
congratulations on
connection between/with
contact between/with
control of
conversation between/with
cost of
criticism of
cure for
danger of
debate about/on
decision about/on
decrease in
delay in
demand for
departure from
dependence on

description of
difference between
difficulty in/with
disadvantage of
disagreement about (something)
disagreement with (someone)
disappearance from
discussion about (something)
discussion between/with (someone)
division between/into
drawing of
dream of/about
drop in
effect of/on
end of
escape from
example of
excuse for
experience of
expert on
failure at/in/of
fall in
fight about (something)
fight between/with (someone)
forgiveness for
help with
hesitation in
hope for/of
improvement in/on
increase in
influence on
information about/on
insistence on
interest in
interview with
introduction to
invitation to
joke about
knowledge about/of
lack of
matter with
meaning of
need for
objection to
opinion about/of
opportunity for
payment for
permission for (something)

permission from (someone)
persistence in
photograph of
picture of
preference for
preparation for
prevention against
price of
pride in
prize for
problem with
protection from
protest about/against
provision for
punishment for
quarrel about (something)
quarrel with (someone)
reaction to
reason for
recovery from
reference to
relationship between/with (someone)
reliance on
reminder about/of
reply to
reputation for
resignation from
respect for
responsibility for
result of
rise in/of
room for
search for
smell of
solution to
success at/in
suspicion of
sympathy for
talent for
taste of
tax on
trouble with
victim of
warning about/against
worry about

Index

The numbers in this index are unit numbers (not page numbers).

A

a bit + comparative	14
a few	6
a great deal of	6
a large number of	6
a little	6
a lot + comparative	14
a lot of	5–6
a/an	1
-able	91
about	81
above	79
absolutely	16
across	79
actually	61
adjective + preposition	83
adjectives	10, 11, 13–14, 43, 50–51, 83, 91, 93–94
adverbial	36
adverbs of degree	16
adverbs of frequency	12, 18
adverbs	11–14, 16–18, 20–22, 36
after all	61
after	27, 60, 63–64, 80
against	79
-al	91
all (of)	7
all	78
along	79
already	21
also	57
although	56, 58
am/is/are + *to*-infinitive	29
among	79
-ance	92
and	56
-ant	91
any	5
anybody	5
anyhow	61
anyone	5
anything	5
anyway	61
articles	1
a/an	1
the	1
zero article	1
as ... as	14
as a result	59
as if	71
as long as	68
as soon as	25, 27, 60
as though	71
as well (as)	57
as	59, 88
assuming (that)	68
at	79–80

B

be able to	33
be about + *to*-infinitive	29–30
be allowed to	35
be going to	27, 30
be/get used to	26
because of	59
because	56, 59
before	27, 60, 63–64, 80
below	79
beneath	79
beside	79
between	79
both (of)	7
both ... and	57
bring	87
but	56, 58
by the way	61
by	73, 79–81

C

can	31–32, 35
can't	32
causative form	76
clauses of cause	59, 64
clauses of concession	58, 62
clauses of contrast	58, 62
clauses of purpose	59
clauses of reason	59, 62, 64
clauses of result	59, 62
clauses of time: see time clauses	
cleft sentences	78
co-	90
come	87
common nouns	2
comparative structures	14
comparison of adjectives	13
comparison of adverbs	13
comparison of quantifiers	13
complement	36
complex sentences	56
compound adjectives	94
compound nouns	95
compound sentences	56
conditionals	65–69
the zero conditional	65
the first conditional	65
the second conditional	66
the third conditional	67
mixed conditionals	69
continuous infinitive	45
coordinating conjunctions	56
coordinating relative clauses	54
could	31–32, 35
countable nouns	3
countryside	89

D

defining relative clauses	52
despite	58, 62
determiners	5
different	14
direct object	36
dis-	90
do	87
due to	29–30, 59
during	80

E

each (of)	7
each other	8
-ed adjectives	93
-ee	92
either (of)	7
either ... or	57
either	39

205

Index

emphasis	40, 78
emphatic forms	40
-ence	92
enough	5, 15
-ent	91
environment	89
-er	92
even if	68
even though	56, 58
ever	20
every	7
exclamations	40

F

fairly	16
far + comparative	14
few	6
finally	57
first conditional	65
first of all	57
first	57
firstly	57
for this reason	59
for	22, 80
formation of adverbs	11
from ... to	79
from	81
-ful	91
fun	89
funny	89
furthermore	56–57
future continuous	28
future forms	27–30
will	27–28
be going to	27
present simple	27
present continuous	27
future continuous	28
future perfect simple	28
future perfect continuous	28
future in the past	30
future perfect continuous	28
future perfect simple	28
future simple: see will	

G

gerunds: see -ing forms	
get something done	76
get	87

give	87
go + -ing	44
go	87
gradable adjectives	16
gradable adverbs	16

H

had better	34, 41
half (of)	7
have been	20
have gone	20
have got to	33
have something done	76
have to	32–33, 41
have	87
-hood	92
how	40
however	56, 58

I

I mean	61
I wish	70
-ian	92
-ible	91
-ic	91
-ical	91
-iety	92
if I were you	66
if only	70
if	50, 56, 65
il-	90
im-	90
imagine (that)	68
impersonal passive	75
in addition	57
in case	68
in order to	59
in other words	61
in spite of	58, 62
in	79–80
in-	90
indirect object	36
infinitive of purpose	43, 59
infinitive without to	41–42, 45
infinitives	41–43, 45, 50–51, 59
-ing adjectives	93
-ing forms	41–42, 44–45
inside	79
into	79

-ion	92
ir-	90
irritable	89
-ish	91
-ism	92
-ist	92
it	43, 51, 77
It was ... that	78
it's time	71
-ity	92
-ive	91

J

journey	89
just	21

L

lastly	57
-less	91
let's	35, 41
like	88
linking expressions in speech	61
little	6
lots of	5–6
-(l)y	91

M

make	87
many	6
may	32, 35
-ment	92
might	32
mis-	90
mixed conditionals	69
modal verbs	31–35
ability	31
possibility	31
degrees of certainty	32
speculation	32
obligation	33
necessity	33
advice	34
recommendations	34
criticism	34
permission	35
requests	35
offers	35
suggestions	35

Index

moreover	57
much	6
much + comparative	14
must	32–34
mustn't	33

N

nature	89
need	33
negative questions	37, 40
neither (*of*)	7
neither ... nor	57
neither	39
nervous	89
-ness	92
never	12, 20
next to	79
nobody	5
no one	5
no	5
non-defining relative clauses	53
none	5
nor	39
not nearly as ... as	14
nothing	5
noun + preposition	85
noun clauses	50–51
nouns	2–4, 85, 92

O

object pronouns	8
object questions	37
object	36
on the contrary	61
on the one hand	58
on top of	79
on	80–81
once	60
one another	8
one	8
opposite	79
or else	68
or rather	61
or	56
-or	92
otherwise	68
ought to	34
out of	79
outside	79
over	79
over-	90
owing to	59

P

participle clauses	55, 62–64
passive infinitive	45
passive *-ing* form	45
passive voice	73–75
past continuous	24
past participle adjectives	93
past participle clauses	55, 64
past perfect continuous	25
past perfect simple	25
past simple	20–25
past	79–80
perfect infinitive	45
perfect *-ing* form	45
perfect passive infinitive	45
perfect passive *-ing* form	45
phrasal verbs	86
plenty	5
plural nouns	4
position and order of adjectives	10
position and order of adverbs	12
position of words in a sentence	36
possessive *'s*	9
possessive *of*	9
possessives	9
prefixes	90
prepositional phrases	55, 82
with *at*	82
with *by*	82
with *for*	82
with *from*	82
with *in*	82
with *on*	82
with *out of*	82
with *to*	82
with *under*	82
prepositional-phrasal verbs	86
prepositions of movement	79
prepositions of place	79
prepositions of time	80
present continuous	18, 27
present participle adjectives	93
present participle clauses	55, 62–63
present perfect continuous	23
present perfect	20–23
present simple	18, 27
pronouns	8
subject pronouns	8
object pronouns	8
reflexive pronouns	8
one	8
each other	8
one another	8
proper nouns	2
provided (*that*)	68
providing (*that*)	68

Q

quantifiers	6
question forms	37
question tags	38
quite	16

R

rather	16
re-	90
really	16
recently	12, 21
reduced relative clauses	55
reflexive pronouns	8
relative clauses	52–55
defining relative clauses	52
non-defining relative clauses	53
coordinating relative clauses	54
reduced relative clauses	55
reply questions	38
reported commands	48
reported questions	48
reported requests	48
reported speech	46–49
reported statements	46–47
reported commands	48
reported questions	48
reported requests	48
reporting verbs	49
reported statements	46–47
reporting verbs	49

S

second	57
second conditional	66
secondly	57
sentence adverbs	17
sentence types	36

207

Index

several	6
shall	27, 35
-ship	92
should	34
similar to	14
since	22, 59, 80
singular nouns	4
slightly + comparative	14
so ... that	15
so as to	59
so long as	68
so that	59
so	39–40, 59
some	5
somebody	5
someone	5
something	5
state verbs	19
sub-	90
subject pronouns	8
subject questions	37
subject	36
subordinating conjunctions	56, 58–60
such ... that	59
such	40
suffixes	91–92
suppose (*that*)	68
supposing (*that*)	68

T

take	87
-th	92
that clause	50
that	50–53
the same as	14
the	1
there is	77
therefore	56, 59
third	57
third conditional	67
thirdly	57
though	56, 58
through	80
till	60, 80
time clauses	60
time expressions with future forms	27, 28
time expressions with past perfect simple	25
time expressions with past simple	24
time expressions with present continuous	18
time expressions with present perfect	20–22
time expressions with present simple	18
to-infinitive	41–43, 45, 50–51, 59
too many	6
too much	6
too	15, 39, 57
travel	89
trip	89

U

un-	90
uncountable nouns	3
under	79
under-	90
underneath	79
unless	56, 68
until	27, 60, 63–64, 80
used to	26

V

verb + preposition	84
very	15–16

W

way	89
well	61
what if	68
what	40, 78
what's ... like?	88
whatever	40
wh- clause	50–51
when	24, 27, 52–53, 60, 63–65
where	52–53
whereas	58
whether	48, 51
which	52–54
while	24, 58, 60
who	52–53
whole (*of*)	7
whom	52–53
whose	52–53
wh- questions	37
why	52
will	27–28, 35
with	81
word order	36, 72
would like	41
would love	41
would prefer	41
would rather	41, 71
would	26, 35

Y

-y	92
yes/no questions	37
yet	21

Z

zero article	1
zero conditional	65

Answer key

Unit 1
1a
1 a, a, the 2 the, the 3 a, a 4 the, the, the 5 a, a, The, the 6 a, the, the 7 the, a, an 8 the, the
1b
1 – 2 – 3 the 4 the 5 – 6 – 7 the 8 the 9 – 10 the 11 – 12 the 13 –
1c
1 The 2 a 3 A 4 the 5 –

Unit 2
2
1 It's open to visitors daily in the summer, from August to September.
2 I took the train to London and then the underground/Underground to Victoria Station. It's a short walk from there.
3 Fortunately, I speak German so I was able to join a group of tourists from Germany, who were being shown round by a guide.
4 Have you met my sister Jane? She's studying at the University of Manchester.
5 She's coming home for Christmas and then she's returning to Manchester for New Year's Eve.
6 Would you like to come with us to see *Titanic* at the Odeon Cinema on Wednesday?
7 Did you hear about Grace's promotion? She's taken over as head of the European division of the company.
8 That's great news! Does this mean she'll be moving to Paris before the autumn?

Unit 3
3a
1 a glass, a cloth 2 a university education, experience 3 cloth 4 a noise, an experience 5 a room 6 glass
3b
1 work 2 an appointment 3 a time 4 valuable advice 5 progress 6 up-to-date equipment 7 swimming 8 classes 9 exercise 10 information

Unit 4
4a
1 men, women, children 2 opportunities 3 series 4 leaves 5 glasses, knives, forks 6 armies 7 species 8 people, arms
4b
1 phenomena 2 are 3 conditions 4 have 5 are 6 resources 7 a 8 crisis
4c
1 is 2 are 3 are 4 have 5 have 6 are

Unit 5
5a
1 somebody/someone, anybody/anyone 2 no 3 anything 4 nothing 5 some 6 anybody/anyone 7 nobody/no one 8 any
5b
1 any 2 nothing 3 none 4 nothing 5 some 6 some 7 None 8 anything 9 anybody/anyone 10 somebody/someone 11 no 12 any
5c
1 None of, no 2 any, None 3 any/some, none 4 enough, plenty/some 5 any of, some of 6 enough/any, Plenty, some

Unit 6
6a
1 little, a few, much 2 a few, a little 3 much, How much 4 many, many of 5 too much, too few 6 a great deal of, many 7 how many, A few 8 several of
6b
1 a little 2 little 3 a few 4 little 5 few 6 a little 7 a few 8 few
6c
1 of 2 – 3 of, of 4 of 5 of 6 – 7 of 8 –
6d
1 deal 2 many 3 Some 4 great 5 few 6 little 7 few

Unit 7
7a
1 every 2 Each 3 both, both 4 a tenth of 5 all of 6 whole
7b
1 is 2 Does (every child) get, gets 3 is, reports 4 is, is 5 Are
7c
1 neither 2 either 3 both 4 each 5 every 6 whole 7 both 8 all 9 Every 10 each 11 whole 12 every

Unit 8
8a
1 yourselves, ourselves 2 one 3 themselves, it, them 4 one another 5 I, me 6 They, oneself 7 itself 8 one another 9 himself 10 yourself/yourselves 11 herself 12 ones, me
8b
1 yourself 2 you 3 you 4 yourself 5 you 6 they 7 them 8 They 9 oneself 10 one 11 oneself 12 themselves 13 they 14 one

Unit 9
9a
1 the first chapter of the book 2 Jane and Mark's, Nathan and Alison's, friends of my parents' 3 the key of the front door 4 the dentist's 5 the university's policy on handing in late assignments
9b
1 audience's reaction 2 parents' wedding anniversary 3 women's changing room 4 friend's cottage 5 Next year's sales figures, this year's 6 James'/James's daughter 7 boys' teacher 8 city's problems of crime and unemployment 9 two weeks' holiday, a week's time 10 dog's tail

209

Answer key

9c
1 daughter's friends, children's party   2 kitchen window
3 centre of the city   4 top of the page   5 table leg   6 computer screen

Check 1
1
1 C   2 A   3 C   4 B   5 A   6 D   7 B   8 D   9 B   10 A   11 C   12 D
2
13 The, the   14 –, –, –, –   15 A, an, a   16 a   17 The   18 –   19 –
3
20 Is Thailand a Buddhist country?
21 What do you think of the President of France?
22 I'd love to buy (some) new furniture for my home.
23 He felt like a king when he won first prize!
24 Are the binoculars yours?
25 Physics is my worst subject.
26 Have you ever watched a game of American football?
4
27 plenty/enough   28 anything(/what)   29 any   30 himself
31 everyone/everybody   32 all   33 Each
5
34 an hour's wait   35 the history of Turkey   36 three weeks' holiday   37 belongings   38 the girls' mothers   39 dress themselves   40 Helmut and Trudy's

Unit 10
10a
1 Alice's hair is beginning to turn grey.
2 That beef stew smells delicious.
3 I'll meet you outside the main entrance.
4 Eric and Mary have an indoor swimming pool.
5 The neighbours' party kept me awake all night.
6 Mark looks upset about something.
7 They gave me a gorgeous round silver-plated photograph frame.
8 Mia bought a beautiful old Chinese carpet.
9 Samuel is a well-respected and wealthy/wealthy and well-respected businessman.
10 Julie wore a pink and brown/brown and pink silk dress.

10b
1 charming whitewashed stone   2 small Greek   3 lovely and warm/warm and lovely   4 traditional outdoor   5 round wooden   6 clean white linen   7 amazing antique Chinese
8 black and gold/gold and black wooden   9 restful and enjoyable/enjoyable and restful

Unit 11
11a
1 well   2 truthfully   3 political   4 easily   5 lonely   6 in a lively way   7 late   8 hard, hardly
11b
1 sincerely   2 noisily   3 economically   4 sensibly   5 nationally
6 foolishly   7 in a friendly way   8 fast
11c
1 free   2 lately, high   3 freely   4 highly   5 wide, late

11d
1 mistakenly   2 eventually   3 widely   4 sadly   5 politely
6 Luckily   7 hard   8 stubbornly   9 fast   10 confidently

Unit 12
12a
1 Ross ran quickly to the bus stop.
2 I worked hard for months in order to get good exam results.
3 The children played happily outside today.
4 I thought you explained your ideas very well in the meeting last week.
5 She slept soundly in the chair all afternoon.

12b
1 As we become busier at home and at work, many of us don't have the time to eat sensibly or exercise as often as we should.
2 Many fashionable diets promise you will see results quickly without working hard to achieve them.
3 However, these diets often involve cutting out certain types of food completely.
4 Many diet pills which advertisers claim have been tested scientifically are either dangerous or ineffective.
5 In fact, the only way to lose weight safely and permanently is to eat less and exercise more.

12c
1 across the fields   2 badly   3 completely   4 for some days
5 slowly   6 often   7 directly   8 suddenly   9 often   10 always

Unit 13
13a
1 best   2 better   3 The worst   4 less polluted   5 less stressful
6 more soundly   7 more interesting   8 less varied   9 safer
10 highest   11 the farthest/furthest   12 most beautiful
13b
1 less   2 the least   3 more   4 fewer   5 more   6 more, the least
7 the most, the fewest   8 more, less
13c
1 more alarming   2 oldest   3 less expensive   4 the most important   5 more efficient   6 better   7 more worrying
8 more effectively   9 better

Unit 14
14a
1 by far the most popular   2 not as expensive as, better
3 nearly as much money as, far happier   4 the same mark as
5 very similar to   6 completely different from   7 less, less
8 The older, the more
14b
1 much more weakly   2 far more   3 much colder   4 largest
5 the coldest   6 a little warmer   7 almost as quickly as   8 by far the best

Unit 15
15a
1 such a, so   2 so, such a   3 such, such a   4 so, so   5 such
15b
1 It wasn't warm/hot enough for us to go swimming.
2 The old lady was too weak to stand up.

210

Answer key

3 They aren't going fast/quickly enough to get there on time.
4 The music is so loud that I can't hear you.
5 The children aren't old enough to travel long distances.

15c
1 very   2 enough   3 such   4 that   5 not   6 enough   7 too
8 too   9 to   10 such   11 that   12 very/so

Unit 16
16a
1 extremely, very   2 really   3 very, really   4 really   5 fairly
6 absolutely   7 extremely   8 absolutely, very   9 really   10 very

16b
1 quite, highly   2 quite   3 absolutely, really   4 utterly
5 entirely   6 completely   7 extremely, very   8 extremely, highly
9 utterly, absolutely   10 highly

16c
1 quite, quite/rather   2 quite, quite/rather   3 quite, rather/quite   4 quite, rather   5 quite/rather, quite

Unit 17
17a
1 The disease was possibly caused by lead poisoning.
2 I certainly didn't expect this to happen.
3 Surely she knew the money was stolen.
4 Obviously, he's very attracted to you. / He's obviously very attracted to you.
5 Clearly, there are no easy answers to the problem. / There are clearly no easy answers to the problem.

17b
1 certainly   2 Personally   3 Anyway   4 definitely   5 By the way
6 luckily   7 Fortunately   8 Naturally

Check 2
1
1a ✓   2a ✓   3b ✓   4b ✓   5a ✓

2
6 My family and I live in a large stone farmhouse.
7 It rarely gets this hot in my country. / In my country it rarely gets this hot.
8 I have always wanted to go to Paris.
9 Our new sofa is green and blue/blue and green.
10 She bought an expensive new digital camera.

3
11 furious   12 hopefully   13 certainly   14 freely
15 economically

4
16 less   17 more   18 bit/little/lot   19 nearly   20 way

5
21 more you study, the better   22 looks/is (very) similar to
23 is too complicated for me   24 isn't as big as   25 is the most imaginative writer   26 so quickly that   27 isn't warm enough
28 fewer mistakes than

6
29 A   30 C   31 B   32 B   33 D   34 B   35 A   36 A   37 D   38 D
39 C   40 C

Unit 18
18a
1 lock   2 plays, isn't playing   3 does Evan come, live
4 begins, ends   5 takes, races, crosses   6 are you doing, 'm waiting, 's running   7 're always leaving, remind   8 are forgetting   9 aren't watching   10 causes

18b
1 are studying   2 are learning   3 remain   4 are gaining
5 offers   6 organises   7 perform   8 go on

18c
1 occupy   2 is destroying   3 live   4 provides   5 is developing
6 is opening up   7 exports   8 is increasing

Unit 19
19a
1 tastes   2 has   3 appears   4 're being   5 're having   6 come
7 's appearing   8 does (an adult African elephant) weigh

19b
1 has   2 is thinking   3 does (he) think   4 see   5 'm seeing
6 includes   7 contains   8 matter   9 are hoping   10 sounds
11 means   12 don't think

Unit 20
20a
1 's had, 's gone   2 have been, was   3 left   4 Have you seen
5 visited   6 've never eaten   7 've tried, talked, put   8 've ever read   9 Have you ever worked, worked, didn't like   10 's ever lost   11 've always dreamed   12 's only been

20b
1 has happened   2 've met   3 met   4 've started
5 encouraged   6 invited   7 started   8 found   9 've always wanted   10 had   11 've ever had

20c
1 has ever done   2 has never flown/hasn't flown   3 have gone
4 is the second time   5 have never/haven't forgotten   6 have been to   7 you have ever told

Unit 21
21a
1 've already met, met   2 hasn't told, told   3 've passed, didn't pass   4 have just arrived, arrived   5 Have you found, found
6 's broken, broke   7 's hurt, hurt   8 've just seen, saw

21b
1 You've just missed him.
2 Have you tasted the chocolates yet? / Have you already tasted the chocolates? / Have you tasted the chocolates already?
3 The film's already started. / The film's started already.
4 They haven't repaired the washing machine yet.
5 Have you finished your homework yet?
6 I've just heard the news.
7 I've already had three cups. / I've had three cups already.
8 Have you seen her recently?

21c
1 've been   2 went   3 's offered   4 've looked   5 've filled in
6 've already seen   7 've just bought   8 stood   9 've given
10 took   11 has already improved   12 's just come   13 ordered

211

Answer key

Unit 22

22a
1 have you been married   2 since they (last) saw their parents
3 haven't slept for two days   4 he's felt more relaxed   5 since
Vanessa (last) went to/was at the cinema   6 worked as a
waiter for a month   7 haven't visited their grandparents for
many years   8 did Belinda and Roderick get married   9 's
known them since she was a child   10 haven't been paid for
two months

22b
1 Have you talked, didn't come/hasn't come, 's been
2 increased/have increased   3 were you, waited, was   4 Did
the package arrive, didn't arrive/hasn't arrived   5 haven't seen

22c
1 've kept   2 haven't seen   3 phoned   4 suggested   5 caught
6 've been   7 introduced   8 have caught   9 (have) collected
10 has dropped

Unit 23

23a
1 've e-mailed, hasn't answered   2 've been expecting   3 Have
you finished, 've been working   4 's been looking   5 's been
learning, 's started   6 've been watching, 've seen   7 's moved
8 've been asking, 've asked

23b
1 've been running   2 have you run   3 's happened   4 've just
passed   5 've been practising   6 's been giving   7 have you
been   8 haven't been feeling/haven't felt   9 Have you been
working   10 's done   11 've been trying   12 've only managed

23c
1 has (also) made/has (also) been making   2 has been
sticking   3 has been doing   4 has (also) been watching   5 has
been avoiding   6 (has been) eating   7 has lost   8 have paid
off   9 have ordered   10 have invited

Check 3

1
1 's being   2 do you think   3 're having   4 's just come
5 haven't seen   6 's already sold   7 have you known   8 was
9 've been trying, haven't returned   10 've been reading,
haven't finished   11 's been painting   12 haven't started

2
13 has survived   14 warned   15 has dominated   16 are putting
up   17 are ruining   18 visited   19 doesn't appear   20 include

3
21 has risen   22 turn   23 are   24 are offering   25 usually
combine   26 is becoming   27 disagree   28 have been using
29 claim   30 haven't seen   31 are also gaining
32 Have you ever tried

4
33 did you move   34 have been cooking for   35 since I (last)
saw   36 has already paid back   37 has just told   38 have been
working since   39 they have ever been   40 have you known

Unit 24

24a
1 were relaxing   2 was reading   3 was dozing   4 were looking
5 arrived   6 looked   7 went   8 thought   9 met   10 were living
11 was renting   12 was staying   13 had   14 was waiting
15 was washing   16 got on   17 were planning   18 was   19 was
sitting   20 went off   21 looked   22 saw   23 were racing
24 were running   25 was turning   26 forced   27 told

24b
1 told   2 was sleeping   3 heard   4 opened   5 heard   6 was
rolling   7 expected/was expecting   8 ran/was running   9 was
swinging   10 annoyed/was annoying   11 got up   12 closed
13 found   14 went

Unit 25

25a
1 'd been, heard   2 'd done   3 was, 'd already appeared   4 had
just started, arrived   5 had never left   6 had already left

25b
1 had, 'd been decorating   2 'd been driving, decided   3 hadn't
been living, began   4 Had you been waiting, arrived   5 'd been
saving, didn't have   6 'd been expecting, pulled

25c
1 found   2 left   3 sailed   4 left/had left   5 wore   6 had already
met   7 heard   8 had sunk   9 decided   10 needed
11 persuaded   12 went   13 didn't find   14 turned

25d
1 had just sold   2 began   3 captured   4 had been chasing
5 had found   6 had been looking   7 decided   8 sailed
9 drove   10 struck   11 sank   12 swam   13 had been travelling
14 had decided   15 had been waiting   16 went

Unit 26

26a
1 used to   2 would   3 would   4 didn't use to   5 Did (you) use
to, used to

26b
1 used to   2 'm/'ve got used to   3 'm/'ve got used to   4 used
to   5 wasn't used to   6 'm/'ve got used to

26c
1 used to/would stop   2 used to/would complete   3 used
to/would rush   4 weren't used to walking   5 used to/would
spend   6 used to/would go   7 used to/would light   8 used to
have   9 used to be   10 used to have

Check 4

1
1 would often   2 started   3 used to   4 took   5 weren't used to
living   6 had been driving   7 did you use to   8 used to argue

2
9 phoned   10 didn't answer   11 were you doing   12 heard
13 was having   14 did you want   15 was clearing   16 found

3
17 had rained/had been raining   18 smelled   19 had gone
20 had arrived   21 had talked/had been talking   22 had only
been

212

Answer key

4
23 was walking 24 slipped 25 broke 26 became 27 had been carrying 28 rescued 29 appeared 30 had dropped 31 had also lost 32 treated 33 had been missing 34 recovered

5
35 used to hate 36 'm/'ve got used to 37 get used to 38 used to hold 39 never used to go 40 used to spend

Unit 27

27a
1 's going to visit 2 'll phone 3 will be 4 's going to be 5 're going to see 6 'll join 7 'll pick 8 are you going to see 9 're going to see 10 'll probably go 11 'll see

27b
1 'm meeting 2 are you going 3 Are you coming 4 'm taking 5 'm going to ask 6 's going to crash 7 's going to need 8 'm playing 9 's going to rain

27c
1 arrive 2 're going/go 3 're having/have 4 are going 5 don't want 6 're meeting 7 're taking 8 starts 9 finishes 10 leaves

27d
1 Shall we invite 2 will look, won't feel 3 're going to cry 4 're leaving, aren't coming 5 'm not going to do, leaves 6 's going to travel, finishes 7 will address 8 're going to change, will start, 'll be

Unit 28

28a
1 'll phone 2 Will you be 3 'll be doing 4 'll have 5 'll be earning 6 'll probably be working 7 'll give 8 'll be playing 9 'll be

28b
1 Scientists will have discovered life on other planets.
2 The Earth's climate will have become much hotter than it is today.
3 We won't be using fossil fuels like coal and oil.
4 Doctors won't have found a cure for the common cold.
5 People will have been living on the moon for several years by then.
6 The Internet will have replaced television as our main source of entertainment.

28c
1 will have become 2 will live/will be living 3 will undoubtedly have found 4 will have 5 will also have invented 6 will help 7 Will there be 8 will be living 9 will look 10 will have taken

Unit 29

29a
1 doesn't intend to spend 2 are about to announce 3 on the point of announcing 4 hopes to travel 5 doesn't plan to write 6 are not to begin 7 are about to stop 8 is due to have

29b
1 hopes/'s hoping to have 2 're about to make 3 isn't due to arrive 4 'm on the point of calling 5 do (you) intend/are (you) intending to pay 6 's due to open 7 intends to finish 8 hope/'m hoping to find 9 don't plan/'m not planning to go

Unit 30

30a
1 was due to 2 was going to cry 3 was getting 4 was to 5 were going to 6 was going to 7 was about to 8 was going to buy 9 would 10 was about to

30b
1 was taking 2 was due to arrive 3 were going 4 was about to pull away 5 'd be/were going to be 6 were just about to check in 7 wasn't leaving/wasn't going to leave 8 was planning/planned

Check 5

1
1 'm going 2 'm going to tell 3 're going to faint 4 aren't doing, 'll stay 5 Will you help

2
6 was due 7 was going to move 8 intends 9 are 10 would write

3
11 were about to leave 12 on the point of leaving 13 is due to finish 14 are not to write 15 do they plan to get 16 was meeting 17 was going to ring 18 would see

4
19 will 20 plans to use 21 are to build 22 will be 23 is 24 will produce 25 will begin 26 will have completed 27 will be supplying 28 were hoping 29 will have to 30 will have

5
31 'll have finished 32 'll be taking 33 'll be leaving 34 leaves 35 will have gone 36 Shall I bring 37 Will you have eaten 38 'll be having 39 'll have been working 40 won't feel

Unit 31

31a
1 could, was able to 2 could have died 3 can 4 was able to get 5 couldn't, wasn't able to 6 managed to 7 being able to 8 Can you, Will you be able to 9 eventually succeeded in 10 've been able to 11 can 12 will be able to

31b
1 is unable to see 2 will be able to understand 3 can be bad-tempered 4 succeeded in persuading 5 was able to get 6 could have left

Unit 32

32a
1 might 2 can't 3 may not 4 could 5 might not 6 must 7 could 8 have to

32b
1 She must be a nurse.
2 he may/might/could be outside
3 She must have forgotten our appointment.

213

Answer key

4 he couldn't/can't have forgotten about it
5 I think it may/might/could rain this afternoon
6 She might have been feeling tired.
7 Mickey must be going out.
8 That can't/couldn't have been Davina you saw last night.
9 Our neighbours must be going away.
10 Some scientists believe there may/might/could/must/can't be life on other planets.

32c
1 could get   2 might be playing   3 must realise   4 can't be
5 could have been/could be   6 must have cost   7 must have been running

32d
1 might have killed   2 must have collided   3 may have been
4 can't be   5 can't have caused   6 might provide   7 may have caused   8 could have destroyed   9 may not have died out
10 could be

Unit 33
33a
1 have to   2 needn't   3 must   4 Did you have to   5 doesn't need to   6 having to   7 don't have to   8 needn't have worried
9 must have forgotten   10 won't have to   11 didn't need to wait   12 had to

33b
1 don't have to stay   2 had to run   3 must/have to be
4 having to do   5 don't/won't have to work   6 must/have to ring   7 Did you have to wear   8 mustn't be   9 doesn't/didn't/won't have to save   10 's had to see   11 mustn't forget   12 did they have to leave

33c
1 have got to make   2 don't need to buy/needn't buy   3 didn't have to be   4 must not park   5 needn't have spent   6 has had to cancel   7 she need to book

33d
1 must   2 must   3 had to/needed to   4 have to/need to
5 mustn't   6 must   7 had to/needed to   8 didn't have to/didn't need to   9 had to/needed to   10 needn't have   11 don't have to/don't need to

Unit 34
34a
1 ought to have/should have called   2 ✓   3 'd better not go
4 ✓   5 should have called   6 should/ought to have been
7 'd better ask   8 ✓

34b
1 must come   2 shouldn't be having   3 shouldn't have told
4 must try   5 should have been working   6 shouldn't have bought   7 mustn't speak   8 should dye, should (I) leave
9 must visit   10 should be training

34c
1 (You) mustn't sunbathe more than once a day.
2 (You) shouldn't have more than ten tanning sessions in two weeks.
3 (You) must wear protective goggles and keep your eyes closed if you use a sun bed.
4 (You) must use a sun cream that protects you against ultraviolet rays.

5 (You) should use skincare products after tanning as well.
6 (You) must check with your doctor that it is safe to tan if you are taking medication.

Unit 35
35a
1 Shall   2 Would   3 Will   4 Let   5 Could   6 May
1 c   2 e   3 g   4 f   5 d   6 a

35b
1 Shall I take   2 would you like   3 would you mind taking off
4 is allowed to smoke   5 couldn't keep   6 May I park   7 Can I get   8 Can I have   9 How about going

Check 6
1
1 ought   2 should have said   3 could   4 could/may/might
5 should

2
6 Why   7 Shall   8 can/may   9 was   10 better   11 mind
12 having   13 being

3
14 don't need to bring/needn't bring   15 mustn't park
16 didn't need to introduce   17 don't need to get up/needn't get up   18 must see   19 needn't have done   20 mustn't forget

4
21 could   22 able   23 been   24 were   25 to   26 must
27 have   28 could/may/might   29 have   30 Could   31 could/might/may   32 can

5
33 can be cold   34 to be able to speak   35 could have gone
36 succeeded in opening   37 think I should call
38 didn't have to work   39 you like me to make   40 about going somewhere different

Unit 36
36a
1 complement   2 adverbial phrase   3 indirect object   4 direct object   5 direct object   6 adverbial phrase   7 complement
8 complement

36b
1 Although they disliked one another at first/Although at first they disliked one another, they soon started to work together.
2 Page and Brin started the Google business in a friend's garage in 1998. / In 1998 Page and Brin started the Google business in a friend's garage.
3 They had been working on a search engine called 'Backrub' since 1996. / Since 1996 they had been working on a search engine called 'Backrub'.
4 When Page and Brin started to work together, they weren't interested in making money.
5 They wanted to share their ideas with the world.
6 Millions of people use Google today/Today millions of people use Google and the company is worth several billion dollars.

Answer key

Unit 37
37a
1 Should he fix the car this weekend?
2 Has she looked everywhere for her keys?
3 Does Conrad want to borrow this book?
4 Had they given the money to Vince?
5 Were you watching a play last night?
6 Will she have finished the book by then?

37b
1 What colour is the new carpet?
2 What/What subject/Which subject did you enjoy most?
3 How often/How many times a week do they play?
4 How many eggs did he buy?
5 Who met Keith at the cinema?
6 Who did Eva meet at the cinema?
7 Whose electric guitar did you borrow?
8 What did Paul leave on the sofa?

37c
1 Who hasn't got one?
2 Why didn't you get ready sooner?
3 Haven't you got anything better to do?
4 Why don't you put it here?
5 Didn't the garage do a great job?

Unit 38
38a
1 aren't I   2 have we   3 shall we   4 will you   5 didn't she
6 aren't they   7 do you   8 didn't it

38b
1 Won't there?   2 Did I?   3 Couldn't you?   4 Isn't he?   5 Does she?   6 Have they?   7 Aren't there?   8 Can you?

38c
1 haven't   2 Did   3 didn't   4 shall   5 Have   6 have   7 will
8 can

Unit 39
39a
1 So   2 not   3 Neither/Nor   4 so   5 do   6 does
7 think/believe   8 either   9 have

39b
1 Neither have I.   2 So am I.   3 I did too.   4 Nor do I.   5 So am I.   6 Neither do I.   7 I couldn't either.   8 I will too.

39c
1 I'm going to ~~have lunch~~   2 we should ~~stop somewhere for something to eat~~   3 I will ~~sit down~~   4 she did ~~pick me up at six~~   5 I did ~~pay for them~~   6 Will you ~~be attending the conference~~

Unit 40
40a
1 How   2 That   3 Lucky you   4 What   5 Why on earth   6 Didn't
7 However   8 Do

40b
1 (How) strange (the birds are!)
2 (They) have such rude children!
3 (What) difficult poems (she writes!)
4 (She's) such a beautiful (woman!)
5 (The problem) is so complicated!

Check 7
1
1 Although the meal didn't look very good, it was quite tasty.
2 Why didn't you call me as soon as you arrived at the hotel?
3 Have you been waiting here for a long time?
4 Sylvia is leaving next month and so am I.
5 Lance left his briefcase on the bus yesterday. / Yesterday Lance left his briefcase on the bus.

2
6 Haven't you?   7 the letter to her   8 Don't you   9 Will you?
10 such an

3
11 What   12 neither/nor   13 so   14 such   15 her   16 could
17 will   18 do   19 shall   20 Do

Unit 41
41a
1 to offend   2 smoking   3 having   4 writing   5 to learn
6 helping   7 to study   8 travelling   9 getting   10 to accept

41b
1 to tell   2 telling   3 having   4 to have   5 to concentrate
6 drinking   7 acting   8 to act   9 to close   10 closing

Unit 42
42a
1 helped   2 stay   3 allow   4 made   5 allows   6 forced
7 expects   8 going

42b
1 Police are advising motorists to avoid that section of the motorway.
2 Rescue services are helping injured people to get to hospital.
3 Police are anxious to stop people panicking.
4 Police are encouraging people to call a special number for more information.
5 Police are preventing motorists (from) approaching the scene of the accident.

42c
1 making/make   2 feeling/to feel   3 taking   4 beginning/begin   5 moving/move   6 to leave   7 rolling/roll   8 drinking/to drink   9 continue   10 watching/watch   11 staring
12 drinking   13 to pour   14 to be

Unit 43
43a
1 to keep   2 to be   3 to travel   4 to understand   5 to be   6 to work   7 to spend   8 to stay   9 to look   10 to leave   11 to love
12 to agree

43b
1 (He)'s keen to move to Italy next year.
2 (It's) rude to interrupt people all the time.
3 (Her) intention is to start up her own business.
4 (It's) my ambition to take part in the Olympic Games one day.
5 (He bought) a DVD to watch this evening.
6 (I was) the only person to disagree with him.

215

Answer key

43c
1 easy to work   2 complicated to work out   3 important (for me) to get   4 great to have   5 aim (is) to save   6 time to apply   7 someone to replace   8 place to stay   9 welcome to share   10 sure to be

43d
1 to receive your letter   2 to heat this house   3 to have interests outside work   4 very quick to learn   5 to cook this fish   6 to see him

Unit 44
44a
1 working, sitting   2 measuring   3 feeling   4 eating   5 giving   6 finding   7 being   8 arguing, getting   9 shopping   10 doing

44b
1 was worth paying   2 couldn't face the thought of it getting   3 'm busy taking   4 moving   5 go swimming   6 trouble studying   7 a waste of time asking   8 's always great to hear/hearing

Unit 45
45a
1 to show   2 being asked   3 to be relaxing   4 being annoyed   5 to be asked

45b
1 being told   2 saying/having said   3 being/having been looked after   4 to go   5 to be given   6 to have lost   7 to be getting

Check 8
1
1 crying   2 to do   3 living   4 to carry   5 to close
2
6 for   7 go   8 to   9 in   10 waste   11 allow   12 bear/face/stand   13 help
3
14 to improve   15 studying   16 following   17 to turn   18 finding   19 to give   20 to live
4
21 to be   22 allowed me to use   23 taking   24 to get   25 to get   26 doing   27 working   28 to become   29 to have   30 to do   31 training   32 sitting
5
33 to be offered   34 being asked to do   35 to have left   36 to be studying   37 having lied   38 surprised to hear   39 attempts to sail   40 somewhere to have

Unit 46
46a
1 couldn't   2 was   3 would   4 hadn't   5 said   6 told   7 that   8 had to   9 had to   10 hadn't

46b (Suggested answers)
1 Derek said (that) I/we could leave my/our things in the wardrobe if I/we liked.
2 'We/They're leaving tomorrow,' said Beth.
3 Bea told Ted (that) it wasn't far from there to her office.
4 'I saw the bank robbery this morning,' Evan told the police officer.
5 Hannah said (that) we/they had to be patient.
6 Nanette told Ian (that) she'd been to the restaurant once before.
7 'I didn't like the film but I enjoyed the book,' Miguel told Gloria.
8 Eva said (that) she might have left her bag on the bus that morning.
9 'We/You ought to get some flowers for Penny's birthday,' said Alan.
10 Lydia told her mother (that) she wouldn't be gone long.

Unit 47
47a
1 (Joan said that) when the project started, there had been/was a lot of interest in it.
2 (Josh said that) he'd been living in France when he met Nora.
3 (Ali tells me that) it's pouring with rain there.
4 (Natalie said that) she'd been hoping to meet me for lunch but her car had broken down/broke down.
5 (Maria told me that) the taxi had already arrived when she rang me.

47b
1 spent   2 had wanted   3 had learnt   4 had gone   5 had loved   6 had taken up   7 has done   8 moves/moved   9 won't/wouldn't be going   10 is/was planning   11 wants/wanted

Unit 48
48a
1 (She asked her husband) to see who was at the door.
2 (He asked them) not to make so much noise.
3 (She told me) to e-mail her if I needed any help.
4 (Janet wanted to know) how many people were coming that night.
5 (Daryl asked them) if/whether they'd enjoyed themselves at the concert.
6 (The doctor enquired) if/whether I'd been eating properly.
7 (Logan asked them) why they hadn't gone to the meeting.
8 (Brenda asked me) to check the information for her.
9 (Hasan asked us) if/whether we'd be travelling far.
10 (Martin told Joanna) not to leave her bag on the floor.

48b
1 if/whether there were   2 how we could make   3 to be   4 not to use   5 how formal we should be/how formal to be   6 if/whether people sent   7 not to use   8 why companies monitored

Unit 49
49a
1 (Her tutor advised) her to finish her degree first.
2 (Her mother begged) her to think carefully before she took such a big step.
3 (Her father warned) her that she'd never find a good job if she dropped out.
4 (He threatened) to stop/that he'd stop paying her rent if she left university.

Answer key

5 (Her best friend offered) to let her stay at her flat until she found a place to live.
6 (Her sister suggested) that she should ask her tutor for advice.
7 (Her grandmother promised) to buy/that she'd buy her a car when she graduated.

49b
1 He refused to discuss the problem with me.
2 She complained about not being invited to the meeting. / She complained that she hadn't been invited to the meeting.
3 The police officer warned me/us not to do it again or they'd fine me/us.
4 She accused me/us of reading her e-mails.
5 He reminded me to apply for a new passport. / He reminded me that I had to apply for a new passport.
6 She apologised for the trouble she'd caused.
7 The doctor advised me to stay home for a few days.

Check 9

1
1 couldn't 2 said 3 'd 4 're having 5 there 6 'd gone
7 asked 8 you hadn't called 9 her 10 's feeling

2
11 (Malcolm said that) he'd been watching television when they arrived.
12 (Amy says that) she'll be there/here in an hour.
13 (Ulrich said that) Niels hadn't left when he rang an hour ago.
14 (Astrid asked me) where I'd left the newspaper.
15 (Leslie asked me) not to say anything to Beatrice.
16 (Jack wondered) if/whether he should ask Sophie out for a meal.
17 (Milos asked) if/whether we/they had to stay there all evening.
18 (Dieter asked Eve) if/whether she was going out that evening.
19 (Sian says that) she's been living in Cardiff for ten years.
20 (Rodney told Winnie) that he'd love her for ever.

3
21 advised me to rest 22 reminded him to book 23 not to go
24 invited me to have 25 congratulated me on passing
26 asked her son to clear 27 told the man not to 28 admitted taking/that he had taken

4
29 B 30 C 31 D 32 A 33 C 34 A 35 B 36 C 37 D 38 D 39 A 40 D

Unit 50
50a
1 how 2 if/whether 3 were 4 would 5 that 6 why 7 what 8 that

50b
1 I couldn't believe that he expected us to work on Sunday!
2 Have you forgotten that Anja's coming round tonight?
3 I'm hoping that the car will be fixed by Friday.
4 I used to think that football is/was boring.
5 Do you realise that you're an hour late?
6 I suppose that it's too late to apply for the job.
7 I understood that the treatment may/might not work.
8 I suddenly remembered that it's/it was my father's birthday on Sunday.

50c
1 where I left my bag 2 if/whether he's left his contact details
3 if/whether we'll get there on time 4 why you don't listen to me 5 when she arrived 6 what time the class starts
7 if/whether he'll recognise us after all these years 8 how many people turned up

50d
1 how to send 2 how to complete 3 where to catch 4 how to assemble 5 where to put

Unit 51
51a
1 We should be grateful (that) she hasn't made a complaint.
2 She seems very angry (that) he didn't tell her the truth.
3 She promised (that) she'd/she'll write to us.
4 I'm sure (that) he's lying to you.
5 I don't like the thought that we might not get a pay rise.
6 My problem is (that) I don't know where to go on holiday.
7 It was my understanding that we were going to meet outside the club.
8 They're concerned (that) they won't have enough money to pay their bills this month.

51b
1 That you're not happy about the decision is clear.
2 The idea that all people are equal is important in many societies.
3 Whether you give me the information now or later is not important.
4 The result gave me hope that our team could win the championship.
5 I'm surprised that no one was there to meet us.
6 I have a promise that the job will be mine if I apply for it.
7 That I didn't pass all of my exams is disappointing.
8 That we didn't notice anything was not surprising in the circumstances.

51c
1 worried (that) she's ill 2 a possibility that the letter got lost
3 doubtful if/whether they'll offer 4 whether or not he'll be
5 the theory that there's life 6 her ambition is to become

51d
1 or not they broke 2 he lied about his whereabouts 3 to cancel the event is 4 whether to accept/I should accept
5 thought that I made 6 my belief that we will 7 he has emotional problems is 8 not certain how to solve

Check 10

1
1 (I don't know) if/whether she's passed her exams.
2 (Have you forgotten) (that) Tursun's coming round this evening?
3 (Do you know) how Hannah is?

217

Answer key

4 (I don't know) how many people are coming to the meeting.
5 (She still) holds on to the belief that he isn't dead.
6 (The suggestion) that she lied to you is ridiculous.

2
7 whether   8 that   9 if/whether   10 that   11 how   12 sure/certain/confident

3
13 don't understand what   14 how to solve   15 taught him how to write   16 whether or not   17 thought that we   18 the accident happened is not   19 surprise that they are getting   20 doubtful if/whether he will accept

Unit 52

52a
1 which/that   2 which/that   3 whom   4 whose   5 which/that   6 which/that   7 which/that   8 where

52b
1 The family who/that live next door moved here from Ireland.
2 The woman whose job I'm doing is coming back to work soon.
3 This is the job I've always wanted.
4 It was during my first year of university when/that I first met Bernard.
5 The hotel which/that overlooks the sea is the most expensive in the area.
6 That's the house where we lived when we were university students.

Unit 53

53a
1 Their e-mail, which I received yesterday, says they'll be staying for a week.
2 My fiancé, who/whom they haven't met, is looking forward to their visit.
3 Naturally, my parents want to meet my fiancé, whose parents want to meet mine.
4 My mother is also planning to visit Scotland, where she was born.
5 She wants to go in August, when the heather blooms.

53b
1 when   2 who   3 which   4 which   5 who/whom   6 when   7 where

53c
1 Pablo Picasso, whose paintings are some of the most famous in the world, suffered from dyslexia.
2 William Shakespeare, who wrote about thirty-seven plays, is considered to be one of the greatest playwrights of all time.
3 Muhammed Ali won the world heavyweight boxing title in 1964, when he defeated Sonny Liston.
4 In the 1980s Brad Pitt moved to Los Angeles, where he took acting classes and worked as a chauffeur.
5 Cleopatra, who married two of her brothers, is one of the most famous rulers in history.
6 Bill Clinton, whose father died three months before he was born, was the forty-second President of the United States.
7 Although he was born in Bonn, Ludwig van Beethoven moved to Vienna in 1792, where he soon established a reputation as a piano virtuoso.

Unit 54

54
1 My grandmother runs five miles every day, which is impressive for a woman of her age.
2 She's going to take a month off work, which will give her the rest she needs.
3 He spent a lot of money on a car he couldn't afford, which was an expensive mistake.
4 The weather there is very cold at this time of year, which means you should pack lots of warm clothing.
5 She arrived a day earlier than we expected, which was a surprise for everyone.
6 My nephew had to go into hospital suddenly, which was frightening for my sister and her husband.
7 He suddenly got very red in the face, which was a sign that he was getting angry.
8 The children ate too much cake at the party, which made them ill.

Unit 55

55a
1 We have already watered the flowers at the front of the house.
2 Clara is the girl with blond hair and green eyes.
3 Hester brought us some vegetables from her garden.
4 Alan is the tall man in the uniform.
5 We play tennis at the courts opposite the park.
6 Our players are the ones in/with the red and white shirts.

55b
1 The dog took the baby, wrapped in a dirty cloth, and put it next to her puppies.
2 A witness said he heard a baby crying.
3 Another witness said she saw a dog carrying a baby across a road.
4 A homesick Chinese cat given away by its owner walked forty days and a hundred miles to return home.
5 The cat's owner is a woman with a small flat in Beijing.
6 She gave the cat to a friend living in the country.

55c
1 ✓   2 suggesting that there may be water   3 on the planet
4 ✓   5 once thought to be lifeless

Check 11

1
1 who/that   2 which   3 where   4 which/that   5 whose   6 who   7 which   8 when   9 which   10 where

2
11 I discussed the problem with my cousin, who is a lawyer.
12 This is Will, whose sister I've known since we were children.
13 Last year we moved back to the town where I was born.
14 The Richardsons are the people (who/whom/that) we met on holiday last year.
15 The children refused to eat the food (which/that) their mother had prepared.
16 Elli called her brother, who/whom she hadn't spoken to for weeks. / Elli called her brother, to whom she hadn't spoken for weeks.

218

Answer key

17 We walked to the top of the hill, where we had a picnic.
18 Do you know the people who/that live next door?
19 They moved in 1997, when their first child was born.
20 I put my contact details on the Internet, which was a mistake.

3
21 that shows   22 which is not enough   23 which is the recommended average   24 controlling appetite   25 who get less than eight hours a night   26 which we can then access   27 conducted on two groups of people   28 they had seen   29 in which one group slept   30 who had had a good night's sleep   31 who had not slept   32 he or she can help you with

4
33 searching for a diamond necklace   34 believed to have sunk with the famous ship   35 with a photograph of a woman   36 wearing the necklace   37 called Rose Dawson Calvert   38 in the photograph   39 played by Kate Winslett   40 with a lot of money

Unit 56
56
1 so   2 or   3 and   4 Although   5 moreover   6 however   7 Because   8 but

4 Although a Rolls Royce is a beautiful car, it's expensive to maintain.
5 They installed a new security system; moreover, they hired extra guards.
6 We've cut costs and increased production; however, we're still not making a profit.
7 Because he wasn't feeling well, I offered to do the shopping for him.

Unit 57
57a
1 as well/too   2 Also   3 both   4 First/First of all, Next/Then   5 nor   6 as well/too   7 Either, or   8 As well as   9 Also/In addition   10 furthermore/moreover

57b
1 neither   2 nor   3 as   4 First   5 Second/Secondly/Furthermore/Moreover   6 Either   7 or   8 too   9 addition

Unit 58
58a
1 while   2 Whereas   3 Despite   4 and   5 In spite of   6 However   7 On the one hand   8 On the other hand

58b
1 Even though her doctor told her to rest, she went to Spain. / She went to Spain even though her doctor told her to rest.
2 In spite of joining the company only a year ago, she's been promoted already. / She's been promoted already in spite of joining the company only a year ago. / In spite of the fact that she joined the company only a year ago, she's been promoted already. / She's been promoted already in spite of the fact that she joined the company only a year ago.

3 He hasn't got any experience. However, he's keen to learn. / He hasn't got any experience; however, he's keen to learn. / He hasn't got any experience. He's keen to learn, however. / He hasn't got any experience; he's keen to learn, however. / He hasn't got any experience. He is, however, keen to learn. / He hasn't got any experience; he is, however, keen to learn.
4 While I'd like to eat out, I should be saving money.
5 I thought he looked ill but I wasn't completely sure.
6 Despite the rain/Despite the fact that it was raining, we went out for the day. / We went out for the day despite the rain/despite the fact that it was raining.
7 Whereas the government spent money on weapons, it neglected education.

Unit 59
59a
1 therefore   2 so that   3 because   4 as   5 Since/As   6 as a result   7 in order to

59b
1 because of the driver's   2 in order to become   3 in order not to hurt   4 has a test tomorrow so   5 since his health was   6 so that we (can/will) avoid

Unit 60
60a
1 While he's working, she'll be lying on the beach. / She'll be lying on the beach while he's working.
2 Once you tell/'ve told me what really happened, I'll help you. / I'll help you once you tell/'ve told me what really happened.
3 As soon as Jake finishes/'s finished the report he's writing, he'll come over to my place. / Jake will come over to my place as soon as he finishes/'s finished the report he's writing.
4 After Petra and Otto do/have done the washing up, they'll go swimming. / Petra and Otto will go swimming after they do/'ve done the washing up.
5 When I see Helen, I'll give her your regards. / I'll give Helen your regards when I see her.
6 Gareth will keep looking for his wallet until he finds it. / Until he finds his wallet, Gareth will keep looking for it.
7 Before you can get a driving licence, you have to pass a driving test. / You have to pass a driving test before you can get a driving licence.
8 When she adds/'s added some herbs to the dish, it will taste better. / The dish will taste better when she adds/'s added some herbs (to it).

60b
1 start   2 finished/'d finished   3 leave/'ve left   4 chose   5 came   6 gave/'d given   7 look   8 'll see   9 have   10 think   11 get/'ve got

Unit 61
61
1 After all   2 Actually   3 or rather   4 Well   5 In other words   6 On the contrary   7 Well

Answer key

Unit 62

62a
1 While hating the job   2 Having plenty of time to spare
3 Having been out all day   4 Having failed one of my exams
5 Being good friends   6 Being happy with my exam results
7 While/In spite of/Despite wanting them to like me   8 Being scared of spiders

62b
1 Having been wounded, Inman deserts the army.
2 Wanting to return home to the woman he loves, he journeys through the Appalachian Mountains.
3 Facing many dangers, he struggles to stay alive.
4 Looking at war and its effect on people, *Cold Mountain* is a deeply moving novel.
5 Being a powerful love story, it appeals to a wide readership.
6 Having read the book and seen the film, I would strongly recommend either.

Unit 63

63a
1 He set off on his journey carrying only one small bag. / Carrying only one small bag, he set off on his journey.
2 I've changed my job since last writing to you. / Since last writing to you, I've changed my job.
3 Before giving you an answer, I need to discuss the situation with my parents. / I need to discuss the situation with my parents before giving you an answer.
4 Having left school, he worked in a restaurant for a year.
5 Switching on her computer, she started to work.
6 Turning the corner, we saw a huge traffic jam ahead of us.
7 Having bought the painting, he discovered that it was a fake.
8 Having had a big argument, we never saw one another again.

63b (Suggested answers)
1 Throwing back the bedcovers, I rushed downstairs to the kitchen.
2 Having made some coffee, I went back upstairs to have a shower and get dressed.
3 I put on my best suit and tie before noticing that my jacket had a coffee stain down the front.
4 Changing my clothes quickly, I rushed to the station to catch the train.
5 On reaching the train station, I saw my train pulling away from the platform.
6 Reaching for my mobile so that I could ring and say I'd be late for the interview, I noticed that someone had left a message.
7 Reading the message, I laughed out loud with relief.
8 After buying myself some breakfast at the station, I sat down to plan how to get to the interview on time the following day.

Unit 64

64 (Suggested answers)
1 Abandoned by his parents at an early age, Peter took to stealing.
2 Since being promoted, I've had no time to go out.
3 After being released from prison, Richard couldn't find a job anywhere.
4 On being caught, she confessed to the crime.
5 If allowed to do so, I would like to present my side of the argument.
6 Hidden in the cellar, the money wasn't discovered for many years.
7 Unless treated with more respect, he will leave the company.
8 (If) given the opportunity, I know I can make a success of the project.
9 Saddened by the death of her father, Linda needed to spend time alone.
10 Although written many years ago, the book is still relevant today.
11 Before being allowed to enter the building, you will be searched.
12 (Being) scared of the dark, she switched on all the lights.

Check 12

1
1 as soon as   2 until   3 Having finished   4 Since leaving   5 but

2
6 After all   7 anyway   8 Actually   9 Well   10 too

3
11 Although/Though   12 whereas/while   13 First   14 However
15 addition   16 as   17 In   18 neither   19 nor   20 If   21 before
22 so

4
23 however   24 Having failed   25 in order to   26 When
27 Attracted   28 and   29 As a result   30 Inspired   31 also
32 after   33 because of   34 so

5
35 Having nothing better to do, I decided to go into town.
36 Not wanting to disturb anyone, we moved quietly.
37 While wishing I could help you, I can do very little.
38 Being so conscientious, Hal rarely leaves the office early.
39 Hearing a suspicious noise, Bettina called the police.
40 On being admitted to hospital, all patients are examined. / All patients are examined on being admitted to hospital.

Unit 65

65a
1 'll be, doesn't get   2 book, 'll be lying   3 call, need   4 hasn't read, won't hear/won't be hearing   5 eat, break out/'ll break out   6 's been raining, 'm not going to cut/won't be cutting

65b
1 can   2 stand up   3 will   4 If   5 should   6 does   7 feel   8 are   9 try   10 leaning   11 be

Unit 66

66a
1 were   2 thought   3 'd   4 could live   5 were   6 'd buy   7 to ask   8 might win   9 Were   10 wasn't working

Answer key

66b
1 discovered 2 'd keep 3 could borrow 4 'd definitely go
5 could earn/could be earning 6 wanted 7 knew 8 'd try
9 were 10 'd call 11 had 12 wouldn't complain

Unit 67
67a
1 wouldn't have been 2 hadn't seen 3 would probably have died 4 had arrived 5 would have been 6 might have been
7 hadn't had 8 wouldn't have opened 9 might not have survived 10 had injected 11 could have died

67b
1 (We)'d have got there in time if you'd phoned us.
2 (I might) have been able to help you if you'd explained the problem to me.
3 (They might) have understood what she was saying if they'd been listening carefully.
4 (If) he could have phoned her, he could have told her what was happening.
5 (If) you'd come round earlier, you'd have seen him.
6 (If) you hadn't taken me to your friend's party, I wouldn't have met Kazuko.
7 (She might not) have married him if she'd known how selfish he was.
8 (Had) the management agreed to a pay rise, there wouldn't have been a strike.

Unit 68
68
1 Don't consider running a marathon unless you are in good physical condition. / Unless you are in good physical condition, don't consider running a marathon.
2 Don't leave training until just before the marathon in case you injure yourself.
3 Take time off from running every week; otherwise, your body will not have a chance to rest.
4 As long as you train carefully, you can avoid injury. / You can avoid injury as long as you train carefully.
5 Assuming (that) you are sensible, you should run a marathon safely and successfully. / You should run a marathon safely and successfully assuming (that) you are sensible.

Unit 69
69a
1 hadn't died, would be 2 didn't work, wouldn't have been
3 hadn't wasted, could be 4 were, wouldn't have upset
5 wanted, would have moved 6 had worked, wouldn't be
7 wouldn't be doing, had known 8 hadn't been delayed, would be 9 hadn't forgotten, would be boarding 10 had followed, might not be

69b
1 wouldn't have 2 were 3 wouldn't have had 4 'd taken out
5 wouldn't be sitting 6 'd set off 7 'd be 8 'd told 9 'd have set 10 'd begun 11 wouldn't weigh 12 'd (also) be

Unit 70
70a
1 'd started 2 could study 3 hadn't done 4 lived 5 would stop 6 were

70b
1 only he had called 2 I hadn't left 3 you would stop criticising 4 we could afford 5 only we had 6 I had finished

Unit 71
71
1 were 2 didn't go 3 's 4 hadn't said 5 told 6 'd won
7 didn't leave, learnt 8 grew 9 booked 10 went

Check 13
1
1 If 2 If only 3 Unless 4 I hope 5 Assuming that
2
6 D 7 B 8 D 9 D 10 C 11 B 12 D 13 B 14 A 15 C 16 C
17 A
3
18 (Had) the authorities known there was a threat, they would have issued a warning.
19 (If) my car hadn't broken down, I wouldn't have been late for work.
20 (If) it hadn't been raining, the event wouldn't have been cancelled.
21 (If) I'd known you were coming, I'd have met you at the station.
22 (If) the taxi had arrived on time, he wouldn't have missed his flight.
4
23 'd help 24 had 25 wouldn't help 26 didn't want 27 'd worked 28 wouldn't have 29 hadn't agreed 30 had
31 hadn't taken 32 wouldn't have
5
33 wish he had accepted 34 were you, I would keep 35 in case she wants 36 if it doesn't rain 37 time you found
38 would rather we stayed 39 wish I could lose 40 they to offer him

Unit 72
72a
1 (Seldom) have I heard such an inspiring speech.
2 (No sooner) had I started my lunch than a client arrived to see me.
3 (Only) later did her words seem important.
4 (Never) have I been so confused by a lecture (before).
5 (Not once) did she ask me how I felt about the accident.
6 (Under no circumstances) should you sign those papers.
7 (Little) did I know that I would be facing such big changes at work.
8 (Rarely) do my parents argue about anything.

72b
1 Comedies I (do) like. 2 My first car that was. 3 This morning they arrived. 4 Soon it will be dark. 5 But the gist I (do) want.

221

Answer key

Unit 73
73a
1 The windows haven't been cleaned for weeks.
2 He was made redundant a year ago.
3 Her health was being affected by the pressures of work.
4 The fire was put out before it did much damage.
5 If it hadn't rained so much, the job would have been finished on time.
6 Our car is being repaired.
7 He was hit on the head with a heavy instrument.
8 I hope I'll be chosen for the basketball team.

73b
1 can be understood 2 are (usually clearly) defined 3 have been fought 4 is called 5 is/has been/was reared 6 is determined 7 may be divided 8 are allowed

Unit 74
74a
1 they aren't allowed to use the computer after eight
2 it needs to be washed/it needs washing
3 we'll be shown the sights by a local guide when we get there
4 I was made to wait for hours to see a doctor
5 she was seen to leave shortly after her arrival
6 he's also been promised a bonus
7 he was helped to cross the street by a kind passer-by
8 it must be handed out to all employees

74b
1 are/were allowed to borrow 2 were lent a sum 3 were given to people 4 needs to be faced 5 should not be given to people

Unit 75
75a
1 is thought to be living 2 is expected that 3 is said to have left 4 is thought that 5 is believed to have been 6 that the accident was caused

75b
1 (It) is said that the fire is still burning.
  (The fire) is said to be still burning.
2 (It) is thought that the fire started in the kitchen.
  (The fire) is thought to have started in the kitchen.
3 (It) is believed that fifteen people have been taken to hospital (by ambulances).
  (Fifteen people) are believed to have been taken to hospital (by ambulances).
4 (It) is reported that seven people are in a serious condition.
  (Seven people) are reported to be in a serious condition.
5 (It) is believed that the fire was started by a cigarette.
  (The fire) is believed to have been started by a cigarette.
6 (It) is expected that the cause of the blaze will be investigated (by the police).
  (The cause of the blaze) is expected to be investigated (by the police).

Unit 76
76
1 had his nose broken 2 having/getting my shoulders massaged 3 get/have the invitations sent out 4 haven't had it repaired 5 should have had it serviced 6 'll have/get it removed

Unit 77
77a
1 It 2 it 3 There 4 It 5 there 6 there 7 It

77b
1 it will be 2 Is there 3 does/did/will it take, Is/Was it 4 There seems/seemed/appears/appeared 5 It's/It was 6 There are/were, they're/they were

77c
1 (It) isn't easy saying goodbye after all this time.
2 (It)'s important (for us) to be there when he arrives.
3 (It) isn't clear when exactly they'll be sending us the papers to sign.
4 (It)'s amazing that you still remember me.
5 (It) was difficult contacting her by phone so I sent an e-mail.
6 (It) isn't known how they committed the crime.

Unit 78
78a
1 that 2 What 3 is 4 It 5 that 6 was 7 that 8 What 9 was

78b
1 (What) children need is love and affection.
2 (It)'s the way he keeps changing his mind that worries me.
3 (All) (that) I'm asking for is a little respect.
4 (What) I really hate is getting up when it's still dark.
5 (All) (that) I need is a hammer and some nails.
6 (It)'s me (who/that) you should be talking to.
7 (What) we should do is ring someone for help.
8 (It)'s a less stressful life that they want more than anything else.

Check 14
1
1 I was made to wait for hours at the hospital.
2 Rene was helped to finish the report by a/his colleague.
3 I am never allowed to leave work early (by my boss).
4 The police should have been called when the accident happened.
5 He is believed to have lied about the scandal.

2
6 (No) sooner had she left than I realised she had taken my car keys by mistake.
7 (Never) have I felt so confused (before).
8 (Gulay) is thought to be selling the company.
9 (What) disappointed us was the result of the match.
10 (The new plane) is said to be fuel-efficient.
11 (The butler) is believed to have inherited her money.
12 (There) must be someone at the door.
13 (What) we'll do is leave them a note so they don't worry.

Answer key

14 (It) takes twenty hours (for us) to fly to New Zealand.
15 (It) was/is only a few minutes ago that I heard the news report.

3
16 is Franco (who/whom/that) you should   17 (they) need to be cleaned   18 is believed to have made   19 is considered (to be)   20 does Renata eat   21 no circumstances are you to   22 that matters to me is   23 haven't had my teeth

4
24 being   25 are   26 there   27 be   28 was   29 been   30 be   31 Not   32 but   33 are   34 it   35 What

5
36 get it finished   37 were having/were getting your hair cut   38 've just had my wallet stolen   39 should have/get a new engine put in   40 Have you had your eyes tested

Unit 79
79a
1 onto   2 over, to/into   3 between, into, among   4 on top of, in/inside   5 in, below/beneath   6 below   7 by/past   8 from, to, beside/by   9 next to, opposite   10 inside, across   11 at, opposite   12 over   13 against   14 along/beside, at

79b
1 across   2 at   3 in   4 in   5 at/on/by   6 over   7 from   8 to   9 along   10 into/in/inside

Unit 80
80a
1 at, in   2 during, for   3 for, Until   4 during, Before   5 by, in   6 on, until

80b
1 in   2 at/after   3 at   4 on   5 after/past   6 until/till   7 in

80c
1 In   2 in   3 for   4 by   5 After   6 until   7 during   8 Since   9 for   10 during

Unit 81
81a
1 with   2 on   3 about   4 from   5 by   6 with   7 about   8 from   9 by   10 about

81b
1 with   2 from   3 from   4 with   5 on   6 by   7 with   8 by

Unit 82
82a
1 in the end   2 on the way   3 At least   4 at the end   5 At last   6 in the way   7 at the latest   8 in time

82b
1 on   2 in   3 at   4 by   5 At   6 on   7 by   8 on   9 to   10 from   11 on   12 in   13 of   14 by   15 at   16 in   17 On   18 At   19 at

Check 15
1
1 In   2 On   3 from   4 by/with   5 at   6 In/During   7 on   8 by   9 about   10 from   11 Since   12 from

2
13 by   14 across   15 opposite   16 on   17 outside   18 in   19 for   20 with

Unit 83
83a
1 A   2 A   3 C   4 B   5 C   6 B   7 B   8 C

83b
1 from   2 for   3 about   4 about/at   5 with   6 to/towards   7 to   8 at   9 on   10 of   11 about   12 with

83c
1 with racing   2 in making   3 of owning   4 in driving   5 in getting   6 at winning   7 for building   8 to

Unit 84
84a
1 in   2 on   3 at   4 on   5 at   6 with   7 for   8 to   9 about   10 after   11 of   12 into   13 to   14 of

84b
1 –   2 –   3 to   4 for   5 on   6 in   7 with   8 on   9 to

84c
1 for   2 from   3 to   4 with   5 of   6 for   7 to   8 from

Unit 85
85a
1 A   2 C   3 B   4 B   5 C   6 C   7 B   8 A   9 C   10 A

85b
1 between   2 for   3 for   4 with   5 of   6 for   7 of   8 between   9 with   10 of   11 for

85c
1 discussion about   2 increase in   3 reason for   4 fall in   5 change in   6 solution to

Unit 86
86a
1 on   2 out   3 up   4 away   5 on   6 out   7 in   8 down   9 up   10 away   11 down   12 in

86b
1 She carried on working even after she'd had a heart attack.
2 They waited for him for over an hour before he finally turned up.
3 We stayed up (later than usual) because we wanted to watch the film.
4 After several tries I succeeded in getting through to her on the telephone.
5 It will take them ages to fill in all these forms/fill all these forms in.
6 We can put you up for the night in the spare room.
7 Please stop making up excuses/making excuses up for why you won't go out with me.
8 If you don't know the meaning of a word, you can look it up in a dictionary.
9 The machine's broken down so they'll have to call in someone to repair it.
10 She worked out (a solution to) the problem.

223

Answer key

86c
1 took up 2 grew up 3 was brought up 4 didn't get on with
5 back down 6 ended up 7 gave up 8 knocked out

Unit 87
87a
1 take 2 bring 3 did 4 doing, making 5 give 6 going 7 got to know 8 take 9 gets 10 coming

87b
1 going 2 take 3 making 4 know 5 get 6 get 7 do/be doing 8 Do 9 make 10 Make 11 take 12 get to know 13 do

Unit 88
88
1 as 2 as 3 Like 4 as 5 like 6 as 7 like 8 As 9 like 10 Like

Unit 89
89a
1 way 2 funny 3 trip 4 nature, countryside 5 journey 6 irritable

89b
1 environment 2 countryside 3 nature 4 nervous 5 trip 6 fun

Check 16
1
1 fun 2 countryside 3 journey 4 like 5 nervous 6 as 7 gave 8 with 9 of 10 on

2
11 doesn't look like 12 is responsible for training 13 as a waiter 14 are proud of 15 a solution to 16 borrow that book from 17 succeeded in convincing 18 approves of

3
19 C 20 D 21 B 22 A 23 D 24 D 25 B 26 A 27 D 28 C 29 B 30 A

4
31 for 32 have 33 got 34 about/at 35 in 36 for 37 round/by 38 from 39 up 40 forward

Unit 90
90
1 co-star 2 miscalculated 3 Over-exposure 4 inseparable, undergraduates 5 disrespectful

Unit 91
91a
1 guilty 2 courageous 3 imaginative 4 truthful 5 national

91b
1 Regional 2 weekly 3 professional 4 homeless 5 important 6 famous 7 independent 8 political

Unit 92
92
1 ability 2 discovery 3 invention 4 developments 5 civilisation 6 communication(s) 7 information 8 destruction 9 pollution 10 scientists 11 politicians 12 solutions

Unit 93
93a
1 interested 2 respected 3 challenging 4 expanding 5 related 6 exciting 7 completed

93b
1 embarrassing 2 dried 3 continuing 4 changing 5 stolen 6 parked 7 broken 8 loving

Unit 94
94a
1 (hard-)working, (easy-)going 2 (level-)headed 3 (middle-)aged, (well-)built 4 (hand)made 5 (left-)handed 6 (world)wide

94b
1 (blue-)eyed 2 best(-selling) 3 (fast-)moving 4 (modern-)day 5 old(-fashioned) 6 (air-)conditioned 7 brand(-new) 8 (high-)rise

Unit 95
95a
1 Air conditioning 2 Job sharing 3 Software 4 Feedback 5 burglar alarm

95b
1 pain(killer) 2 traffic (light) 3 computer (game) 4 food (poisoning) 5 opening (hours)

Check 17
1
1 ability 2 organisation 3 surprised 4 competitor 5 unable 6 effective 7 disappointing 8 solution(s) 9 action 10 important

2
11 unemployment 12 misunderstood 13 reunited 14 frozen 15 incompetent

3
16 (television) series 17 (long-)running 18 (front-)row 19 power (dressing) 20 (lateral) thinking